# WHEN CHRISTIANS
# FACE PERSECUTION

'Exactly what constitutes persecution for being a Christian from the Bible's perspective? What were all the reasons why it happened in New Testament times? What was the range of appropriate responses? How do we apply them today? If any of these questions interest you, Chee-Chiew Lee's New Testament theology of suffering is a must read. If they don't, given our world's current religious climate, they should! An excellent resource.'
**Craig L. Blomberg**, Distinguished Professor of New Testament, Denver Seminary, USA

'Dr Chee-Chiew Lee's book of well-researched scholarship combines a rich exploration of New Testament theology regarding how to face persecution, the diverse Christian response to persecution in the Greco-Roman world, and how the different authors in the New Testament encourage readers to persevere in faith during persecution. The epilogue is a must read as Dr Lee presents her own personal reflections on how to apply a theological understanding of persecution to our current contemporary context. Lee's appeal for readers to *empathize with the persecuted* is certainly the book's grand finale.'
**The Revd Dr Patrick Fung**, General Director, OMF International

'At its best, biblical scholarship brings out the teaching of Scripture for the edification of the people of God. This such a work. By reading the text carefully, Dr Lee traces the various responses to persecution seen in the New Testament. No study is ever done without context; in this study, Dr Lee uses her context to bring the issue of persecution into a renewed and sharp focus. Recommended to every Christian – and biblical scholar – who wants to reflect seriously on how persecution shaped early thinking in the church.'
**Dirk Jongkind**, Academic Vice Principal, Tyndale House, Cambridge

'This well-researched work of careful scholarship addresses a topic of vital importance to the global church. Lee engages this theme throughout the New Testament, examining the many passages in their first-century setting and showing the relevance of the early Christian writers' wisdom for analogous situations today.'
**Craig S. Keener**, F. M. and Ada Thompson Professor of Biblical Studies, Asbury Theological Seminary, USA

# WHEN CHRISTIANS FACE PERSECUTION

Theological perspectives
from the New Testament

Chee-Chiew Lee

APOLLOS (an imprint of Inter-Varsity Press)
36 Causton Street, London SW1P 4ST, England
Email: ivp@ivpbooks.com
Website: www.ivpbooks.com

*First published 2022*

**British Library Cataloguing-in-Publication Data**
A catalogue record for this book is available from the British Library.

ISBN: 978-1-78974-268-8
eBook ISBN: 978-1-78974-269-5

Set in 10/13.25pt Minion Pro
Typeset in Great Britain by CRB Associates, Potterhanworth, Lincolnshire
Printed and bound in Great Britain by Ashford Colour Press Ltd,
Gosport, Hampshire

Produced on paper from sustainable sources.

Inter-Varsity Press publishes Christian books that are true to the Bible
and that communicate the gospel, develop discipleship and strengthen
the church for its mission in the world.

IVP originated within the Inter-Varsity Fellowship, now the Universities
and Colleges Christian Fellowship, a student movement connecting Christian
Unions in universities and colleges throughout Great Britain, and a member
movement of the International Fellowship of Evangelical Students.
Website: www.uccf.org.uk. That historic association is maintained, and all senior
IVP staff and committee members subscribe to the UCCF Basis of Faith.

# Contents

# Foreword

The early Christian experience of persecution has attracted a long history of scholarship. It was the subject of both ardent devotion and significant dispute since antiquity. This occurred not only vis-à-vis hostile outsiders, but also between Christians sharply divided over whether one should seek martyrdom or flee persecution, and how to restore those whose confession crumbled under duress.

Ironically, most modern critical study of the subject (since, say, Edward Gibbon, 1737–1794) has been carried out by scholars of the North Atlantic world who were themselves untroubled by any recent or personal experience of religious persecution, and whose political cultures had for the most part erected legal protections that seemed at least for the time being to render the colourful and exaggerated ancient testimonies wholly implausible. Until very recently, there have been scholars keen to cultivate publicity around assertions that Christian claims of persecution, then or now, are wholesale 'myth', 'invented' for purposes of political convenience.

Across many parts of Asia, however, the oppression of Christians is shockingly real today, as indeed it was repeatedly in antiquity and in later centuries: the BBC in 2019 reported 'near genocide' levels of violence, abuse and harassment against believers.

For these and many other good reasons, it is a privilege to welcome this volume by Chee-Chiew Lee, one of Southeast Asia's leading female biblical scholars and an associate professor of New Testament in the Chinese programme of Singapore Bible College. She offers here a constructive engagement with existing scholarship to explore the diverse causes of, and responses to, persecution in the New Testament, showing how its authors offer an empathetic theology of perseverance that has the potential to empower a response contextually suited for afflicted Christians in Asian and African settings today.

Markus Bockmuehl
University of Oxford

# Preface

'It takes a village to raise a child.' Similar to this African proverb, to publish a book involves the help and support of many people. Consistent interactions with students from regions with significant Christian persecution first motivated me to study and write on this topic more than a decade ago. Its fruition began when Langham Partnership extended their invitation for me to apply for their postdoctoral fellowship. The month-long research residencies over three years provided a conducive environment, from which four articles were eventually published in journals and cited in this book. During these residencies, interactions with fellow Majority World scholars and the senior academic mentors of this postdoctoral cohort have greatly enriched this project in many ways. Although the COVID-19 pandemic halved the original six-month residency at Cambridge's Tyndale House and Ridley Hall, I am thankful to God to have written a large portion of the book prior to returning to Singapore.

Therefore, I am immensely grateful to the following people for being part of this 'village'. Langham Partnership, their partners (especially Asbury Theological Seminary; Ridley Hall and Tyndale House, Cambridge; Wycliffe Hall, Oxford) and their donors for investing their resources and facilitating Majority World scholars to do research and contextual theological reflections for the church. Dr Ian Shaw (Langham Postdoctoral Projects Director) for his firm but kind direction in the project. Dr Dirk Jongkind (Vice Principal of Tyndale House) for his encouragement, feedback and suggestions as my senior academic mentor. Dr Clement Chia (Principal of Singapore Bible College) for the College's fulfilment of their commitment with Langham Partnership in this project and for his relentless support in allowing me to include time for research and writing concurrent with my regular teaching and administrative duties. All my friends and students who have enhanced my understanding of persecution with their real-life experiences in various regions. Dr Philip Duce and the team at Inter-Varsity Press (UK) for their professional help in the publication process. My home church, Bethesda Katong Church, for blessing me in this project through their prayer. My beloved husband, Vincent; my son, Ray; and my daughter, Min, who have been constantly with me, loving and supporting me, even during the times when we have to be physically apart. There are more people than I am able to mention here and I thank my God for all of you for your partnership in the gospel (Phil. 1:3–4). Last, but not least, I thank God for putting this research project into my heart and for providing all that is necessary for it to come to fruition for the edification of his people.

Chee-Chiew Lee
Singapore

# Abbreviations

| | |
|---|---|
| *1 En.* | *1 Enoch* |
| 1QH<sup>a</sup> | *Hodayota* (Thanksgiving Hymns) copy A from Qumran Cave 1 |
| 1QM | *Milḥamah* (War Scroll) from Qumran Cave 1 |
| *2 Bar.* | *2 Baruch* |
| 2Q23 | apocrProph from Qumran Cave 2 |
| א | Codex Sinaiticus or Aleph (01) |
| א* | Codex Sinaiticus, original reading |
| א² | Codex Sinaiticus, second corrector |
| A | Codex Alexandrinus (02) |
| AB | Anchor Bible |
| *AcT* | *Acta theologica* |
| AH | Ancient History |
| ANE | ancient Near East(ern) |
| ANTC | Apostasy in the New Testament Communities |
| AYB | Anchor Yale Bible |
| B | Codex Vaticanus (03) |
| BAC | Bloomsbury Academic Collections |
| *BBR* | *Bulletin for Biblical Research* |
| BDAG | Bauer, W., F. W. Danker, W. F. Arndt and F. W. Gingrich, *Greek-English Lexicon of the New Testament and Other Early Christian Literature*, 3rd edn, Chicago: University of Chicago Press, 1999 |
| BECNT | Baker Exegetical Commentary on the New Testament |
| BETL | Bibliotheca Ephemeridum Theologicarum Lovaniensium |
| BHGNT | Baylor Handbook on the Greek New Testament |
| *Bib* | *Biblica* |
| *BibInt* | *Biblical Interpretation* |
| BIS | Biblical Interpretation Series |
| BNTC | Black's New Testament Commentaries |
| *BTB* | *Biblical Theology Bulletin* |
| BTCP | Biblical Theology for Christian Proclamation |

| | |
|---|---|
| Byz | Byzantine codices |
| C | Codex Ephraemi Rescriptus (04) |
| CBC | Cornerstone Bible Commentary |
| CBNTS | Coniectanea Biblica: New Testament Series |
| *CBQ* | *Catholic Biblical Quarterly* |
| co | all Coptic versions |
| CS | Cornerstones Series |
| *CTTSJ* | *Central Taiwan Theological Seminary Journal* |
| Cyr | Cyril of Alexander |
| D | Codex Bezae (05) and Codex Claromontanus (06) |
| EBS | Essentials of Biblical Studies |
| EC | Epworth Commentaries |
| ECCA | Early Christianity in the Context of Antiquity |
| EPRO | Études préliminaires aux religions orientales dans l'Empire romain |
| ESV | English Standard Version |
| EUS | European University Studies |
| FCCGRW | First-Century Christians in the Graeco-Roman World |
| FCNTECW | Feminist Companion to the New Testament and Early Christian Writings |
| HB | Hebrew Bible |
| HNT | Handbuch zum Neuen Testament |
| *HTR* | *Harvard Theological Review* |
| *HTS* | *HTS Theological Series* |
| ICC | International Critical Commentary |
| *IJRF* | *International Journal for Religious Freedom* |
| *Int* | *Interpretation* |
| *JBL* | *Journal of Biblical Literature* |
| *JETS* | *Journal of the Evangelical Theological Society* |
| JSJSup | Journal for the Study of the Pseudepigrapha: Supplement Series |
| *JSNT* | *Journal for the Study of the New Testament* |
| JSNTSup | Journal for the Study of the New Testament: Supplement Series |
| *Jub.* | *Jubilees* |
| L&N | Louw, J. P. and E. A. Nida (eds.), *Greek-English Lexicon of the New Testament: Based on Semantic Domains*, 2nd edn (New York: United Bible Societies, 1989) |

| | |
|---|---|
| latt | the entire Latin tradition |
| LBT | Library of Biblical Theology |
| LCL | Loeb Classical Library |
| LEC | Library of Early Christianity |
| *LMM* | *Lutheran Mission Matters* |
| LNTS | Library of New Testament Studies |
| LXX | Septuagint |
| MBPS | Mellen Biblical Press Series |
| MNTS | McMaster New Testament Studies |
| MT | Masoretic Text |
| NABPRSSS | National Association of Baptist Professors of Religion Special Studies Series |
| NAC | New American Commentary |
| *Neot* | *Neotestamentica* |
| NET | New English Translation |
| NICNT | New International Commentary on the New Testament |
| NICOT | New International Commentary on the Old Testament |
| NIGTC | New International Greek Testament Commentary |
| NIV | New International Version |
| NLT | New Living Testament |
| *NovT* | *Novum Testamentum* |
| NovTSup | Supplements to Novum Testamentum |
| NRSV | New Revised Standard Version |
| NTL | New Testament Library |
| *NTS* | *New Testament Studies* |
| OCM | Oxford Classical Monographs |
| OTL | Old Testament Library |
| P | Codex Guelferbytanus A (024) and Codex Porphyrianus (025) |
| 𝔓 | New Testament papyri |
| *P.Lond.*1912 | Papyrus copy of Letter of Claudius to the Alexandrians |
| PNTC | Pillar New Testament Commentaries |
| PS | Pauline Studies |
| Ψ | Codex Athous Laurae (044) |
| *Pss Sol.* | *Psalms of Solomon* |
| PTMS | Princeton Theological Monograph Series |
| RBS | Resources for Biblical Study |
| *ResQ* | *Restoration Quarterly* |

| | |
|---|---|
| RGRW | Religions in the Graeco-Roman World |
| RNTS | Reading the New Testament Series |
| RSF | Religious Freedom Series |
| SBLAcBib | Society of Biblical Literature Academia Biblica |
| SBLMS | Society of Biblical Literature Monograph Series |
| SBLSymS | Society of Biblical Literature Symposium Series |
| SCJ | Studies in Christianity and Judaism |
| SHBC | Smyth & Helwys Bible Commentary |
| SJLA | Studies in Judaism in Late Antiquity |
| SNTSMS | Society for New Testament Studies Monograph Series |
| STAC | Studien und Texte zu Antike und Christentum |
| sy | the entire Syriac tradition |
| *TAPA* | *Transactions of the American Philological Association* |
| *T. Gad* | *Testament of Gad* |
| THNTC | Two Horizons New Testament Commentary |
| Θ | Codex Coridethianus (038) |
| *T. Job* | *Testament of Job* |
| tr. | translated |
| *TynBul* | *Tyndale Bulletin* |
| W | Codex Washingtonianus (032) |
| WBC | Word Biblical Commentary |
| WEAGIS | World Evangelical Alliance Global Issues Series |
| WUNT | Wissenschaftliche Untersuchungen zum Neuen Testament |
| ZECNT | Zondervan Exegetical Commentary on the New Testament |

# Introduction

Opposition to the Christian faith to the extent of persecution has been a concern to Christians ever since the beginning of Christianity until today. What are the sociopolitical and theological factors that led to the persecution of Christians as described in the New Testament and how did these Christians justify their responses to it? How do the New Testament authors interpret, develop and reapply the gospel traditions of Jesus regarding persecution to their context? This book is an attempt to describe a New Testament theology of facing persecution as a basis for further theological reflections for various contemporary contexts.

## Understanding persecution: definition and scope

While we might have come across the word 'persecution' quite often, it is necessary for us to clarify what we mean by 'persecution' in this study. According to the *Cambridge English Dictionary*, 'persecution' involves 'unfair or cruel treatment over a long period of time because of race, religion, or political beliefs'.[1] From this definition, I will discuss the various aspects of persecution as follows. First, it entails action, not just attitude.[2] Second, the action is deemed to be unfair or cruel. 'Unfairness' entails discrimination while 'cruelty' involves inflicting some form of suffering (physical or psychological). Discrimination implies unjust treatment. It is important to note that 'justice' is perspectival: what may be perceived as 'unjust' by the persecuted may be deemed 'just' for the persecutor. Therefore, as this study seeks to describe the New Testament

---

[1] 'Persecution', in the *Cambridge Advanced Learner's Dictionary and Thesaurus* <https://dictionary.cambridge.org/dictionary/english/persecution>, accessed 8 August 2021. See also Cunningham, who adopts a very similar definition in terms of harm inflicted by opponents due to beliefs and not because of any crime committed by the afflicted. Scott Cunningham, *'Through Many Tribulations': The Theology of Persecution in Luke–Acts*, JSNTSup 142 (Sheffield: Sheffield Academic Press, 1997), p. 139.

[2] Charles L. Tieszen, 'Towards Redefining Persecution', *IJRF* 1.1 (2008), p. 69.

authors' view, I will adopt the perspective of the persecuted.[3] Also, opposition may not always constitute persecution, unless it can be established that unjust treatment results from the opposition.

Third, from a modern perspective, it is possible to separate racial, religious and political motives behind the persecution. However, in the first century all three aspects are knitted closely together and not easily segregated, as we will see in chapter 1 below. For the purpose of our study, persecution of Christians in the New Testament refers to the unjust treatment meted out to people due to their faith in Jesus Christ as their God, and their Lord and Saviour. Tieszen's definition below aptly captures the various aspects: 'Any unjust action of varying levels of hostility, perpetrated primarily on the basis of religion, and directed at Christians, resulting in varying levels of harm as it is considered from the victim's perspective.'[4]

Fourth, persecution includes violent (verbal or physical) opposition as a reaction provoked by Christians' words or deeds (e.g. Stephen's speech and martyrdom in Acts 7), as well as a systematic seeking out of Christians to mete out punishments (e.g. Saul's persecution in Acts 8:3). Whether sporadic incidents in the former or systematic persecution in the latter, both would have occurred over a reasonably long period of time. While persecution is a form of opposition, opposition in itself does not necessarily lead to persecution and should not simply be identified with

---

[3] For examples of differing perspectives between the persecutor and persecuted, see ibid., p. 70.

[4] Ibid., p. 69. Penner defines 'persecution' as 'suffering for doing what is good, more specifically, because of one's allegiance to the living God' or 'a situation where Christians are repetitively, persistently and systematically inflicted with grave and serious suffering or harm and deprived of (or significantly threatened with deprival of) their basic human rights because of a difference that comes from being a Christian that the persecutor will not tolerate', while Kelhoffer defines it as the 'undeserved penalty or punishment – whether real, imagined, anticipated, or exaggerated – that is said to be incurred in the course of the Christian life'. See Glenn M. Penner, *In the Shadow of the Cross: A Biblical Theology of Persecution and Discipleship* (Bartlesville: Living Sacrifice, 2004), p. 41; James A. Kelhoffer, *Persecution, Persuasion, and Power: Readiness to Withstand Hardship as a Corroboration of Legitimacy in the New Testament*, WUNT 270 (Tübingen: Mohr Siebeck, 2010), p. 8. Penner's definition is taken from the organization The Voice of the Martyrs in Canada and is quite close to Tieszen's. While I agree with Kelhoffer regarding the perspective of the Christian ('whether real, imagined, anticipated, or exaggerated'), both his ('the course of the Christian life') and Penner's ('suffering for doing what is good') definition seems too broad as it does not clearly distinguish between undeserved treatments suffered by Christians in general or due to their faith. E.g. a person who exposes the wicked deeds of others to bring them to justice and prevent them from further harming others (i.e. doing good) may face retaliation for doing so, whether or not they are Christians or acted out of Christian convictions.

persecution. For example, although Elymas the magician opposed Paul, Luke did not suggest that Elymas used any physical or verbal violence (Acts 13:8). Thus, it would be too simplistic to identify Elymas as a persecutor. Similarly, rejection of the gospel message in itself does not constitute persecution, unless it becomes a violent rejection towards those who proclaim the message.

The above definition distinguishes persecution from suffering for Christ in general and from conformity due to social pressure. In the former, the suffering is not caused directly due to one's confession of faith in Jesus Christ (e.g. Paul's shipwreck experience and encounter with bandits in 2 Cor. 11:25–26 in his missionary travels).[5] In the latter, there is no explicit order externally to comply but the person yields to group pressure (e.g. some Corinthians participating in cultic meals at private or public gatherings).[6] Persecution is also to be distinguished from martyrdom, in that the latter is an outcome of persecution, but not all persecution results in martyrdom.[7]

The term 'Christian' was first used by 'outsiders' at Antioch to designate Jesus' followers (Acts 11:26),[8] while the terms used by 'insiders' to designate themselves include disciples (e.g. Matt. 28:19; Acts 6:1), believers (e.g. Acts 5:14; 1 Thess. 1:7), saints (e.g. Acts 9:13; 1 Cor. 1:2; Rev. 13:7), brothers/sisters (e.g. 1 Cor. 7:15; Jas 2:15), the elect (e.g. Titus 1:1; 1 Peter 1:1; 2 John 1) and the church (e.g. Matt. 18:7; Acts 8:3; Gal. 1:2; Heb. 12:23; Rev. 1:4).[9] In this study, I will be using the term 'Christian' to refer to 'one who believes in, or professes or confesses Jesus Christ as Lord and Saviour, or is assumed to believe in Jesus Christ'.[10]

---

[5] See also Charles L. Tieszen, 'Minding the Gaps: Overcoming Misconceptions of Persecution', *IJRF* 2.1 (2009), pp. 67–69. As Tieszen (p. 68) notes, 'while those who are persecuted suffer, those who suffer are not necessarily persecuted'.

[6] Andrew M. Colman, 'Conformity', in *Dictionary of Psychology*, 4th edn (Oxford: Oxford University Press, 2015), p. 158.

[7] Tieszen, 'Minding the Gaps', pp. 69–70.

[8] The term 'Christian' as a self-designation appears only once in the New Testament (1 Peter 4:16).

[9] See also Paul R. Trebilco, *Self-Designations and Group Identity in the New Testament* (Cambridge: Cambridge University Press, 2012), pp. 16–297.

[10] David B. Barrett, George T. Kurian and Todd M. Johnson (eds.), *World Christian Encyclopedia: A Comparative Survey of Churches and Religions in the Modern World*, 2nd edn (Oxford: Oxford University Press, 2001), p. 655. See also Trebilco (*Self-Designations*, pp. 297, 313–314), who argues that it is valid to use the designation 'Christian' to describe early followers of Jesus in the New Testament.

This study has a few specific focuses. First, it concentrates on describing how the New Testament authors attain the goal of encouraging their Christian audience to persevere in faith despite facing persecution, thus a 'theology of facing persecution' rather than a broader 'theology of persecution'. As such, the persecution of Jesus will be the background cause of Christian persecution, rather than the foreground of our discussion. Second, it is primarily a biblical-theological study of the New Testament, rather than a historical study of early Christianity.[11] Therefore, we will concentrate on texts within the twenty-seven books of the New Testament canon that clearly address persecution, but will not include other non-canonical Christian texts such as those of the apostolic fathers. Also, we will concentrate on looking at the first-century historical, political and cultural context as background to the study, rather than on a historical analysis of 'what happened' as foreground. Nonetheless, we will also briefly look into the century before to understand various causes leading up to the first-century context, as well as explore possible areas of continuities into the next few centuries.[12] Third, we will also focus on conflicts with outsiders, rather than intra-Christian conflicts (e.g. disagreements between Paul and other Jewish Christians).

---

[11] Some may argue that a study of first-century Christianity should include other non-canonical early Christian writings of the first century, because the present New Testament canon reflects only the fourth-century portrayal of orthodox Christianity. See the discussion in James D. G. Dunn, *New Testament Theology: An Introduction*, LBT 3 (Nashville: Abingdon, 2009), pp. 4–5. While their observation is true and I also acknowledge that a number of these non-canonical early Christian writings were highly regarded by the early church, this is a study of the New Testament authors' theology, rather than that of the broader 'first-century' Christian theology. On the legitimacy of studying New Testament theology within its canon, see Udo Schnelle, *Theology of the New Testament*, tr. M. Eugene Boring (Grand Rapids: Baker Academic, 2009), pp. 48–49.

[12] As such, Jewish writings reflecting persecution of the Jews and their responses (e.g. martyrdom or adaptation) during the Second Temple period function as a background to how early Christians might have been influenced by these traditions. I use the term 'Jewish writings' to refer broadly to the Jewish literature existing during the Second Temple period that include writings later categorized as canonical (essentially equivalent to the Christian Old Testament) and non-canonical (e.g. apocrypha, pseudepigrapha, Philo, Josephus, Qumran). Other non-canonical writings (e.g. Roman writings such as those of Suetonius, Tacitus and Pliny; early Christian writings such as those of Ignatius and Polycarp) reflecting persecution of Christians and their responses will inform us of how certain views of the New Testament authors continued to influence subsequent Christians.

# Let the New Testament authors speak for themselves: methodology

In describing the theological view(s) of the New Testament authors, our task is to allow the New Testament authors to speak for themselves first, before we compare their similarities and differences, and then synthesize them to formulate a New Testament theology of facing persecution.[13] It is important for us to exercise caution not to read the view of one into another (e.g. the view of Luke, Paul, 1 Peter, and Revelation with regard to the role that ruling authorities played in the persecution of Christians). Scholars engaging in biblical theology usually acknowledge that biblical authors can be diverse in their theological views, but it is still possible to find some commonalities among these authors that unite these writings across the present canon.[14] On the one hand, it is understandable that evangelical Christians need to emphasize the unity of the New Testament in its message in response to those who claim otherwise.[15] On the other

---

[13] Due to constraints of space, there is always a tension between comprehensive interaction with the vast amount of secondary literature with extensive documentation and the presentation of my interpretation of the New Testament authors' theology. See also Robert H. Gundry, *Matthew: A Commentary on His Handbook for a Mixed Church Under Persecution* (Grand Rapids: Eerdmans, 1994), p. 1. Following the practice of most other works on biblical theology, I have kept the interactions with secondary literature minimal and mostly to the footnotes.

[14] For a list of these scholars, see Schnelle, *Theology of the New Testament*, pp. 49–51; Thomas R. Hatina, *New Testament Theology and Its Quest for Relevance: Ancient Texts and Modern Readers* (London: Bloomsbury T&T Clark, 2013), pp. 156–160.

[15] Hatina (ibid., pp. 58, 62) provides a helpful analysis of the presuppositions underlying the assumption that the New Testament can be unified into a single theology: (1) there is a pure form of 'proto-orthodox' Christianity that may reflect certain differences but not contradictions among its leaders; (2) this unified theology can be recovered by using a 'proper method' (i.e. historical-critical method) and has an authority that is above later doctrinal formulations; and (3) the divine inspiration of Scripture requires consistency and unity. Hatina also notes that scholars understand unity in various ways: 'Some hold to an understanding of unity that includes internal contradictions and a scepticism about an author's creative role in the establishment of a coherent governing purpose, whereas others assume an understanding of unity wherein conflicting data can be harmonized or synthesized in accordance with an overriding purpose cleverly orchestrated by an author.' As evangelical Christians hold to some form of doctrine of inspiration, they would usually argue that there is some degree of unity in New Testament theology. Those who argue against the possibility of unity are e.g. Rudolf Bultmann, *Theology of the New Testament*, tr. Kendrick Grobel, 2 vols. (Waco: Baylor University Press, 2007), vol. 2, pp. 237–240; Hatina, *New Testament Theology*, pp. 67–79. Bultmann argues against a kind of unity in terms of a 'once-for-all' Christian dogmatics, as reflected by Hatina's points (1) and (2) above, because he understands New Testament theology as part of a continuum of theological reflections in history, while Hatina attempts to show that early Christianity had always been diverse, sometimes intentionally, as exhibited in the New Testament and non-canonical Christian writings. While I agree with Bultmann regarding the recovery

hand, we need to be careful not to flatten out and lose sight of the individual authors' distinctives, because both similarities and differences are equally important for us to have a well-rounded and comprehensive understanding of the New Testament's teachings with regard to facing persecution. As Dunn notes:

> the unity of the NT can be conceived and grasped only as a unity in diversity, that is, a unity that is like the unity of the body, a single identity composed of and made possible by the integration and interaction of the diverse parts.[16]

In order to do the above, we first need to understand these New Testament writings in their context: historical, cultural and literary. Nonetheless, biblical theology is inevitably a hermeneutical enterprise, both for the New Testament authors and for biblical scholars involved in it. The New Testament authors interpret the sayings of Jesus and the historical events (e.g. with regard to persecution) for their theological significance and relevance for their own context. Biblical scholars interpret the New Testament authors' writings (e.g. with regard to facing persecution for the purpose of this study) and inevitably present them in terms of their own hermeneutical presuppositions and context (modern/postmodern concerns).[17] This is not just inevitable but also necessary, as Schnelle notes, because 'a theology of the New Testament must both (1) bring the thought world of the New Testament writings into clear focus and (2) articulate this thought world in the context of a contemporary understanding of reality'.[18]

---

(note 15 *cont.*) of a 'pure' and 'authoritative' form of New Testament theology as overly reductionistic and with Hatina regarding his observations on diversity, this study will show that there are still similarities among the New Testament authors that can form some degree of unity in their theology of facing persecution.

[16] Dunn, *New Testament Theology*, p. 8.

[17] Schnelle, *Theology of the New Testament*, pp. 26–29. By 'modern' concerns I refer to the quest for some level of objective understanding as possible (e.g. the New Testament authors' theology of facing persecution) while not denying the influence of subjectivity. By 'postmodern' concerns I refer to the welcomed correction of the overly optimistic quest of absolute objective knowledge and thus the appreciation of pluralistic perspectives. Different perspectives of the same matter can be complementary or contradictory. An appreciation of the former helps us to have a more well-rounded view and the existence of the latter helps us to be aware that not all perspectives are equally valid. As Hatina (*New Testament Theology*, pp. 16–17) notes, 'postmodernism' is better understood as an 'extension' and 'reaction' to 'modernism' ideals, rather than two distinct periods in history.

[18] Schnelle, *Theology of the New Testament*, p. 25.

While this study strives towards a descriptive approach as much as possible, I fully acknowledge that the framework of my presentation reflects some of our contemporary concerns.[19] For example, insiders' and outsiders' perspectives of understanding why Christians face persecution reflect our postmodern concern for plurality of perspectives and our interest to uncover the sociopolitical reasons behind the persecution of Christians as reflected in the New Testament. However, the New Testament authors may be more concerned with the theological reasons behind the persecution than with the sociopolitical reasons. Nonetheless, as our purpose for doing biblical theology is not solely as an academic exercise, but for its relevance and appropriation for contemporary contexts,[20] the framework of my presentation here will help us with our contemporary reflections and appropriation. The appropriation of biblical-theological knowledge is not just for those who hold the teachings of Scripture as their standard of faith and practice. Even for those who do not confess faith in Jesus Christ, insights gleaned from such knowledge are helpful for contemporary reflections and appropriation, in the same way we could appropriate insights gleaned from studies of other fields of knowledge.[21]

This study will be mindful of the relationship between the literary and historical nature of the text. All historical accounts reflect the perspective of the narrator. As in all historical studies, we will need to assume the truthfulness of these accounts unless proven otherwise.[22] As this study focuses on how New Testament authors encourage their audience to persevere in their faith despite facing persecution, we will look at the text by asking the following: (1) In the narrative or discourse, how does the author portray the early Christians' responses to persecution and what is the author's evaluation of these responses? (2) How does the author directly exhort the audience or use direct exhortations of Jesus and other early Christian leaders, and combine these portrayals and exhortations

---

[19] Ibid.; Hatina, *New Testament Theology*, p. 30.

[20] Schnelle, *Theology of the New Testament*, p. 40; Hatina, *New Testament Theology*, p. 19.

[21] See e.g. the appropriation of New Testament theology for inter-religious dialogue in Hatina, *New Testament Theology*, pp. 181–183.

[22] Truthfulness is not identical to accuracy. A truthful witness may not be entirely accurate in all the details, but an untruthful witness may falsify certain facts. A detailed discussion of this is beyond the scope of this study. For extended discussions on reliability of eyewitnesses, historiography and historical reliability, see e.g. Richard Bauckham, *Jesus and the Eyewitnesses: The Gospels as Eyewitness Testimony*, 2nd edn (Grand Rapids: Eerdmans, 2017); Craig S. Keener, *Acts: An Exegetical Commentary*, 4 vols. (Grand Rapids: Baker Academic, 2012–15), vol. 1, pp. 3–319.

with literary and rhetorical devices to attain the goal of encouraging perseverance? (3) What theology of facing persecution surfaces from the approach taken by the author?

This study will take a literary approach for narrative texts and a redactional approach for the Synoptic Gospels. For the former, literary order plays an important role in narratives and discourses, by which the author develops characters, plots and logical arguments to bring across theological messages.[23] For the latter, noting the emphases of the author will help bring to the surface unique theological perspectives of the individual Gospel.[24] Using a redactional approach in analysing characterization in narratives is especially helpful in this respect.[25] While this study presents a theology of persecution thematically, I will also note significant instances when literary order or redactional emphasis sheds light on our understanding of the author's message.

On the authorship of the Gospels, while they are technically anonymous in the text, I will refer to their authors according to the superscription traditionally attributed to them. For the New Testament epistles, I will assume the authors of these epistles to be who they claim to be, whether Pauline or the general epistles.[26] For the purpose of our study, even for those writings whose attributed authorship some scholars dispute, it should suffice that these writings will still reflect their author's own perception of and responses to persecution or their interpretation of the attributed author's perception and responses in accord with their tradition. Thus, it

---

[23] For an introduction to how narrative criticism of the New Testament can help with understanding the meaning of the text as a whole, see James L. Resseguie, *Narrative Criticism of the New Testament: An Introduction* (Grand Rapids: Baker Academic, 2005).

[24] Gundry, *Matthew*, p. 3; Mark L. Strauss, *Four Portraits, One Jesus: An Introduction to Jesus and the Gospels*, 2nd edn (Grand Rapids: Zondervan, 2020), pp. 80–86. Although many scholars argue for or assume Markan priority, others hold to Matthean priority. Since we do not have absolute evidence of either, this study takes the approach of comparing the Synoptic Gospels to bring to the surface certain editorial emphases of each Gospel without assuming direct literary dependence on a particular Gospel or 'changes' made to the text of one Gospel by another evangelist.

[25] See e.g. the characterization of Joseph of Arimathea on pp. 83–87 below.

[26] The argument for the authenticity of all the New Testament epistles is beyond the scope of this study. For detailed arguments, see e.g. Terry L. Wilder, 'Pseudonymity and the New Testament', in David Alan Black and David S. Dockery (eds.), *Interpreting the New Testament: Essays on Methods and Issues* (Nashville: B&H, 2001), pp. 296–355; Kent D. Clarke, 'The Problem of Pseudonymity in Biblical Literature and Its Implications for Canon Formation', in Lee Martin McDonald and James A. Sanders (eds.), *The Canon Debate* (Peabody: Hendrickson, 2002), pp. 440–468; Stanley E. Porter, 'Pauline Chronology and the Question of Pseudonymity of the Pastoral Epistles', in Stanley E. Porter and Gregory P. Fewster (eds.), *Paul and Pseudepigraphy*, PS 8 (Leiden: Brill, 2013), pp. 65–88.

should suffice that we present, for example, a theology of facing persecution as reflected in the Gospel of Matthew or the Pauline epistles, in which 'Matthew' is the shorthand for 'the author of the Gospel of Matthew' while 'Paul' is the shorthand for the 'author' or 'attributed author' of the epistle.

## Theology of persecution in modern scholarship: a brief overview

Many have written regarding the persecution of Christians. Some take the historical approach, chronicling the persecution of Christians in the early church (first to third century),[27] while others engage in theological reflections.[28] As this study seeks to describe a theology of the New Testament authors with regard to facing persecution, the following will survey only biblical theological works pertaining to persecution. A number of scholars have also written on specific books of the New Testament regarding persecution.[29] However, in this survey, we will concentrate on those who have worked through the entire New Testament.

The most extensive monograph written on persecution in the New Testament using a socio-rhetorical and biblical-theological approach is

[27] E.g. Herbert B. Workman, *Persecution in the Early Church: A Chapter in the History of Renunciation* (London: Epworth, 1906; repr. Oxford: Oxford University Press, 1980); W. H. C. Frend, *Martyrdom and Persecution in the Early Church: A Study of a Conflict from the Maccabees to Donatus* (Oxford: Blackwell, 1965; repr. Cambridge: James Clarke, 2008); I. Lesbaupin, *Blessed Are the Persecuted: Christian Life in the Roman Empire, AD 64–313*, tr. R. R. Barr (Maryknoll: Orbis, 1987); Jakob Engberg, *Impulsore Chresto: Opposition to Christianity in the Roman Empire c. 50–250 AD*, tr. Gregory Carter, ECCA 2 (Frankfurt am Main: Peter Lang, 2007); Candida R. Moss, *The Myth of Persecution: How Early Christians Invented a Story of Martyrdom* (New York: HarperOne, 2013); Eckhard J. Schnabel, 'The Persecution of Christians in the First Century', *JETS* 61.3 (2018), pp. 525–547. We will not be responding to Moss's claims here as it is beyond the scope of this study. For scholarly reviews of her work, see e.g. Anne Thayer, review of *The Myth of Persecution: How Early Christians Invented a Story of Martyrdom*, by Candida Moss, *Int* 68.1 (2014), pp. 81–83, and W. Shelton, review of *The Myth of Persecution: How Early Christianity Invented a Story of Martyrdom*, by Candida Moss, *JETS* 57.1 (2014), pp. 210–214.

[28] E.g. Thomas Schirrmacher, *The Persecution of Christians Concerns Us All: Towards a Theology of Martyrdom*, 3rd edn, WEAGIS 5, repr. (Eugene: Wipf & Stock, 2018); Christof Sauer and Richard Howell (eds.), *Suffering, Persecution and Martyrdom: Theological Reflections*, RSF 2 (Johannesburg: AcadSA, 2010).

[29] E.g. J. S. Pobee, *Persecution and Martyrdom in the Theology of Paul*, JSNTSup 6 (Sheffield: JSOT Press, 1985); Gundry, *Matthew*; Cunningham, *Through Many Tribulations*; Douglas R. A. Hare, *The Theme of Jewish Persecution of Christians in the Gospel According to St. Matthew*, SNTSMS 6 (Cambridge: Cambridge University Press, 2005); Travis B. Williams, *Persecution in 1 Peter: Differentiating and Contextualizing Early Christian Suffering*, NovTSup 145 (Leiden: Brill, 2012); Lian Wang, 'Johannine View of Persecution and Tribulation', *LMM* 25.2 (2017), pp. 359–370.

Kelhoffer's *Persecution, Persuasion, and Power*. Kelhoffer argues that the New Testament authors viewed persecution theologically as a corroboration of legitimate Christian standing and thus attached value (in the form of cultural, social and symbolic capital) to such suffering. Kelhoffer is to be commended for his excellent work on describing a New Testament theology of persecution. Yet, he acknowledges that there is more to be done and challenges his readers for further reflections and tasks.[30] Thus, this study seeks to provide alternative or complementary perspectives to Kelhoffer's and contribute to the conversation on the ethical implications arising from the study.

Penner (2004) and Harrod (2018) attempt to trace a biblical theology of persecution from the Old and New Testaments.[31] Both of them attribute the reason behind the persecution of Christians to the conflict between the serpent and the offspring of the woman in Genesis 3:15.[32] Penner discusses the relevant scriptural passages by corpus,[33] but does not derive an overarching motif from these passages. Nonetheless, his unique contribution lies in describing how the New Testament authors appropriated the psalms with regard to persecution.[34] Although Penner attempts to connect persecution with discipleship, this connection is underdeveloped in the second half of his book.

Harrod, on the other hand, uses 'promise' as an overarching motif. He traces how 'the offspring of the woman' develops as the promised Abrahamic offspring and the promised Davidic offspring, and is eventually fulfilled in Jesus Christ. Throughout the process, Harrod highlights the concept of the spiritual conflict between the serpent (i.e. Satan) and the Son of God (cf. John 15:18–21; Rev. 12), and how it is manifested through opposition and sometimes outright persecution when the gospel is proclaimed (e.g. Acts 13:10, 50; 14:19). Although Christ is depicted as victorious over Satan through the cross (Rev. 12), the conflict between the two will end only in the new heavens and new earth

---

[30] Kelhoffer, *Persecution, Persuasion, and Power*, p. 386.

[31] Penner, *Shadow of the Cross*; Kenneth Harrod, *Promise and Persecution: A Biblical Theology of Suffering for Christ* (Orpington, Kent: Release International, 2018).

[32] Penner, *Shadow of the Cross*, pp. 22–27; Harrod, *Promise and Persecution*, pp. 28–33.

[33] The corpus divisions are as follows: Pentateuch, Historical, Wisdom, Prophets, Gospels, Acts, Epistles and Revelation grouped under 'Teaching of the Apostles'. See Penner, *Shadow of the Cross*, pp. 3–6.

[34] Ibid., pp. 48–55.

(Rev. 21 – 22).[35] Harrod concludes with implications for contemporary Christians.[36]

# Answering the relevant questions: overview of this book

As an attempt to describe a New Testament theology of facing persecution, this study seeks to answer the questions raised at the beginning of this introduction as follows.[37] Chapter 1 begins by asking why it all began. After surveying the religious world views of the New Testament period, we will examine the texts to see who persecuted the Christians and why they did so. I will not only describe the insiders' (the New Testament authors') perspectives but will also attempt to work out the outsiders' (non-Christians') perspectives. Chapter 2 asks, 'What was happening?' After detailing the various forms of persecution these early Christians faced, I will describe the diverse Christian responses the New Testament depicts. Chapter 3 asks how to stand firm to the end and examines how the New Testament authors persuaded their audiences to persevere in their Christian faith despite facing persecution. The concluding chapter will not only synthesize the similar theological perspectives among the New Testament authors, but will also highlight their individual distinct perspective on certain issues. Finally, in the epilogue, I will reflect on how such a New Testament theology of facing persecution relates to contemporary churches facing persecution for their faith in Christ.

---

[35] Harrod, *Promise and Persecution*, pp. 39–90, 93–114, 124–126.

[36] Ibid., pp. 134–138.

[37] See p. 1 above.

# 1

# Why it all began: exploring the reasons

In the Greco-Roman world, people could worship many different gods. Why then were the early Christians persecuted for worshipping Jesus? This chapter will first describe the historical background of the first century, specifically how the social, religious and political aspects of people's world view were tightly intertwined. With this historical background in mind, I will then discuss who persecuted the early Christians, so as to appreciate why they were persecuted, from both the insiders' and outsiders' perspective. From there, I will then describe a theology of why Christians face persecution according to the New Testament authors.

## Historical background

During the Greco-Roman period, Jews commonly referred to other non-Jews as 'the Gentiles' (*ta ethnē*; cf. Ezra 6:21 LXX; Rom. 3:29). Both Jews and Christians were the minority, living among other people who practised polytheistic worship. In accord with the scholarly convention, I will refer to these 'other people' as 'pagans'. Since Jewish monotheism stands in stark contrast to pagan polytheism in the Greco-Roman world, I will broadly classify the first-century religious world view as 'Greco-Roman' and 'Jewish' when I discuss the historical setting from which Christianity arose, particularly those elements in both these world views that lead to their conflict with Christians.

### Greco-Roman religious world view

In the Greco-Roman world, polytheism was the norm. Different people groups in various cities and regions had their patron gods (e.g. Artemis was the patron goddess of Ephesus; cf. Acts 19:27–35). In antiquity, religion was pragmatic, rather than faith-based. Therefore, it was common for people to worship many gods for various purposes. For example, Asclepius for their health and Aphrodite for fertility and love.[1] Performing rituals was key in religious practices.[2] As such, worship practices are referred to as 'cult', which Rothaus defines as 'activity directed toward or in relationship to a deity or deities by an identifiable and self-recognizing group of individuals in a form identifiable to both participants and non-participating observers'.[3]

Among the many pagan cults, the imperial cult – worship of the Roman emperor – is of special relevance to our study. Therefore, I will first examine the pagan cult in general and then the imperial cult in detail.

## Pagan cult

In antiquity, the patron–client relationship extends to the gods as patrons and people as clients.[4] People sought the favour of the gods for the former's general well-being and prosperity, from their personal life, such as good health and a successful business, to their collective well-being, such as a good harvest or a successful military campaign. Thus, religion permeated all aspects of life, both private and public: household, economic, political, military, administration, and so on. As religion was pragmatic, people could include additional gods in their pantheon without having to renounce other gods.[5]

People believed their well-being was a favour obtained from the gods. As clients receiving such benefactions, they were obliged to reciprocate by performing rituals and offering sacrifices to the gods, as a form of expressing their gratitude and giving honour to the gods. Conversely, people believed disasters (e.g. poor business, famine, earthquake) were

---

[1] Graf Fritz, 'Asclepius', in Simon Hornblower, Antony Spawforth and Esther Eidinow (eds.), *The Oxford Classical Dictionary*, 4th edn (Oxford: Oxford University Press, 2012), doi: 10.1093/acref/9780199545568.013.0853, and Pirenne-Delforge Vinciane and André Motte, 'Aphrodite', in ibid., doi: 10.1093/acref/9780199545568.013.0582.

[2] Harry O. Maier, *New Testament Christianity in the Roman World*, EBS (New York: Oxford University Press, 2018), p. 34.

[3] Richard M. Rothaus, *Corinth, the First City of Greece: An Urban History of Late Antique Cult and Religion*, RGRW 139 (Leiden: Brill, 2000), p. 6.

[4] Maier, *New Testament Christianity*, pp. 34–35.

[5] David P. Nystrom, 'We Have No King but Caesar: Roman Imperial Ideology and the Imperial Cult', in Scot McKnight and Joseph B. Modica (eds.), *Jesus Is Lord, Caesar Is Not: Evaluating Empire in New Testament Studies* (Downers Grove: InterVarsity Press, 2013), p. 29; Ralph Anderson, 'New Gods', in Esther Eidinow and Julia Kindt (eds.), *The Oxford Handbook of Ancient Greek Religion* (Oxford: Oxford University Press, 2015), pp. 309–323.

the result of the gods' displeasure or anger, usually attributing such disasters to wrongly performed or neglected rituals.[6]

As the Roman Empire conquered more territories, the Roman senate usually allowed conquered people to continue with their local cults.[7] Nonetheless, as Keener notes, Romans in the early republic believed their gods would punish them for admitting new deities (Dionysius of Halicarnassus, *Antiquitates Romanae* 3.35.2) and would instruct their citizens to worship only Roman gods using only Roman cultic practices (Livy, *History of Rome* 4.30.9–11). However, this exclusiveness became unpractical when the empire expanded.[8] Eventually, the Romans admitted certain foreign cults into their religious system. According to Orlin, this phenomenon is closely associated with their political decisions to 'incorporate new territories and new peoples within the body politic of the Roman people'.[9] Proper religious practice was essential to the Romans, who attributed their success in territorial expansion to their ability to maintain 'peace among the gods' (*pax deorum*).[10]

For the Romans, 'religious people' (*religiosi*) were those 'who have chosen to fulfil or pass over religious observances in accordance with the custom of the state and who do not involve themselves with alien cults (*superstitiones*)'.[11] In contrast to 'true religion' (*religio*), *superstitio* was used to refer to non-traditional religious practices that had been 'carried to extremes', 'without understanding' or might even be 'base or evil'.[12] As summarized by Martin, '*superstitio* could be used to cover all sorts of religious practices, including suspicious divination, foreign rituals, and magic, that were perceived as maleficent and threatening to Roman society and the state'.[13]

---

[6] Maier, *New Testament Christianity*, p. 35; Engberg, *Impulsore Chresto*, p. 31.

[7] Alan Watson, *The State, Law, and Religion: Pagan Rome* (Athens, Ga.: University of Georgia Press, 1992), p. 62. However, the Roman senate sometimes forbade their citizens from participating in certain foreign cults.

[8] Keener, *Acts*, vol. 3, p. 2473.

[9] Eric M. Orlin, *Foreign Cults in Rome: Creating a Roman Empire* (Oxford: Oxford University Press, 2010), p. 4.

[10] Ibid., p. 24.

[11] Festus, s.v. 'Religiosus', cited in Watson, *State, Law, and Religion*, p. 60.

[12] Dale B. Martin, *Inventing Superstition: From the Hippocratics to the Christians* (Cambridge, Mass.: Harvard University Press, 2004), pp. 126, 128, 130. Cf. Cicero, *Nature of the Gods* 1.42.117, 2.28.71; Seneca, *Moral Epistles* 95.35.

[13] Martin, *Inventing Superstition*, p. 134; James R. Harrison, 'The Persecution of Christians from Nero to Hadrian', in Mark Harding and Alanna Nobbs (eds.), *Into All the World: Emergent Christianity in Its Jewish and Greco-Roman Context* (Grand Rapids: Eerdmans, 2017), p. 279.

Furthermore, Gradel notes that *religio* refers to reverence for those with higher authority, frequently used for gods, but can also include people.[14] Therefore, people offered worship as a form of highest honour due to the power and status of their object of worship, rather than for ontological reasons.[15] This form of worship was common, and can be traced to the pre-classical period (prior to the fifth century BC) among the Greeks, who would give 'equal divine honours' (*isotheoi timai*) to both rulers and gods.[16] Since people regarded the Roman emperor as the most powerful ruler, they accorded divine honours to him. Furthermore, people in antiquity also believed gods could come to them in human form (cf. Acts 12:11; 14:11; 28:6). Thus, it is no surprise that they would also regard rulers as vicegerents of the gods or even as gods.[17] With this concept in mind, I continue our discussion on imperial cult below.

## Imperial cult

In line with honouring the gods by performing rituals (e.g. offering prayers and sacrifices) to them, the general populace and local authorities also did the same to honour the Roman emperor and to show their loyalty to him. The rationale was the same: the Roman Empire brought peace and prosperity, albeit after bloody military conquests. Thus, the Roman emperor was the patron and benefactor of the people; and more so for the local authorities, who received direct benefits from the emperor such as their offices, honour and financial benefits.[18] As clients, people were expected to reciprocate with honour, loyalty and service, as well as to seek continued benefactions from the emperor, using traditional and customary means.[19]

---

[14] '*Religio* meant reverence, conscientiousness, and diligence towards superiors, commonly, but not exclusively the gods.' See Ittai Gradel, *Emperor Worship and Roman Religion*, OCM (Oxford: Clarendon, 2002), p. 4. Cf. Festus, s.v. 'Religiosus'.

[15] Ibid., p. 101; Michael Peppard, *The Son of God in the Roman World: Divine Sonship in Its Social and Political Context* (Oxford: Oxford University Press, 2011), p. 31. This does not imply that people in antiquity did not distinguish between the nature of humans and gods. As Levene points out, it is rather that the worship of emperors occurred in contexts where the distinction did not matter. See D. S. Levene, 'Defining the Divine in Rome', *TAPA* 142.1 (2012), pp. 72–76.

[16] Duncan Fishwick, *The Imperial Cult in the Latin West: Studies in the Ruler Cult of the Western Provinces of the Roman Empire*, 2nd edn, EPRO 108 (Leiden: Brill, 1993), p. 21.

[17] Gradel, *Emperor Worship*, pp. 100–102, 191.

[18] Peter Garnsey and Richard P. Saller, *The Roman Empire: Economy, Society and Culture*, 2nd edn (London: Bloomsbury Academic, 2014), pp. 174–175.

[19] Traditional and customary means are important, because the people held that properly performed rituals were crucial to please the gods (see p. 14 above) and, by extension, the emperor, the absence of which could lead to disastrous consequences. New cultic practices were frowned upon as they had not been attested to be acceptable to the gods.

Conversely, the emperor, as a patron who received (divine) honour from clients, was obliged to reciprocate with further benefactions by ruling well.[20] In a culture framed by the patron–client relationship and steeped in honour and shame, failure to reciprocate using traditional and customary means was regarded as ingratitude and shameful.[21] Therefore, imperial cults served as a form of power negotiation for both the emperor and his subjects.[22]

Both Hillard and Winter have noted three types of cultic activities associated with this reciprocation between the Roman emperor and his subjects, and thus propose that this phenomenon be termed collectively as 'imperial *cults*', rather than '*the* imperial cult'.[23] In order to seek continued blessings on the empire for peace and prosperity, first, the people prayed to and made sacrifices to the gods for the safety and well-being of the emperor. Second, they performed these rituals directly to the emperor because they also regarded him as a divine being. Third, the emperor was regarded as the 'high priest' (Latin: *pontifex maximus*; Greek: *ho archiereus*) between the gods and the empire and also performed these rituals to the gods for the peace and prosperity of the empire (which included the well-being of the people).[24]

Imperial cults were practised at multiple levels: state, municipal and private.[25] Even though the Romans usually restricted their worship only to emperors who were deceased, non-Romans (especially in the eastern part of the empire) also worshipped living emperors. There is archaeological

---

[20] Gradel, *Emperor Worship*, p. 370. Gradel (p. 287) notes that emperors who ruled well were eventually deified posthumously by the senate as a form of ultimate honour (*apotheosis*), while those who failed to do so (e.g. Nero) had their statues destroyed and their names erased from inscriptions as a visible form of condemnation.

[21] Cf. Seneca, *On Benefits* 1.10.4; Cicero, *On Duties* 1.48.

[22] Jacob A. Latham, '"Honors Greater Than Human": Imperial Cult in the Pompa Circensis', in *Performance, Memory, and Processions in Ancient Rome: The Pompa Circensis from the Late Republic to Late Antiquity* (Cambridge: Cambridge University Press, 2016), p. 106.

[23] Bruce W. Winter, 'Divine Imperial Cultic Activities and the Early Church', in Mark Harding and Alanna Nobbs (eds.), *Into All the World: Emergent Christianity in Its Jewish and Greco-Roman Context* (Grand Rapids: Eerdmans, 2017), p. 240; Tom W. Hillard, in Matthew Dillon (ed.), 'Vespasian's Death-Bed Attitude to His Impending Deification', in *Religion in the Ancient World: New Themes and Approaches* (Amsterdam: A. M. Hakkert, 1996), pp. 197–198. Emphasis according to Winter.

[24] This concept of the ruler as 'priest king' can also be found in ANE cultures. While the Akkadians regarded the ruler as a human agent of the gods but not divine, the Egyptians regarded their king as divine. See William H. Stiebing and Susan N. Helft, *Ancient Near Eastern History and Culture*, 3rd edn (London: Routledge, 2017), pp. 39, 74–78, 122–125.

[25] Gradel, *Emperor Worship*, p. 13; Gwynaeth McIntyre, *Imperial Cult*, AH (Leiden: Brill, 2019), p. 65.

evidence that the worship of living emperors was a common practice among the populace throughout the empire.[26]

It is important to note that imperial cults were more a movement from the people than a directive from Rome.[27] The motives behind the populace and the local authorities were not identical. At the risk of oversimplification, perhaps a positive motivation would be to seek the common well-being of the people and a negative motivation would be to avoid the social pressure of shame. For some local authorities, rendering of divine honours to the emperor was also a means to ingratiate themselves with the Roman rulers.[28] In addition, failure to show loyalty to the empire in acceptable ways was to run the risk of being accused of treason, which had dire consequences should this invite Roman suppression.

## Christians among other persecuted groups: a bigger picture

Although the Roman senate, on behalf of the state, eventually admitted new (foreign or local) deities as part of their official religion, not every foreign deity made it into their pantheon, depending on the nature of the religion.[29] For the Romans, the performance of correct rituals was important, because incorrectly performed or inappropriate forms of rituals might anger the gods and could cause disasters to come upon the state.[30] Therefore, the Romans were strict in observing the 'customs of the ancestors' (*mos maiorum*) and forbade any introduction of new or foreign cults or rites in public or private without official approval (see Cicero, *De legibus* 2.8, 12, 37).[31]

---

[26] Gradel, *Emperor Worship*, pp. 13, 77; Peppard, *Son of God*, p. 32.

[27] Other than a few exceptions (e.g. Caligula; Domitian's case is debatable), most emperors did not demand to be worshipped. Gradel, *Emperor Worship*, pp. 140–161. However, we must be cautious of the other extreme of limiting imperial cults exclusively to being initiated provincially or locally, because Winter has shown that proconsuls, who were governors sent directly by the emperor, also promoted the imperial cult on behalf of Rome. Bruce W. Winter, *Divine Honours for the Caesars: The First Christians' Responses* (Grand Rapids: Eerdmans, 2015), pp. 29–47.

[28] Murray J. Smith, 'The Book of Revelation: A Call to Worship, Witness, and Wait in the Midst of Violence', in Mark Harding and Alanna Nobbs (eds.), *Into All the World: Emergent Christianity in Its Jewish and Greco-Roman Context* (Grand Rapids: Eerdmans, 2017), p. 338.

[29] Eric M. Orlin, *Temples, Religion, and Politics in the Roman Republic* (Boston: Brill Academic, 2002), p. 12; Harrison, 'Persecution of Christians', pp. 276–278.

[30] Maier, *New Testament Christianity*, p. 35; Harrison, 'Persecution of Christians', p. 277.

[31] Harrison, 'Persecution of Christians', pp. 277, 279; Watson, *State, Law, and Religion*, p. 58. Cf. Cicero, *De legibus*, 2.8, 12; Orlin, *Temples, Religion, and Politics*, p. 61.

Among those religions that were rejected were, for example, the Volsinian goddess Nortia, the Egyptian goddess Isis and the Bacchanalian cult; the latter two were not only rejected but outlawed and suppressed.[32] While the Bacchanalian cult had been outlawed due to sexual immorality and crimes associated with it (Livy, *History of Rome* 39.13.13), the Isis cult had been rejected for political reasons.[33]

It is worthwhile to note that Christians were not the only group of religious people rejected and suppressed by the Roman Empire.[34] While the suppression of the Bacchanalian cult may be seen as just and thus should not be regarded as persecution, the actions against the adherents of the cult of Isis (e.g. expulsion from Rome) may be regarded as unfair treatment from the perspective of the adherents and thus regarded as persecution. In addition, although the Jewish religion was officially a legal religion, anti-Jewish sentiments from the populace were nevertheless strong in many parts of the empire for reasons that we will see below.

## Jewish religious world view

Having discussed the Greco-Roman religious world view, we will now look into the Jewish religious world view. Technically speaking, during the Greco-Roman period, the term 'Jews' was not a purely ethnic category because Gentiles, though a small number, could be admitted into the community through proselytism. Thus, 'Jewish religious world view' during the first century refers to that which was largely shaped by the contemporaneous traditions and interpretations of the Jewish Scriptures.[35] The early church began as a movement within Judaism and consisted of both Jewish and Gentile followers of Jesus. Therefore, in this section, we

---

[32] Orlin, *Foreign Cults in Rome*, pp. 203–207; Orlin, *Temples, Religion, and Politics*, p. 12, n. 4; Richard A. Bauman, 'The Suppression of the Bacchanals: Five Questions', *Historia* 39.3 (1990), pp. 334–348.

[33] Sarolta A. Takács, *Isis and Sarapis in the Roman World*, RGRW 124 (Leiden: Brill, 1995), pp. 56–58; Orlin, *Foreign Cults in Rome*, p. 205.

[34] As noted in 'Persecution', in *The Concise Oxford Dictionary of World Religions* <https://www.oxfordreference.com/view/10.1093/acref/9780192800947.001.0001/acref-9780192800947-e-5576>, accessed 9 August 2021, 'Adherents of virtually all religions have suffered persecution for their faith at some point in their history.' For modern-day examples of ethnic and religious persecutions, see Tieszen, 'Towards Redefining Persecution', pp. 70–73.

[35] 'Jewish Scriptures' refers to the HB and its Greek translation the LXX. Scriptural citations in the New Testament reflect renderings that are (1) essentially similar to both HB and LXX; (2) similar to HB but not quite the same as LXX; e.g. Rom. 11:35; (3) similar to LXX but not quite the same as HB; e.g. Heb. 10:5, 38; and (4) not apparent in extant HB and LXX manuscripts; e.g. Matt. 2:23.

will explore elements of the Jewish religious world view from which the Christian movement developed and diverged: messianic expectations, monotheism, resurrection, Gentile inclusion as God's people and eschatology. These elements also became the cause of contention and conflict with pagans and non-Christian Jews. As these individual elements are interrelated in many ways, I will be discussing them in an integrated manner.

Prophetic literature in the Jewish Scriptures speaks of an ideal Davidic king who will come and rule over God's people, with some of these texts referring to the gathering of God's people from the diaspora and re-establishing the nation in the ancestral land (e.g. Isa. 9:7; 16:5; Jer. 23:25; Ezek. 37:24–25; Hos. 3:5). In some royal psalms, this ideal king holds both a priestly office and rules over all other nations (e.g. Pss 72; 110). In Daniel 7:13–14 (cf. Dan. 2:44–45; 9:25–27), this coming ruler of all nations is portrayed as a heavenly figure who will come at the eschaton and establish eternal rule. These scriptural passages provided trajectories from which the concept of the Messiah was developed further during the Second Temple period.[36] The word 'Messiah' ('the Anointed One'; *christos* in Greek), which appears in Daniel 9:25–26, began to take on more connotations than before. Nonetheless, as Grabbe notes, Second Temple literature exhibits a variety of views with regard to messianic expectations that defy a single coherent Second Temple messianic theology.[37]

According to Grabbe's analysis, some messianic expectations took on strong political overtones, fuelling Jewish revolts against foreign rule, beginning with the religious oppression by Antiochus Epiphanes (early second century BC), with occasional uprisings during the early first century (cf. Acts 5:36–37; 21:38), culminating in the first Jewish revolt in Palestine (AD 66–70), with sporadic uprising among the Jewish diaspora in Egypt and Mesopotamia (AD 115–117), until such an idea was put to an end during the failed Bar Kochba revolt in Palestine (AD 132–135).[38]

---

[36] For a survey of how these trajectories developed from the Jewish Scriptures during the Second Temple period, see Herbert W. Bateman, Darrell L. Bock and Gordon H. Johnston, *Jesus the Messiah: Tracing the Promises, Expectations, and Coming of Israel's King* (Grand Rapids: Kregel, 2012), pp. 37–329. On the development of a heavenly figure in the Second Temple literature, see Lester L. Grabbe, *An Introduction to Second Temple Judaism: History and Religion of the Jews in the Time of Nehemiah, the Maccabees, Hillel and Jesus* (London: T&T Clark, 2010), pp. 103–105.

[37] Grabbe, *Second Temple Judaism*, p. 80. For examples of various messianic views, see ibid., pp. 81–83.

[38] Ibid., pp. 80, 84.

Therefore, as Jewish messianic expectation claims were frequently associated with revolts, the Christian proclamation of Jesus the Jew as the Messiah would therefore also be easily perceived as resistance to Roman rule.

During the Second Temple period, Jewish apocalypticism, developed mostly from prophetic traditions in the Jewish Scriptures,[39] brought together several ideas such as (1) God's special revelation to his prophets through visions and explained by his angelic mediators; (2) the Messiah will come to execute final judgment, bringing the world to an end through cosmic cataclysm and establishing God's eternal kingdom; and (3) resurrection and life after death.[40] Similar to messianic expectations, there were also different views among Jewish sects with regard to these ideas; especially resurrection. It is well known that the Sadducees did not believe in the afterlife and resurrection, but lesser known that Ben Sira is likewise, while Wisdom 3.1–9 mentions immortality of the soul without mentioning resurrection.[41] While many Jews at that time might have believed there is a resurrection, they might differ in details as to the form (bodily or spiritually) and when resurrection will occur (at the present time or at the eschaton).[42] Therefore, the Christian proclamation of Jesus' bodily resurrection became one of the contentions with Jewish leaders.

In addition, the cataclysmic end of the world was usually portrayed as the destruction of the present ruling empire, represented by the form of a beast (e.g. Dan. 7:19–27; 8:19–25; *4 Ezra* 11 – 12). Revelation 13:1–18 and 19:11–21 also develop this tradition. Thus, such apocalyptic ideas presented strong resistance to foreign rule by predicting its eventual destruction.

Another important element is Jewish monotheism. Although certain scriptural texts seem to indicate sole devotion to only one God without denying the existence of other gods (e.g. Exod. 20:3; Deut. 5:7), other texts seem to deny that there are other gods except Yahweh (e.g. Deut. 32:39; Isa. 43:10). Nonetheless, during the Greco-Roman period, a number of pagan historical sources described the Jews as devoted only to their own

---

[39] There may be other influences, such as ANE cultures, Persian Zoroastrianism and mantic wisdom. Apocalypticism is not unique to the Jewish religious world view and can be found in other Hellenistic cultures. See ibid., pp. 89–91.

[40] See also ibid., p. 88.

[41] Ibid., pp. 93, 95.

[42] E.g. 2 Macc. 7 and *2 Bar.* 49–51 seem to expect a bodily resurrection, but *Jub.* 23.20–22 seems to expect a spiritual resurrection. In John 11:21–27, Martha expected resurrection to take place at the eschaton, but Jesus said resurrection can occur now.

God and rejecting images as representations of god(s).[43] This distinctive apparently set them apart from the pagans.[44] As such, most Jews refused to participate in pagan and imperial cults, because of (1) their exclusive devotion to only their God as the only true God; (2) their rejection of pagan gods and idolatry; and (3) their rejection of divine claims for a human emperor. Since most of the first Christians were Jews, early Christians were similar to the Jews in this respect. In fact, the Jews also faced similar social pressures for not participating in the imperial cult, as well as from pagan opposition in the diaspora.[45] Nonetheless, the imperial edicts by Julius Caesar, Augustus and Claudius granted Jews the right to perform their *mos maiorum*, thus their status as an 'approved religion' (*religio licita*).[46] While all other associations could meet at most only once a month in order to curb the possibility of political dissensions arising from such meetings, the Jews were granted exemption for their weekly meetings.[47]

Josephus (*Antiquities of the Jews* 17.42; [Marcus and Wikgren LCL]) recorded that 'the whole of the Jewish people affirmed by an oath that they would be loyal to Caesar and to the king's government' during the time of Herod the Great. As such, from the time of Caesar Augustus, the Jews

---

[43] For details on these pagan sources, see James F. McGrath, *The Only True God: Early Christian Monotheism in Its Jewish Context* (Urbana: University of Illinois Press, 2009), pp. 26–29, 35–36.

[44] Scholars are divided as to whether Jews of the first century were truly monotheistic. Although most agree that Jews held to the uniqueness of their God over other gods, they disagree on whether the practice of veneration of intermediary agents of God (angels, patriarchs) among some Jews differed from their worship of God, and whether veneration of these agents played a part in forming the understanding of divine Christology among early Christians. See e.g. Richard Bauckham, *Jesus and the God of Israel: God Crucified and Other Studies on the New Testament's Christology of Divine Identity* (Grand Rapids: Eerdmans, 2008); McGrath, *Only True God*; Larry W. Hurtado, *One God, One Lord: Early Christian Devotion and Ancient Jewish Monotheism*, 3rd edn, CS (London: Bloomsbury, 2015).

[45] See Erich S. Gruen, *Diaspora: Jews Amidst Greeks and Romans* (Cambridge, Mass.: Harvard University Press, 2002), pp. 8–9; Miriam Pucci Ben Zeev, 'Jews Among Greeks and Romans', in John J. Collins and Daniel C. Harlow (eds.), *The Eerdmans Dictionary of Early Judaism* (Grand Rapids: Eerdmans, 2010), pp. 245–254; Ritter Bradley, 'The Stasis in Alexandria in 38 CE and Its Aftermath', in *Judeans in the Greek Cities of the Roman Empire*, JSJSup 170 (Leiden: Brill, 2015), pp. 132–183. Although the Jews did not seek to proselytize others, their apparent success of attracting some Gentiles to become adherents of Judaism (as proselytes or God-fearers) also became one of the causes for anti-Jewish sentiments. See John G. Gager, *The Origins of Anti-Semitism: Attitudes Toward Judaism in Pagan and Christian Antiquity* (New York: Oxford University Press, 1983), pp. 59–62.

[46] E. Mary Smallwood, *The Jews Under Roman Rule: From Pompey to Diocletian*, 2nd edn, SJLA 21 (Leiden: Brill, 1981), p. 539; Harrison, 'Persecution of Christians', p. 280.

[47] O. F. Robinson, *The Criminal Law of Ancient Rome* (London: Duckworth, 1995), p. 80. For primary sources, see p. 80, n. 77.

adapted the first type of imperial cultic activities by offering daily sacrifices and prayers to their God at the Jerusalem temple for the welfare of the emperor and the people of the empire.[48] Thus, the Romans tolerated the Jews with this 'special form' (*sui generis*) of honouring the emperor as a substitute to offering worship or sacrifices directly to the emperor's statue, based on their respect for the Jewish *mos maiorum*.[49] Diaspora Jews also adapted their practices to offer honours to the emperor by (1) contributing to the Jerusalem temple sacrifices through paying temple tax; and (2) offering prayers and honorific inscriptions for the emperor in their synagogues.[50] Therefore, even though the Jews did not participate in imperial celebratory processions because that would involve pagan rites performed under the first and second types of imperial cults, they were not regarded as seditious.[51] By doing so, the Jews fulfilled the civic obligations of the imperial cults but within the framework of and without compromising their monotheism.[52] When such sacrifices and prayers ceased at the temple from AD 66, it was clearly a defiant act of resistance by the Jews in Judea and perceived as such by the Romans, leading to the first Jewish rebellion and the bloody Roman suppression between 66 and 70.[53]

The emphasis on monotheism during the Second Temple period can be reckoned as a post-exilic response to the polytheistic practices of many pre-exilic Jews. According to the Jewish Scriptures, the exile was God's judgment meted out on the Israelites, because they and their ancestors were unfaithful to their God in their covenantal relationship by *following the nations* in worshipping other gods and not obeying the covenantal stipulations (e.g. 2 Kgs. 17:7–23; Ezek. 20:1–44; Dan. 9:1–19). As such, in repentance, post-exilic Jewish leaders such as Ezra and Nehemiah were resolute in their commitment to God by obeying the law of Moses and by separating themselves from *the nations* (the Gentiles) (e.g. Ezra 9 – 10; Neh. 8 – 9). As idolatry is defilement (Ezek. 36:25; 37:23), Gentiles by

---

[48] Philo, *Embassy* 157; Josephus, *Against Apion* 2.77. See p. 16 above.

[49] Winter, *Divine Honours for the Caesars*, pp. 98–109.

[50] For historical evidence, see Justin K. Hardin, *Galatians and the Imperial Cult: A Critical Analysis of the First-Century Social Context of Paul's Letter*, WUNT 2.237 (Tübingen: Mohr Siebeck, 2008), pp. 108–109; Winter, *Divine Honours for the Caesars*, pp. 110–116.

[51] Hardin, *Galatians and the Imperial Cult*, pp. 107–108, 110. See also Winter, *Divine Honours for the Caesars*, p. 113.

[52] See also ibid., p. 131.

[53] Ibid., pp. 117–123.

implication are also unclean due to their idolatry. Thus, one of the likely rationales behind Greco-Roman Jews' dissociation with Gentiles was to keep themselves from defilement (idolatry and unclean food).

While opinions are diverse as to who constitute the people of God in the Second Temple literature, Thornhill notes that (1) the notion that only a portion of the Jews are true people of God (remnant theology) is strong among some; (2) there is an overwhelming emphasis on the 'centrality of the Torah and circumcision' as 'markers of identity'; and (3) most consider Gentiles as 'wicked and sinful', though some consider them possibly to be included as the people of God at the eschaton.[54] Gentile inclusion during the Hellenistic period was possible through proselytization. Sim notes that although there were Gentiles, known as worshippers of God or God-fearers, who were attracted to the Jewish way of life (cf. Acts 10:2; 13:6, 50; 16:14; 17:4, 17; 18:7), they were not considered as the people of God unless they became fully proselytized through (1) exclusive worship of God and abandonment of idolatry; (2) Torah observance (including circumcision of males); and (3) integration into the Jewish community.[55]

# Oppositions during the first century

Having introduced the pagan and Jewish religious world view, we will now look into how and why Christian beliefs clashed so strongly with both of them. We will first examine who persecuted Christians and then look at why they did so.

Although the author of Hebrews addresses the issue of persecution, the text is not explicit with regard to the identity of the persecutors or the reason behind the persecution. Therefore, we will not include Hebrews in our discussion below. Nonetheless, as the author and recipients of Hebrews

---

[54] A. Chadwick Thornhill, *The Chosen People: Election, Paul, and Second Temple Judaism* (Downers Grove: InterVarsity Press, 2015), pp. 146, 184, 255. For details on the relevant Second Temple literature, see Thornhill, *Chosen People*, pp. 99–185. See also David C. Sim, 'Jews, Christians and Gentiles: Observations and Some Concluding Remarks', in David C. Sim and James S. McLaren (eds.), *Attitudes to Gentiles in Ancient Judaism and Early Christianity*, LNTS 499 (London: Bloomsbury, 2015), pp. 261–263.

[55] David C. Sim, 'Gentiles, God-Fearers and Proselytes', in David C. Sim and James S. McLaren (eds.), *Attitudes to Gentiles in Ancient Judaism and Early Christianity*, LNTS 499 (London: Bloomsbury, 2015) , pp. 9–27. Sim traces the development of Gentile inclusion into the covenantal people of God from an apparently exclusively ethnic approach during the post-exilic period to an ethnic and cultural (way of life) approach during the Hellenistic period.

were in the same milieu, we can assume that opponents and reasons behind the persecution were largely similar. In chapter 2 below, we will see how the forms of persecution as described in Hebrews may provide us the clue as to who these opponents might have been.

## Who persecuted the Christians?

In this section, we will be detailing the people who persecuted Christians due to their faith in Jesus, as mentioned in the New Testament. In the gospel traditions, Jesus had warned his disciples that they would be persecuted because of their association with him (Mark 13:13 // Matt. 10:12 // Luke 21:17; John 15:18–21). While Mark and Matthew preserve Jesus' saying that persecution will come even from immediate family members, Luke is unique for including relatives and friends as well (Luke 21:16; cf. Mark 13:12 // Matt. 10:21). Furthermore, Jesus predicted that the disciples would stand trial before ruling authorities such as synagogues, local councils, governors and kings (Mark 13:9 // Matt. 10:17–18 //Luke 12:11; 21:12).[56] In this prediction, no other details are given as to whether the charges brought to non-Jewish ruling authorities against the disciples were by Jews or Gentiles. These ruling authorities might or might not be persecuting the disciples, as we will see below. However, the Gospel of John makes it broad enough to encompass opposition from both Jews and Gentiles by using the phrase 'the world hates you' (John 15:18).[57]

Engberg reminds us that different groups of opponents may vary in their motives and may employ different forms of opposition. Therefore, while we divide the opponents into two broad categories – Jewish and pagan – we also note the spectrum of opponents as Engberg suggests:

---

[56] *Synagōgē* (synagogue) may function as a venue for formal legal hearings. See Kenneth D. Litwak, 'Synagogue and Sanhedrin', in Joel B. Green and Lee Martin McDonald (eds.), *The World of the New Testament: Cultural, Social, and Historical Contexts* (Grand Rapids: Baker Academic, 2013), p. 266; Anders Runesson, 'Synagogue', in Joel B. Green, Jeannine K. Brown and Nicholas Perrin (eds.), *Dictionary of Jesus and the Gospels*, 2nd edn (Downers Grove: IVP Academic, 2013), p. 904. In the Gospels and Acts, *synhedrion* (Sanhedrin) mainly refers to Jewish local authorities, but the term is also broadly used in other Greek literature to refer to local councils, including the Roman senate. Peter J. Rhodes and Beate Ego, 'Synhedrion', in Hubert Cancik and Helmuth Schneider (eds.), *Brill's New Pauly*, vol. 14 (Leiden: Brill, 2019), pp. 26–28. Roman high-ranking provincial officials (e.g. procurators) are often referred to using the term *hēgemōn* ('governor'; e.g. Acts 23:24).

[57] See also Lars Kierspel, *The Jews and the World in the Fourth Gospel: Parallelism, Function, and Context*, WUNT 2.220 (Tübingen: Mohr Siebeck, 2006), p. 127.

(1) central authorities (the emperors);

(2) regional authorities (Roman provincial officials);

(3) local authorities (city councils [including the Jewish council San-hedrin]); and

(4) individual [or group] opponents (relatives and non-relatives of Christians).[58]

From the insiders' perspective, we will then discuss a third category – 'satanic opposition', which is absent from the outsiders' perspectives in external sources.

Although a number of Pauline letters mention that Paul and other believers suffered persecution, the identity of some of these opponents are notoriously difficult to ascertain.[59] There are hints in 1 Corinthians 16:9, 2 Corinthians 1:8–10, Philippians 1:28, Galatians 3:5 and 4:29 that he and the believers there faced opposition and suffered for their faith, but Paul is not explicit as to who these opponents are.[60] They may be Jews or pagans or both. Even when 2 Timothy 4:14 names Alexander as Paul's opponent, it is unclear if this person is a Jew or a Gentile.[61] Therefore, in the following we will discuss only those Pauline passages that clearly indicate the opponents as Jews or pagans.

---

[58] Engberg, *Impulsore Chresto*, pp. 18–19. As Engberg's study deals only with pagan opposition, I have included Jewish opposition where relevant. Non-ruling opponents seldom act individually, though there may be an influential individual leading the opposition (e.g. Saul and Demetrius in Acts 7:58 – 8:3 and 19:24–25 respectively).

[59] See e.g. the history of interpretation in Jerry L. Sumney, 'Studying Paul's Opponents: Advances and Challenges', in Stanley E. Porter (ed.), *Paul and His Opponents*, PS 2 (Leiden: Brill, 2005), pp. 7–58.

[60] Both Jewish and Gentile oppositions are possible for both the Philippians and the Galatians. On Phil. 1:28, see Jerry L. Sumney, *'Servants of Satan', 'False Brothers' and Other Opponents of Paul*, JSNTSup 188 (Sheffield: Sheffield Academic Press, 1999), pp. 174–175; John Reumann, *Philippians: A New Translation with Introduction and Commentary*, AYB 33B (New Haven: Yale University Press, 2008), p. 288. *Paschō* in Gal. 3:5 may refer to the experience of the Holy Spirit (BDAG, p. 785, 1; e.g. Longenecker, Martyn) or sufferings from persecution (e.g. Moo, Schreiner). Although the flow of the argument in Gal. 3:1–5 favours its reference to experience, the possibility of referring to persecution cannot easily be dismissed either (cf. Gal. 4:29; 6:12). Richard N. Longenecker, *Galatians*, WBC 41 (Dallas: Word, 1990), p. 104; J. Louis Martyn, *Galatians: A New Translation with Introduction and Commentary*, AB 33A (New York: Doubleday, 1997), p. 285; Thomas R. Schreiner, *Galatians*, ZECNT (Grand Rapids: Zondervan, 2010), p. 185; Douglas J. Moo, *Galatians*, BECNT (Grand Rapids: Baker Academic, 2013), p. 185.

[61] Scholars have mentioned a few possibilities of this Alexander's identity (e.g. Acts 19:33–34; 1 Tim. 1:20) but none are conclusive. See e.g. William D. Mounce, *Pastoral Epistles*, WBC 46 (Dallas: Word, 2000), p. 593; Raymond F. Collins, *1 & 2 Timothy and Titus: A Commentary*, NTL (Louisville: Westminster John Knox, 2012), pp. 284–285.

## Jewish opponents

After the death and resurrection of Jesus, the followers of Jesus began their ministry among the Jews, and thus it was natural that their first opponents were Jewish. In Matthew and Mark, during the lifetime of Jesus oppositions from the Jews were always directed at Jesus, rather than his disciples. However, Luke at times depicts the Jewish leaders as including the disciples when the former were opposing Jesus (Luke 5:30; 6:2).[62] Similarly, according to John, Jewish leaders had already breathed out threats to expel from the synagogue those who confessed Jesus as the Christ (John 9:22; 12:42).[63]

Nonetheless, in Acts, Luke portrays that the disciples begin to be persecuted by the Jewish local authorities only after they proclaim the resurrected Jesus. These Jewish leaders include Pharisees, scribes (experts in the law), Sadducees, chief priests and elders (e.g. Acts 4:5). These leaders are often also members of the Sanhedrin (consisting of the high priest, chief priests, Sadducees and Pharisees), which is the local ruling authority in Jerusalem, akin to the councils of other cities in the Roman Empire.[64]

---

[62] As Cunningham notes, in contrast to Mark 2:16 and Matt. 9:11, where the Jewish leaders question the disciples why Jesus eats with tax collectors and sinners, Luke portrays them directly confronting the disciples: 'Why do you [pl.] eat and drink (*esthiete kai pinete*) with tax collectors and sinners?' (5:30). Luke also uses the stronger word 'grumble' (*gongyzō*) rather than 'say' (*legō*), as used in Mark and Matthew. In Luke 6:2, the Pharisees accuse the disciples of breaking the sabbath, rather than directing their accusation towards Jesus regarding his disciples' action (Mark 2:24; Matt. 12:2). Cunningham, *Through Many Tribulations*, p. 71. Nonetheless, we need to note that opposition did not lead to persecution here.

[63] Scholars debate whether expulsion from the synagogue in the Gospel of John is historical or is reflected anachronistically. See e.g. Barnabas Lindars, 'The Persecution of Christians in John 15:18–16:4a', in *Suffering and Martyrdom in the New Testament* (Cambridge: Cambridge University Press, 1981), pp. 48–69; J. Louis Martyn, *History and Theology in the Fourth Gospel*, 3rd edn, NTL (Louisville: Westminster John Knox, 2003); Edward W. Klink III, 'The Overrealized Expulsion in the Gospel of John', in Paul N. Anderson, Felix Just and Tom Thatcher (eds.), *John, Jesus, and History*, vol. 2: *Aspects of Historicity in the Fourth Gospel*, SBLSym 44 (Atlanta: SBL, 2007), pp. 175–184; John S. Kloppenborg, 'Disaffiliation in Associations and the Ἀποσυνάγωγος of John', *HTS* 67.1 (2011), pp. 1–16; Jonathan Bernier, *Aposynagōgos and the Historical Jesus in John: Rethinking the Historicity of the Johannine Expulsion Passages*, BibInt 122 (Boston: Brill, 2013); 'Jesus, Ἀποσυνάγωγος, and Modes of Religiosity', in R. Alan Culpepper and Paul N. Anderson (eds.), *John and Judaism: A Contested Relationship in Context*, RBS 87 (Atlanta: SBL, 2017), pp. 127–134; Craig A. Evans, 'Evidence of Conflict with the Synagogue in the Johannine Writings', in R. Alan Culpepper and Paul N. Anderson (eds.), *John and Judaism: A Contested Relationship in Context*, RBS 87 (Atlanta: SBL, 2017), pp. 135–154; J. Andrew Doole, 'To Be "an out-of-the-Synagoguer"', *JSNT* 43.3 (2021), pp. 389–410. However, as mentioned on p. 4 above, this study is describing the perspective of the New Testament authors, rather than investigating the historicity of the events.

[64] Litwak, 'Synagogue and Sanhedrin', pp. 268–270.

Luke continues to portray Jewish opposition in Acts as follows. Peter and John, including other apostles, were arrested and imprisoned by the Jewish authorities when the former attracted attention with their proclamation of Jesus' resurrection (Acts 4:1–3) and when increasing numbers of people became believers due to their proclamation, as well as the signs and wonders they performed (Acts 5:12–18).

It is also noteworthy that, even in the earliest days, opposition also arose among Greek-speaking Jews from the diaspora who were residing in Jerusalem (Acts 6:9). They opposed Stephen and brought him before the Sanhedrin (Acts 6:12). Among these Greek-speaking Jews was Saul of Tarsus (Acts 7:58), who initiated the first wave of severe persecution in Jerusalem (Acts 8:1–3). Saul even requested permission from the Sanhedrin to pursue the disciples who had probably fled from Jerusalem to Damascus (Acts 8:1; 9:1–2). Saul was an individual opponent, who sought the help of higher authorities in his effort to stamp out the Jesus movement. During these earliest days, the apostles were charged and tried by the Sanhedrin at the local level.

After Saul became a believer in Jesus, he surprised the Jews at Damascus when he began to proclaim the very message he had opposed earlier – Jesus is the Messiah and the Son of God (Acts 9:20–22). After leaving Damascus, Paul returned to proclaim the name of Jesus and debated with Greek-speaking Jews there (Acts 9:29), probably the same community he had belonged to earlier. The Jews at Damascus and Jerusalem who opposed Paul plotted to kill him (Acts 9:23, 29).

Subsequently, during his missionary journeys (Acts 13 – 19) wherever Paul proclaimed the gospel to the Jews in the diaspora he would face opposition from some of these Greek-speaking Jews – in Pisidian Antioch (13:45, 50), Iconium (14:1), Thessalonica (17:5), Corinth (18:6) and Ephesus (19:9). These Greek-speaking Jews were highly mobile geographically, for some of them travelled from Pisidian Antioch and Iconium to Lystra (14:19), from Thessalonica to Berea (17:13), and some from Asia were even at Jerusalem (21:27) to oppose Paul.

It was these diaspora Jews who incited the crowd to oppose Paul when he was in the Jerusalem temple, triggering a riot that subsequently caused the Roman 'commander' (*chiliarchos*) to keep Paul in custody (Acts 21:27–34). Although some Pharisaic members of the Sanhedrin did not find Paul guilty of any crime, others disagreed and violent disputes broke out (23:9–10). Later, some Jews conspired with the Sanhedrin to kill Paul, causing the Roman commander to transfer him secretly to the Roman governor at Caesarea (Acts 23:23–35). Representatives of the Sanhedrin attempted to bring charges against Paul before the governor twice to no avail, once during the time of Felix (Acts 24:1–27) and again during the time of Festus (Acts 25:1 – 26:32).

Paul, in his letters, testifies how he previously persecuted followers of Jesus (Gal. 1:13–14, 23; Phil. 3:6; 1 Tim. 1:13–16). A number of his letters also detail the persecution he and other believers suffered at the hands of Jewish opponents. In 1 Thessalonians 2:14–15, Paul mentions that both he and believers in Judea (i.e. Jewish Christians) suffered persecution from their own people. In 2 Corinthians 11:23–26, where Paul gives the most detailed description of the persecutions he suffered, he mentions being whipped five times by the Jews (11:24).[65]

In Galatians, Paul portrays his opponents and persecutors as those who advocate Torah observance and circumcision (Gal. 4:29; cf. Phil. 3:2, 18). These opponents are likely believers in Jesus who hold a different view of how Gentiles can be included as the people of God and thus is an intra-Christian dispute.[66] It is interesting to note that although Luke portrays both Christian and non-Christian Jews as opposing Paul with regard to circumcision and Gentile inclusion (Acts 21:21, 27–28; 22:21–22), he portrays only non-Christian Jews as those who persecute Paul. In contrast, Paul claims that he has been persecuted because he does not preach circumcision (Gal. 5:11), implying both parties are his persecutors. Therefore, Paul is apparently not concerned with differentiating his opponents as Christian or non-Christian Jews. Rather, he regards himself as persecuted by the Jews who disagree with him with regard to Torah observance (e.g. circumcision, observance of days), Gentile inclusion as God's people and his authenticity as God's apostle (e.g. Gal. 1:11–12; 2:1–9; 4:10).

In Revelation there is a group of opponents whom Jesus labels as 'those who say that they are Jews but are not' and as a 'synagogue of Satan'; they

---

[65] These whippings most likely took place in synagogues. George H. Guthrie, *2 Corinthians*, BECNT (Grand Rapids: Baker Academic, 2015), p. 556. See n. 56 above on the function of Jewish synagogues.

[66] Although scholars differ in their opinions as to whether these advocates of Torah observance are Jewish or Gentile, most agree that the opponents are believers in Jesus. A few scholars argue that these opponents were non-Christian Jews. For a comprehensive survey, see Ian J. Elmer, *Paul, Jerusalem and the Judaisers: The Galatian Crisis in Its Broadest Historical Context*, WUNT 2.258 (Tübingen: Mohr Siebeck, 2009), pp. 3–26.

blaspheme the saints in Smyrna and are described as liars (Rev. 2:9; 3:9).[67] Scholars differ in their opinion as to whether this group are ethnic non-believing Jews or Judaizing Gentiles.[68] On the one hand, the narrative of Revelation distinguishes between the faithful followers of Jesus as the implied 'true Jews' who inherit the new Jerusalem and are brought into the presence of God in his temple (cf. Rev. 12:17; 14:1; 21:1–3, 7, 22) and 'those who say they are Jews and are not'.[69] On the other hand, it seems too broad to include all the others (non-believing Jews, pagans and the unfaithful apostates)[70] in the latter group. More likely, this latter group refers to Jews who opposed the followers of Jesus, as indicated by the persecutions suffered by the church in Smyrna and Philadelphia.[71]

---

[67] Similarly, the Qumran community labels their intra-Jewish opponents as the 'assembly of Belial' (*'ădat bĕlia'al*) (1QHa X, 22) and 'assembly of deceit' (*'ădat šāw'*) (1QHa XV, 34). *Yāhad* is often rendered as *synagōgē* in the LXX (e.g. Exod. 12:3; Lev. 4:13; Num. 1:2). See also Craig R. Koester, *Revelation: A New Translation with Introduction and Commentary*, AB 38A (New Haven: Yale University Press, 2014), p. 296.

[68] The various views of whom these 'Jews' might refer to may be summarized as follows: (1) the Jewish community in Smyrna and Philadelphia who opposed the followers of Jesus due to their claims about Jesus (e.g. Koester, Mayo, Beale); (2) opponents within the church such as the Balaam- and Jezebel-followers and Nicolaitans (e.g. Frankfurter, Kraft); and (3) Christians who sought refuge in synagogues to escape persecution (e.g. Wilson, Murray). Koester, *Revelation*, pp. 275–276; Philip L. Mayo, *'Those Who Call Themselves Jews': The Church and Judaism in the Apocalypse of John*, PTMS (Eugene: Pickwick, 2006), pp. 53–62; G. K. Beale, *The Book of Revelation: A Commentary on the Greek Text*, NIGTC (Grand Rapids: Eerdmans, 1999), pp. 240–241, 286–288; David Frankfurter, 'Jews or Not?: Reconstructing the "Other" in Rev 2:9 and 3:9', *HTR* 94.4 (2001), pp. 403–425; Heinrich Kraft, *Die Offenbarung des Johannes*, HNT 16a (Tübingen: Mohr, 1974), pp. 60–61; S. G. Wilson, *Related Strangers: Jews and Christians, 70–170 C.E.* (Minneapolis: Fortress, 1995), p. 163; Michele Murray, *Playing a Jewish Game: Gentile Christian Judaizing in the First and Second Centuries CE*, SCJ 13 (Waterloo, Ont.: Wilfrid Laurier University Press, 2004), pp. 73–81.

[69] See also Steven J. Friesen, 'Sarcasm in Revelation 2–3: Churches, Christians, True Jews, and Satanic Synagogues', in David L. Barr (ed.), *The Reality of Apocalypse: Rhetoric and Politics in the Book of Revelation*, SBLSymS 39 (Atlanta: Society of Biblical Literature, 2006), pp. 137–144; Beale, *Revelation*, p. 241.

[70] 'Apostasy' here denotes a Christian perspective of rejecting the truth or the true God (cf. Titus 1:14; Heb. 12:25). In modern sociological terms, this phenomenon of 'disaffiliating' from one's religious faith is termed as 'deconversion'. See Heinz Streib, 'Deconversion', in Lewis R. Rambo and Charles E. Farhadian (eds.), *The Oxford Handbook of Religious Conversion* (Oxford: Oxford University Press, 2014), pp. 271–296.

[71] Contra Duff, who argues that there is no evidence of persecution from non-believing Jews in Revelation, but John intentionally and artificially constructed the depiction of 'false Jews' and 'synagogue of Satan' in the letters to Smyrna and Philadelphia to discourage believers from seeking relief from persecution by joining Jewish synagogues. Paul Duff, 'The "Synagogue of Satan": Crisis Mongering and the Apocalypse of John', in David L. Barr (ed.), *The Reality of Apocalypse: Rhetoric and Politics in the Book of Revelation*, SBLSymS 39 (Atlanta: SBL, 2006), pp. 147–168. Duff's argument from silence is unconvincing, because there is evidence of Jewish persecution prior to (Acts 13 – 14) and after (Ignatius, Polycarp) the writing of Revelation (assuming a late first-century date) in Anatolia for similar reasons. Thus, it is highly probable that the few decades in between would be similar.

## Pagan opponents

In Acts, the first Gentile to harm the leaders of the church at Jerusalem was Herod (King Agrippa I).[72] He killed James, the brother of John, and managed to put Peter in prison (Acts 12:1–4). However, this persecution did not last long with Peter's miraculous escape from prison and Herod's death (Acts 12:5–32). Conversely, Agrippa I's successor, Agrippa II, showed no signs of hostility towards Paul during a legal hearing and, in fact, found that Paul was not guilty of any crime deserving death or imprisonment (Acts 26).

The narrative plot of Acts depicts Greek-speaking Jews of the cities as the ones who initiated most of the opposition, and they usually stirred up influential Gentiles or crowds to oppose Paul (Acts 13:50; 14:2, 19; 17:5, 13). The first Gentile-initiated opposition against Paul in Acts occurred in Philippi (16:19), the second in Athens (17:32) and the third in Ephesus (19:24–27). Nonetheless, the opposition in Athens was mild, with the Athenians mocking Paul, but not initiating other attempts to stop his proclamation. We will look into the reasons behind these three oppositions in the next section. All these three instances were initiated by individuals who were not official authorities.

1 Peter also shows evidence of Gentile opposition mostly likely initiated by individuals (1 Peter 2:12; 4:3–4).[73] It is likely that some Christians were brought before official authorities by their accusers (cf. 1 Peter 3:15),[74]

---

[72] Although the Idumeans had been circumcised since Hasmonean times and had adopted various Jewish ways of life (Josephus, *Antiquities* 13.257–258), quite a number of Second Temple Jewish sources rejected the Idumeans as Jews even though they were circumcised. See Matthew Thiessen, *Contesting Conversion: Genealogy, Circumcision, and Identity in Ancient Judaism and Christianity* (Oxford: Oxford University Press, 2011), pp. 87–110. Marshak also notes that some scholars argue that the Idumean circumcision was a 'political accommodation' rather than a 'cultural transformation'. Adam Marshak, 'Idumea', in John J. Collins and Daniel C. Harlow (eds.), *The Eerdmans Dictionary of Early Judaism* (Grand Rapids: Eerdmans, 2010), p. 760. Furthermore, the Herodian kings were pagan in their cultic practices, as seen in Herod the Great, who built temples for pagan and imperial cults. See Winter, *Divine Honours for the Caesars*, pp. 96–97.

[73] 1 Peter 2:12 and 4:3 use the term 'Gentiles' (*ethnoi*) to refer to non-believers in general. See Paul J. Achtemeier, *1 Peter*, Hermeneia (Minneapolis: Fortress, 1996), p. 177; Karen H. Jobes, *1 Peter*, BECNT (Grand Rapids: Baker Academic, 2005), p. 267; Williams, *Persecution in 1 Peter*, p. 93. While the behaviour described in 1 Peter 4:4 was common among pagans, it does not mean that no Jews would have indulged in these practices. For probable evidence in primary sources, see Jobes, *1 Peter*, p. 268. Nonetheless, it suffices for our purpose that the 'Gentiles' in 1 Peter mostly comprised pagans.

[74] Williams makes a good case that in Anatolia individual disputes might be brought to the civic court to resolve. The legal process in Roman Anatolia was basically 'set in motion by the private accusations of local inhabitants'. The language of answering accusations need not be restricted to informal occasions, but can extend to legal hearings as well. See Williams, *Persecution in 1 Peter*, pp. 138–178, 303–136.

though it is unclear from the text itself if the official authorities persecuted them as well. The exhortations to slaves and wives (1 Peter 2:18 – 3:6) could indicate that they were under pressure or suffering persecution from their household for their faith in Christ.[75]

Luke's characterization of the Roman (Gentile) authorities in Acts is diverse – from hostile to helpful. The 'leading men' at Pisidian Antioch (Acts 13:50), whom the Jews incited, were likely magistrates of the city with sufficient authority to expel Paul and Barnabas from the city.[76] The 'magistrates' (*stratēgoi*) at Philippi had unduly punished Paul before trial, violating his rights as a Roman citizen (Acts 16:22–24). At Thessalonica, when the mob could not find Paul and Silas, they seized Jason and other believers and brought them before the 'city officials' (*politarches*), who released them after receiving bail from them (Acts 17:5–9). At Corinth, the Jews attempted to press charges against Paul before Gallio the 'proconsul' (*anthypatos*) of Achaia. Gallio dismissed the case because he deemed it to be a religious dispute and not a crime (Acts 18:14–16). Even when the crowd beat Sosthenes, the synagogue ruler, before Gallio, he showed no concern (Acts 18:17).[77] At Ephesus, when Demetrius the silversmith incited the people of the city to oppose Paul, they seized Paul's companions, Gaius and Aristarchus, and brought them to the theatre (Acts 19:23–34). In this episode, some 'provincial officials' (*Asiarches*), who were Paul's friends, tried to prevent him from entering the rioting crowd, and it was the city 'official' (*grammateus*) who calmed and dispersed the crowd (Acts 19:35–41). Lastly, when the crowd and conspiring Jews at Jerusalem tried to harm Paul, the Roman commander Lysias repeatedly protected Paul from harm (Acts 21:31–35; 23:17–23).[78]

Luke's portrayal of the Roman officials in Acts seems to show that they were not inherently against Christians due to the latter's faith in Jesus, but were performing their duties to keep law and order.[79] Even if some of their treatment of prisoners was questionable (e.g. beating without trial), they would have done so to any other people regardless. The plot in Acts

---

[75] See also ibid., pp. 301–303, 317–322.

[76] C. K. Barrett, *A Critical and Exegetical Commentary on the Acts of the Apostles*, ICC (London: T&T Clark, 2004), vol. 1, p. 659.

[77] The identity of Sosthenes and whether he was a Christian is debatable. See Eckhard J. Schnabel, *Acts* (Grand Rapids: Zondervan, 2012), p. 765; Keener, *Acts*, vol. 3, p. 2778.

[78] On officials helping Paul in Ephesus and Jerusalem (Acts 19, 23), see also Cunningham, *Through Many Tribulations*, p. 266.

[79] See also Maier, *New Testament Christianity*, p. 77; Engberg, *Impulsore Chresto*, p. 117.

with regard to the Roman officials moves from hostility to help,[80] with an emphasis towards the end that Paul was not found guilty of any punishable crime. This matches Luke's unique emphasis among the Synoptic Gospels that Jesus was also not found guilty of any punishable crime by the Roman official Pontius Pilate (Luke 23:4; cf. John 18:38).[81] These characterizations of the Roman officials and the plot movement could have been his apologetic move for a Gentile audience (including the Romans). It exhibits his theology that the persecution Christians face is not due to any crime they have done, but is a fulfilment of Jesus' prediction that his followers will be persecuted because of their association with him (Luke 21:17).

In the Pauline epistles, it is clear that the Thessalonian believers, consisting of both Jews and Gentiles, faced persecution from their own countrymen (1 Thess. 2:14) and 2 Corinthians also describes the persecutions Paul suffered from the Gentiles. Three times he was beaten with rods (2 Cor. 11:25; cf. Acts 16:20–22), the usual form of punishment meted out by Roman officials.[82] Once he was stoned, likely by a mob consisting of Gentiles and Jews at Lystra (cf. Acts 14:19–20).[83] Paul also describes his escape from Damascus when he was lowered in a basket through a window in the city wall. However, Paul attributes the Damascus persecution to the governor under King Aretas (a Gentile), while Luke depicts the Jews as the persecutors (Acts 9:23–25). Some scholars note it is likely the Jews colluded with the officials of the city to get rid of Paul, as with most of the cases Luke recounts (e.g. Acts 13:50; 14:5; 17:5–9; 18:12–13), or Paul might also have preached among the Nabateans and triggered their hostility (cf. Gal. 1:17).[84]

---

[80] See also Cunningham, *Through Many Tribulations*, p. 266, who notes that it was the Roman officials who saved the disciples in Ephesus (Acts 19:35–41) and Paul in Jerusalem (Acts 21 – 23). Nonetheless, Engberg notes that the Roman official in Jerusalem saved Paul because Paul was a Roman citizen, rather than because of his beliefs in Christ. See Engberg, *Impulsore Chresto*, p. 121.

[81] Cunningham, *Through Many Tribulations*, pp. 285–286.

[82] Guthrie, *2 Corinthians*, p. 557; Margaret E. Thrall, *A Critical and Exegetical Commentary on the Second Epistle of the Corinthians*, 2 vols., ICC (London: T&T Clark International, 2000), vol. 2, p. 739.

[83] Guthrie, *2 Corinthians*, p. 558; Thrall, *Second Epistle of the Corinthians*, vol. 2, p. 738.

[84] For the former view, see Colin G. Kruse, 'The Price Paid for a Ministry Among Gentiles: Paul's Persecution at the Hands of the Jews', in Michael J. Wilkins and Terence Paige (eds.), *Worship, Theology and Ministry in the Early Church*, JSNTSup 87 (Sheffield: JSOT Press, 1992), p. 266, n. 1; Guthrie, *2 Corinthians*, p. 575. For the latter view, see Keener, *Acts*, vol. 2, pp. 1681–1683. On the possibility of Paul's preaching in Nabatea, see Richard Bauckham, 'What if Paul Had Travelled East Rather Than West?', *BibInt* 8.1–2 (2000), pp. 171–184.

Using symbolic language, in Revelation John mentions four sources of persecution – the enormous red serpent,[85] the two beasts from the sea and the earth respectively, and Babylon the whore (Rev. 12 – 13; 17:1 – 19:3). I will discuss this 'enormous red serpent' under 'Satanic opponents' in the next section. John describes the beast from the sea as being given authority to rule over 'every tribe, people, language and nation', to wage war against the saints and to conquer them (Rev. 13:7). 'All the inhabitants of the earth' worship this beast, while another beast that arises from the earth enforces the worship, such that the beasts can cause all who refuse such worship to be killed. It has been well established that the Jewish Scriptures (e.g. Dan. 7:2–8) and apocalyptic literature (e.g. *4 Ezra* 11.1) use the imagery of beast(s) rising from the sea to symbolize oppressive empires and their rulers.[86] The allusion to Daniel 7:2–8, coupled with the description of 'worldwide' worship of the beast, makes it most likely that the imagery is a symbol for the Roman Empire in terms of its ruler, the imperial cults, and those who promote and enforce the imperial cults. Through this imagery John portrays the imperial rulers and their officials who exhibit these characteristics as persecutors of the saints of God.[87]

The other imagery is Babylon the whore, who is portrayed as being drunk with the blood of the saints and of those who bore witness to Jesus (Rev. 17:6). Not only has she slaughtered the saints and prophets of God, but also all who have been slain on earth (Rev. 18:24). From the narrative's characterization, Babylon the whore stands in contrast and in opposition

---

[85] For the explanation of using 'serpent' rather than 'dragon', see n. 96 below.

[86] See e.g. G. K. Beale, *The Use of Daniel in Jewish Apocalyptic Literature and in the Revelation of St. John* (Lanham: University Press of America, 1984), pp. 220–248; Steve Moyise, *The Old Testament in the Book of Revelation*, JSNTSup 115 (Sheffield: Sheffield Academic Press, 1995), pp. 52–54; Koester, *Revelation*, pp. 568–569.

[87] Scholars have debated whether there is a reference to a specific reign of an emperor (e.g. Nero or Domitian) or only a perceived persecution that does not reflect the historical period of its composition. For a survey and critique of these views, see Pieter G. R. de Villiers, 'Persecution in the Book of Revelation', *AcT* 22.2 (2002), pp. 47–70. De Villiers argues that both views are overly restrictive and do not explain the literary nature of the work. He thus proposes that, while John might have been sparked by the historical circumstances he was in, he was also aware of the long history of how God's people had been persecuted and was thus describing a 'paradigmatic' situation his audience were likely to face then and into the future. As this study focuses on describing the New Testament author's theology, a detailed discussion on the historical reference is beyond our scope. Considering the multivalency of symbols in apocalyptic literature, I agree with de Villiers that John could have 'multi-layered' references that transcend one historical period.

to the bride of the Lamb.[88] Thus, the meaning of the symbol is apparent – all 'the others' who do not belong to and who oppose the faithful followers of the Lamb. While scholars differ in their opinion on who the referent of Babylon the whore may be,[89] it is likely that it is a symbol for 'the others' – the (Greco-Roman) society as a whole that opposes the saints of God.[90] It suffices for our purpose that Gentile opponents and persecutors are included here.

We must note that, in reality, not all of 'the others' are persecutors, but that John uses a dualistic framework and the literary device of contrast to delineate his community from the others.[91] As historical evidence leans towards local and sporadic persecution during the late first century, some scholars have doubted if there was such extensive persecution during John's time as depicted in the images of Revelation.[92] Actually, the persecution mentioned in the seven letters, which likely portrays the audience's current situation, corroborates such historical evidence. However, it is important to note that the nature of apocalyptic literature includes a predictive element, which Revelation itself indicates (Rev. 1:1b; 22:6b).

---

[88] Note especially the literary parallel in Rev. 17:1–3 and 21:9–10. The narrative also contrasts two cities – Great Babylon and the New Jerusalem. Both images of 'woman' and 'city' are symbols for communities of people. For details on similar symbolic meaning in the Jewish Scriptures and the Greco-Roman world, see W. Gordon Campbell, 'Bride-City and Whore-City', in *Reading Revelation: A Thematic Approach* (Cambridge: James Clarke, 2012), pp. 225–260; Adela Y. Collins, 'Feminine Symbolism in the Book of Revelation', in Amy-Jill Levine and Maria Mayo Robbins (eds.), *A Feminist Companion to the Apocalypse of John*, FCNTECW 13 (London: T&T Clark, 2010), pp. 125–126.

[89] For the history of interpretation of Babylon the whore, see Koester, *Revelation*, pp. 637–641.

[90] For details of the argument, see J.-W. Sun, 'Conquering Idolatry: John's Literary Creativity and Purpose in His Depiction of Babylon the Whore', ThM thesis, Singapore Bible College, 2020 (in Chinese).

[91] In this book, I am adopting Bauckham's definition of 'dualism' as 'the various forms that the polarity of good and evil takes in Jewish and Christian literature' and 'duality' as 'forms of thinking that divide reality into two contrasting, but not opposed, categories, such as Creator and creation'. Richard Bauckham, *Gospel of Glory: Major Themes in Johannine Theology* (Grand Rapids: Baker Academic, 2015), p. 123. The adjective 'dualistic' may be used to modify both terms above, and the 'dualistic framework' in Revelation includes both 'dualism' and 'duality'.

[92] E.g. Leonard L. Thompson, *The Book of Revelation: Apocalypse and Empire* (New York: Oxford University Press, 1990), pp. 95–115; Adela Y. Collins, *Crisis and Catharsis: The Power of the Apocalypse* (Philadelphia: Westminster, 1984), pp. 84–110. Thompson argues that there was barely any persecution, while Collins suggests that it is John who perceived the persecution to be such. As deSilva notes, while Thompson is likely correct regarding the 'bottom-up' approach of ascribing divine titles to Domitian, he has 'understated the degree of hostility experienced by Christians'. David A. deSilva, *Seeing Things John's Way: The Rhetoric of the Book of Revelation* (Louisville: Westminster John Knox, 2009), p. 51.

Therefore, while persecution might not have been empire-wide for John's initial audience, John's visions warn them that the situation will escalate in the future.

## Satanic opponents

Satan – sometimes called 'the devil' or 'the evil one' – as the opponent of God and his people is already evident in the gospel traditions. Nonetheless, Satan is portrayed as a tempter influencing believers to oppose the will of God (e.g. Peter's attempt to stop Jesus from dying at the hands of the religious leaders), rather than as an instigator of persecution.[93] In Luke 10:18, Satan is portrayed as being cast down from heaven when the kingdom of God is proclaimed with signs and wonders such as exorcism (Luke 10:1–20). In addition, Luke and John interpret Judas's betrayal as being prompted by Satan.[94] Both Luke and John also portray those who opposed Jesus and the disciples' gospel message as 'children of the devil' (John 8:44; Acts 13:10), while Matthew is unique in portraying pseudo-disciples as belonging to the devil (Matt. 13:24–30, 36–43; 25:41).[95] Paul also associates his opponents with the work of the devil (2 Cor. 11:4; 2 Tim. 2:25–26) and reckons the devil as the one who tempts believers to apostatize (1 Thess. 3:5).

Revelation develops most fully the concept of Satan as the instigator of persecution. While the prophetic tradition in the Jewish Scriptures uses the ANE mythic serpent-like chaos creature as a symbol for the imperial ruler who oppresses God's people (e.g. Jer. 51:34 referring to Nebuchadnezzar; Ezek. 29:3 referring to Pharaoh),[96] this enormous red serpent is identified as the ancient serpent called the devil or Satan (Rev. 12:9). It will be thrown down from heaven when the kingdom of God and the authority of Christ has come (Rev. 12:7–10), a tradition likely associated with the one mentioned in Luke 10:18. It persecutes the woman, her son and the rest of

---

[93] Mark 1:13 (cf. Matt. 4:1–11 // Luke 4:1–13); Mark 4:15 // Matt. 13:19 // Luke 8:12; Mark 8:33 // Matt. 16:23; Luke 22:31. See also Acts 5:3.

[94] Compare Luke 22:3, John 6:70–71, 13:2, 27 with Mark 14:10 and Matt. 26:14–15.

[95] See also Gundry, *Matthew*, pp. 261–265, 271–275, 511–515.

[96] The Hebrew word for this creature is *tannîn* or *liwyātān*, frequently translated as *drakōn* or *ophis* in the LXX (e.g. Ps. 74:13–14 MT // 73:13–14 LXX; Isa. 27:1; Jer. 51:34 MT // 28:34 LXX; Ezek. 29:3). In ANE and Greco-Roman mythology, there are serpent-like creatures similar to this imagery in Rev. 12. See Koester, *Revelation*, pp. 555–559. Thus, I prefer to render *drakōn* in Rev. 12 as 'serpent' rather than 'dragon', because the latter tends to conjure up images of the medieval European dragon or the East Asian dragon (both lizard-like rather than serpent-like) in the mind of modern readers.

her offspring (Rev. 12:4–6, 13–17). This serpent imagery bears similarity to the Jewish prophetic tradition, and forms a likely intertextual connection to give the first hint that even in ancient times before John the oppression of God's people is associated with evil forces behind it.[97]

This serpent is also the one who gives authority to the beast from the sea (Rev. 13:4), who in turn gives authority to the beast from the land (Rev. 13:12). The imagery of seven heads and ten horns shared by the serpent and the beast (Rev. 12:3; 13:1; 17:3) shows their close association. This shared imagery and the receiving of authority ultimately from the serpent together reveal the satanic power and instigation behind the persecution of the saints by the two beasts. Worship of the beast goes hand in hand with worship of the enormous red serpent (Rev. 13:4).[98]

# Why do Christians face persecution? Perspectives of insiders and outsiders

In this section, we will first focus on the insiders' perspective – how the New Testament authors perceive and portray their persecutors. This first perspective will contribute directly to describing their theology of facing persecution. Subsequently, based on both the New Testament and external historical sources, we will attempt to understand the outsiders' perspective – how the opponents portrayed, and the reasons for opposing, Christians. This second perspective will function as a background to help us understand the motives and forms of persecution meted out to Christians, while both perspectives will help us understand the diverse Christian responses (see chapter 2 below).

## Insiders' perspectives

The gospel tradition clearly explains that the disciples will face persecution due to their association with Jesus (Mark 13:13 // Matt. 10:12 // Luke 21:17; John 15:18–21). According to John, persecution stems from the rejection of Jesus' teachings (John 8:37; 15:20). In the Gospels, these rejected teachings mainly revolve around Sabbath observance and Jesus' sayings. His opponents interpreted some of these sayings as Jesus' claims

---

[97] See also Beale, *Revelation*, pp. 632–634, 686.

[98] As Koester notes, the Jews understood worshipping idols as equivalent to worshipping demons (e.g. Deut. 32:17; cf. *1 En.* 19.1; 99.7–9; *Jub.* 22.17; 2Q23 1, 7–8; *T. Job* 3.3–4) and this concept is also reflected in Paul (1 Cor. 10:19–21). See Koester, *Revelation*, p. 571.

to be divine: he is the Son of God and Messiah.[99] For Matthew and Luke, unbelieving Israel will persecute the disciples who proclaim Jesus' kingdom message, in the same way their ancestors persecuted the prophets (Matt. 23:29–35; Luke 11:47–51).[100] Their obduracy to God's appeal to repent through his messengers is the cause of persecution.

In John's Gospel, anyone who confesses Jesus as the Messiah runs the risk of being persecuted by the Jewish authorities (John 9:22; 12:42). All four Gospels note that, for the Jews, such confession amounts to blasphemy and deserves death (Mark 14:61–64 // Matt. 26:63–66 // John 19:7; cf. Luke 23:67–71).[101] Enmity also arose when Jesus publicly denounced the Jewish leaders.[102] In addition, John notes Jesus' explanation of the reason behind the persecution: 'the time is coming when anyone who kills you will think they are offering a service to God. They will do such things because they have not known the Father or me' (John 16:2–3).[103] Verse 3 portrays the insiders' perspective, while verse 2 the outsiders' perspective. While the immediate context refers to Jewish opponents, it is nevertheless also true for pagan opponents, as we will see from the outsiders' perspective below.

In the narratives of Acts, Luke often provides reasons behind the persecution. After the death of Jesus, the disciples (including Paul) began to proclaim the resurrection of Jesus and him as the Messiah whom God promised in the Scriptures.[104] As in the Gospels, this claim of Jesus' messiahship continues to be a main cause of Jewish opposition. In their proclamation, the disciples also made the Jewish leaders guilty of Jesus' death (Acts 3:15b; 7:52; 10:39; 13:27–28; cf. 1 Thess. 2:15). The Jewish

---

[99] On Sabbath controversies, see Mark 2:23 – 3:6; Matt. 12:1–14; Luke 6:1–11; 13:10–17; 14:1–6; John 5:1–16; 7:21–24; 9:14–16. The perceived divine claims include the following: (1) Jesus' ability to forgive sins (Mark 2:7 // Matt. 9:1–3 // Luke 5:21); (2) his pre-existence before Abraham (John 8:59); (3) Jesus himself as the temple, but also perceived as a threat to destroy the existing physical temple (Mark 14:58 // Matt. 26:61; John 2:19–21); (4) Jesus does the work of God his Father (John 5:17–18); (5) admitting to be the Messiah and the Son of God (Mark 14:61–64 // Matt. 26:63–66 // Luke 22:67–71).

[100] Hare argues that Matthew is interested only in portraying the 'obduracy' of Israel as the theological cause of persecution and that 'the dispute over Torah, while clearly perceived by Matthew as a point of friction between the Church and the synagogue, is not treated by him as a cause of the persecution'. Hare, *Jewish Persecution of Christians*, pp. 144–145. This is because, for Hare, Matthew is interested only in presenting the theological, not the sociological, cause of persecution.

[101] See pp. 20–21 above on Jewish monotheism in the first century.

[102] Mark 11:15–18; 12:1–12 (// Matt. 21:33– 46); Luke 4:28; John 8:44.

[103] Unless otherwise indicated, Scripture quotations are from the NIV.

[104] On proclaiming Jesus' resurrection, see Acts 3:13–15a; 4:8–12; 7:2–50; 10:40; 13:29–31; 17:3, 18; 23:6; 24:15; 26:23. On Jesus as the Messiah God promised in the Scriptures, see Acts 3:18–26; 9:20–22; 10:41–43; 13:16–26, 32–41; 17:2–3; 18:28; 26:6, 22; 28:23.

leaders were annoyed by both the message of Jesus' resurrection (Acts 4:1–2) and the accusation of being responsible for his death (Acts 5:28). The Sadducees were not the only ones who did not believe in resurrection (Acts 23:8); some Athenians also did not believe in it (Acts 17:32).

According to Luke, the message of Gentile inclusion as the people of God without receiving circumcision and obeying the law of Moses was unacceptable to many Jews. This was so for both Jews who believed in Jesus (Acts 15:1, 5) and those who did not.[105] Luke mentions rumours that Paul had been teaching diaspora Jews not to practise circumcision or obey the law of Moses (Acts 21:21). This would have provoked Jews who were zealous for the law. Paul's teachings that justification is by believing in Christ and not by works of the law (Gal. 2:15 – 3:29; Rom. 2:1 – 5:2) corroborate Luke's account. In fact, Paul himself thought he had been persecuted because he did not preach circumcision as necessary for justification (Gal. 5:11; cf. 5:6; 6:15). These Jewish opponents could have misconstrued Paul or wilfully twisted his teachings to create opposition against him. At Jerusalem, the crowd quietened down to listen to Paul when he spoke in Aramaic (Acts 21:40), but suddenly began to shout and opposed him when he mentioned that God had sent him to the Gentiles (Acts 22:22–23). This sudden negative reaction showed how averse the Jews were to the idea of Gentile inclusion. From Paul's own perspective in 1 Thessalonians 2:16, his Jewish opponents had prevented him from proclaiming the message of salvation to the Gentiles.

From Luke's perspective, other than the disagreements with regard to Jesus as the Messiah and Gentile inclusion, the Jewish opponents were also jealous of Peter (Acts 5:17) and Paul (Acts 13:45, 50; 17:5) when many people became followers of Jesus.[106] It was not just about losing a substantial number of their adherents to the Jesus community (Acts 13:43; 17:4), but the ramifications – loss of honour and economic benefits, which I will discuss below from the outsiders' perspective.

In contrast to the Jewish opponents, whose motives for persecuting Paul and followers of Jesus were reckoned to be selfish (jealousy, loss of honour and economic benefits), Luke portrays Paul's motive for persecuting followers of Jesus before his encounter with Jesus as being zealous

---

[105] See pp. 22–23 above.
[106] Keener notes that 'jealousy was a common motive to attribute to one's enemies'. For ancient examples, see Keener, *Acts*, vol. 2, pp. 1206–1207, 2094.

for God (Acts 22:3). Luke recounts Paul's personal testimony, in which Paul described himself as convinced that these followers of Jesus were wrong and thus he sought all means to stamp out this movement (Acts 26:9–11). Once again, Paul's own testimony in Galatians 1:13–14 and Philippians 3:6 regarding his former misplaced zeal for the traditions of his ancestors corroborates Luke's account. In addition, 1 Timothy 1:13–16 states Paul's assessment of his former self as a 'blasphemer', a 'persecutor', a 'violent man' and 'the worst of sinners' and his reason for persecution as 'ignorance and unbelief'.

According to Luke's analysis, self-serving political reasons also account for certain Gentile persecutions. Herod in order to please the Jews had persecuted the church and its leaders James and Peter (Acts 12:3).[107] Similarly, Felix, the governor of Judea, also kept Paul imprisoned for a prolonged period in order to grant a favour to the Jews (Acts 24:27). Luke exposed another selfish reason behind this unfair prolonged imprisonment – Felix was hoping that Paul would offer him a bribe to gain release from prison (Acts 24:26).

In 1 Peter the persecution suffered by Christians is attributed to three reasons: (1) accusation of wrongdoing (1 Peter 2:12);[108] (2) the good works they did (1 Peter 2:20; 3:14, 17); and (3) forsaking a former sinful lifestyle (1 Peter 4:4). However, the text does not provide details on what kind of wrong Christians were accused of or what kind of good works led to persecution. It is also noteworthy that 1 Peter presents 'good works' as both the cause of and response to hostility (1 Peter 2:12, 15; 3:16, 4:19). In 2 Timothy 3:12, Paul declares that 'everyone who wants to live a godly life in Christ Jesus will be persecuted'. As a cause of persecution, godly living for Paul is akin to good works in 1 Peter. 'Good works' and 'godly living' from the insiders' perspective could be viewed as evil from the outsiders' perspective. Thus, we will need to examine underlying factors from the outsiders' perspective below. I will also discuss 'good works' as the response of persecution in chapter 2 below.

---

[107] For other probable historical reasons not directly reflected in Acts, see Schnabel, 'Persecution of Christians', pp. 531–534.

[108] We should note that 1 Peter regards suffering punishment from wrongdoing such as theft, murder or other criminal offences as justly deserved (1 Peter 4:15), but sees suffering for the name of Christ and as a Christian as honourable and undeserved (1 Peter 4:14, 16), equivalent to suffering due to 'doing good' (1 Peter 2:20; 3:14, 17). Thus, the latter two can be regarded as persecution according to my definition.

As mentioned above, Revelation is unique in portraying Satan as the instigator of persecution. The defeat of Satan – the serpent – in the cosmic battle and his expulsion from heaven marks the beginning of the persecution of 'the woman' and 'the rest of her offspring' (Rev. 12:13–17),[109] with the latter specifically referring to 'those who keep God's commands and hold fast their testimony about Jesus' (Rev. 12:17 ).[110] The serpent 'wages war' (*poiēsai polemon*) against the saints (Rev. 12:17) because it was 'enraged' due to his failed attempts and inability to foil God's protection of the woman (Rev. 12:14–16). The beast was then able to 'wage war' (*poiēsai polemon*) with the saints and to conquer them, because the serpent gave him the power to do so (Rev. 13:2, 7). This vision clearly portrays the reason behind the persecution from a spiritual perspective.

## Outsiders' perspectives

In order for us to appreciate the New Testament authors' exhortation on how their audience should respond to persecution, it is essential that we understand the outsiders' perspective as a background. From the outsiders' perspective, Christians are to be opposed for the following reasons:

1 Threat to dearly held traditional values.
2 Threat of economic losses.
3 (Alleged) vilification of opponents.
4 Threat of social unrest.

---

[109] Although scholars have differing opinions regarding the referent of 'the woman', it is most likely that 'the woman' is a symbol for God's people throughout the generations. I would argue that 'God's people' is a better term to describe the referent than 'Jews' or 'Israel', because the latter tends to have ethnic and political overtones. Even in the Old Testament, God's people are defined according to their allegiance to Yahweh regardless of ethnic or political affiliations. From the very beginning to the last days, God's people are defined by their faith in Yahweh, rather than their ethnicity, consisting of both faithful descendants of Jacob and 'a community of nations' who have 'joined themselves with Yahweh' (cf. Gen. 35:11; Zech. 2:11; e.g. Ruth). See Chee-Chiew Lee, '*Gôyim* in Genesis 35:11 and the Abrahamic Promise of Blessings for the Nations', *JETS* 52.3 (2009), pp. 467–482.

[110] The concept of cosmic war behind the persecution of God's people stems from the Second Temple Jewish tradition, where war on earth is a manifestation of cosmic war (cf. Dan. 10:1–21), with the archangel Michael as the protector of God's people (Dan. 10:13, 21). On the term 'prince' being applied to angels, see John J. Collins, *Daniel: A Commentary on the Book of Daniel*, Hermeneia (Minneapolis: Fortress, 1993), pp. 374–375; Carol A. Newsom and Brennan W. Breed, *Daniel: A Commentary*, OTL (Louisville: Westminster John Knox, 2014), pp. 332–333. See also the Greek text of Esther: Addition A LXX vv. 1–5 [NRSV 11:1–10]; Addition F LXX v. 4 [NRSV 10:7], in which the vision of the two fighting serpents (*drakontes*) referred to Mordecai and Haman, the latter persecuting the Jews throughout the Persian Empire and the former fighting against him.

These reasons are common to both non-Christian Jews and pagans, although the content of the conflict may take different forms.[111]

### 1 Threat to dearly held traditional values

From the Pauline epistles, Kruse discerns five reasons why Paul suffered persecution from the perspective of his Jewish opponents.[112] First, since Paul was not the only one who attempted to destroy those who proclaimed the faith previously, it is not surprising that those who were like him previously would persecute him when he now preached this same faith. Since he was previously in league with the high priests (Acts 9:1–2), it is no wonder that these Jewish leaders would persecute him because he had switched sides. Second, the things his Jewish contemporaries deemed as essential to faith and identity – circumcision, ethnicity, observance of the law as interpreted by ancestral tradition – Paul now regarded as 'loss' (*zēmia*) rather than 'gain' (*kerdē*) (Phil. 3:7–8). This would have triggered anger and violent opposition. Third, Paul's insistence that works of the law do not lead to justification would have been deemed as causing people to neglect of the law of Moses and promoting sin (cf. Gal. 2:17). Fourth, Paul's denial of 'the necessity of circumcision' for justification would be 'offensive' to the Jews (cf. Gal. 5:11). Finally, immorality among some believers (e.g. 1 Cor. 5:1–2; 6:12–20) could have been deemed to be the result of Paul's law-free gospel that 'relaxed ethical demands' (cf. Rom. 3:7–8).

The second to fourth reasons Kruse suggests reflect how the first-century Jews viewed the Christian message as a threat to traditional values they held dearly. The fifth reason is perceived as a negative consequence of abandoning the law of Moses. The first is their response to such perceived threats. Other perceived threats to dearly held traditional values include the apparent 'questioning' of the contemporaneous traditional Jewish understanding of the temple, the Holy City, and the Sabbath or its Christian reinterpretation, as reflected in the Gospels and other New Testament writings.[113]

---

[111] See also Penner (*Shadow of the Cross*, p. 162), who notes the following reasons: religious, political, social, economic and emotional.

[112] Kruse, 'Price Paid for a Ministry', pp. 267–271.

[113] Hare, *Jewish Persecution of Christians*, pp. 3–6. E.g. Jesus' prediction of the destruction of the temple and Holy City due to the Jews' rejection of him as the Messiah (Luke 19:41–44), the body of Jesus (John 2:19–22) and the community of believers (1 Cor. 3:16–17; 1 Peter 2:4–8) as the temple of God.

From the pagan outsiders' perspective there are a number of reasons for strongly opposing Christians. The primary reason is the Christians' withdrawal from pagan worship (cf. 1 Thess. 1:9, 'turned to God from idols to serve the living and true God'), which would include non-participation in worship of both traditional gods and the emperor (for the secondary reason, see the section below on '[Alleged] vilification of opponents').[114] This reason has further ramifications: I will discuss the first one below and the second one in the section 'Threat of economic losses'.

The first ramification of the Christians' withdrawal from pagan worship is that the denial of other gods is deemed to be highly offensive and dangerous (for the second ramification, see p. 47 below). New gods can be added to the pantheon for worship without much difficulty, but exclusive worship of only one God in denial of others is very dangerous. For the pagans, this would cause dishonour to their revered gods (cf. Acts 19:26–27). In a culture steeped in honour and shame, shame is a 'social catastrophe'; if loss of honour of one member brings dishonour to the whole community,[115] how much more is the whole community dishonoured when its revered gods have been dishonoured. Not only so, but denial of the gods also indicates shameful ingratitude towards the benefactions received from the gods, and will thus anger the gods, bringing punishment to individuals or the community in the form of disasters (natural disasters, illnesses, etc.).[116] Christians could easily be blamed as the cause of these disasters for their non-participation in cultic activities.[117] Similarly, non-participation in the imperial cult and denial of the emperor's divinity amounted to ingratitude (at the least) for the emperor's benefaction, and treason (at the worst) when a 'Lord and God' other than Caesar was proclaimed. For the pagans, ingratitude might lead to withdrawal of benefactions from the patron god or the emperor, a

---

[114] See also Williams, *Persecution in 1 Peter*, pp. 258–275. Williams describes two 'behavioural causes' for the conflict: suffering from social withdrawal and for 'good works'/'doing good'. Social withdrawal includes non-participation in voluntary associations and the pagan (including imperial) cult.

[115] Richard L. Rohrbaugh, 'Honor: Core Value in the Biblical World', in Dietmar Neufeld and Richard E. DeMaris (eds.), *Understanding the Social World of the New Testament* (Milton Park: Routledge, 2009), p. 112.

[116] E.g. Suetonius (*Nero* 56–57; *Domitianus* 15.3–6) reckoned that both Nero and Domitian were punished because of their excessive worship of one deity to the neglect of others (*superstitio*).

[117] See also Williams, *Persecution in 1 Peter*, p. 256. This is reflected in later second-century works; e.g. Tertullian, *Apology* 40.2.

consequence perceived as bad enough. However, treason was worse and highly dangerous, because it invited Roman military suppression and bloodshed. We can imagine why local authorities would be keen to promote the imperial cult and punish those who did not comply (cf. Rev. 13:11–17).

It is important to note that a number of divine titles the early church used of Jesus (e.g. Son of God, great high priest, Lord and God) were nearly identical to those used by the people of the Roman emperor – Augustus and his successors were called '(grand)sons of (a) god' and 'the great high priest' (*pontifex maximus*; rendered as *archiereus* in Greek; cf. Heb. 4:15; 6:20); Claudius was called 'the saviour of all mankind' (cf. John 4:42; 1 Tim. 4:10); Nero was called 'the lord of all the world'.[118]

With this in mind, it is understandable that the crowd and the city officials of Thessalonica were 'in a turmoil' when Paul and Silas were accused of 'defying Caesar's decrees, saying that there is another king, one called Jesus' (Acts 17:7 ).[119] Both Augustus (Dio Cassius 56.25.5–6) and Tiberius (Dio Cassius 57.15.8) had earlier decreed that pronouncements or prophecies of new rulers were prohibited during the reign of the current emperor. In AD 41, Claudius had issued a decree to the Alexandrian Jews to warn them against colluding with Jewish revolutionaries from Egypt or Syria, or face imperial punishment (*P.Lond.*1912, ll. 96–99). These could be the decrees referred to in Acts 17:7. Paul and Silas were accused of inciting the Thessalonians to shift their allegiance from Caesar to Jesus (i.e. rejecting the rule of Caesar), amounting to treason and thus punishable. This accusation was not entirely without basis, as we will see below.

When Paul wrote to the Thessalonians, he mentioned that they had turned 'from idols to serve the living and true God' (1 Thess. 1:9). This would include not just abandoning the worship of traditional gods, but also no longer participating in the imperial cult – an outward expression reckoned as rebellion. Paul also proclaimed that this Jesus is the 'Son from heaven' who will come again (1 Thess. 1:10). In addition, Paul also mentions 'the man of lawlessness' who will exalt himself as God above all other gods

---

[118] For inscriptional and literary evidence, see Winter, *Divine Honours for the Caesars*, pp. 62–77. On the implications of the divine title 'Son of God', see also Peppard, *Son of God*, pp. 31–49.

[119] Keener, *Acts*, vol. 3, pp. 2552–2555.

and be worshipped in God's temple (2 Thess. 2:3–4).[120] Although Paul is not explicit in whom this statement refers to, we can reasonably infer that he was referring to the deification of Roman emperors and possibly especially Caligula's failed attempt to set up his statue in Jerusalem around AD 41.[121] Furthermore, although Paul's eschatology is mainly developed from Jewish apocalyptic imagery, a number of terms he uses overlap with language used in imperial contexts, such as 'coming' and 'manifestation' of Christ (*parousia, epiphaneia*; 1 Thess. 4:15; 2 Thess. 2:8), 'meeting' (*apantēsis*; 1 Thess. 4:17), 'peace and safety' (*eirēnē kai asphaleia*; 1 Thess. 5:3a).[122] Regardless of whether Paul is deliberate in using these terms as a critique of imperial Rome, they can certainly be perceived as such by the audience, who may be sensitive to imperial language. As Winter notes, although these titles and terms used of Jesus are developed mainly from the Jewish Scriptures and tradition, their 'unhappy coincidence' with imperial usage posed a great challenge for early Christians.[123]

Additionally, Winter notes that Paul uses the term 'the so-called' (*hoi legomenoi*) to refer to the pagan gods (2 Thess. 2:4; cf. 1 Cor. 8:5), a term 'also used of kings, philosophers and sophists when false claims were being made of their actual status'.[124] Such a term reflects Paul's theology of monotheism and his understanding that these other gods were wrongly regarded as gods. Similarly, the book of Revelation presents a strong resistance against pagan cults (both traditional gods and imperial cults) and anti-Roman sentiment (Rev. 2:12–29; 13:1 – 14:13).

This perception of Christians as a threat seems to be reflected by later second-century Roman historians (Suetonius and Tacitus) when they recount Nero's persecution of Christians.[125] According to Suetonius (*Life*

---

[120] As Winter notes, this language sounds very similar to that found in official inscriptions, where emperors such as Augustus and Claudius were called 'the greatest' or 'the most divine' god. Winter, *Divine Honours for the Caesars*, p. 261.

[121] James R. Harrison, *Paul and the Imperial Authorities at Thessalonica and Rome: A Study in the Conflict of Ideology*, WUNT 273 (Tübingen: Mohr Siebeck, 2011), pp. 85–95; Gary S. Shogren, *1 and 2 Thessalonians*, ZECNT (Grand Rapids: Zondervan, 2012), pp. 281–282.

[122] For literary and inscriptional sources for the imperial context, see Harrison, *Paul and the Imperial Authorities*, pp. 56–63.

[123] Winter, *Divine Honours for the Caesars*, p. 93.

[124] Ibid., pp. 212–213.

[125] Nero's execution of Christians is regarded as persecution because Christians were unfairly and cruelly treated when Nero made them the scapegoat for the great fire in Rome. Nonetheless, it is clear from Tacitus' description that Nero was not persecuting Christians because of their beliefs, but rather capitalizing on Christians as a community already very much detested by the Roman populace. See also Harrison, 'Persecution of Christians', pp. 288–289.

*of Nero* 16.2 [Rolfe]), Christians were regarded as 'a class of men given to a new and mischievous [*maleficus*: 'wicked, harmful']¹²⁶ superstition [*superstitio*]'. Tacitus (*Annals* 15.44; [Jackson]) mentions that Christians were 'loathed for their vices', and their 'pernicious superstition [*superstitio*]' was like a disease, spreading from Judea to Rome, 'where all things horrible or shameful in the world' became popular; and they were punished eventually on the charge of 'hatred of the human race'.

What could 'wicked, harmful, horrible, and shameful vices' and 'hatred of the human race' refer to? From my analysis of the first-century background and the New Testament texts above, these 'wicked, harmful, horrible, and shameful vices' most likely refer to their abandonment of and non-participation in pagan and imperial cults.¹²⁷ This 'hatred of the human race' most likely refers to (1) the Christians' alienation from society through withdrawal from social life, which mostly involved the pagan cult,¹²⁸ which I will discuss in more detail below; and (2) the perceived danger of angering the gods. To the Romans, Christian practice was a *superstitio – religio* carried to the extreme due to their surpassing reverence for and sole allegiance to one God, thereby denouncing other gods.

From the above we can discern what wrongdoing the recipients of 1 Peter were accused of and what kind of good works (see p. 39 above) could possibly lead to persecution 'because of the name of Christ' (*en onomati Christou*) and 'as a Christian . . . because of this name' (*hōs christianos . . . en tō onomati toutō*)¹²⁹ (1 Peter 4:14, 16).¹³⁰ It is essential for us to understand

---

¹²⁶ James Morwood (ed.), *Pocket Oxford Latin Dictionary: Latin–English*, 3rd edn (Oxford: Oxford University Press, 2005), s.v. 'maleficus'.

¹²⁷ See also Smith, 'Book of Revelation', p. 344, n. 68.

¹²⁸ 'Hatred of the human race' is similar to Tacitus' charge against Jews for their disdain of Gentiles (*Histories* 5.5).

¹²⁹ Byzantine manuscripts read *en tō merei toutō*, 'in this situation' (P 307. 642. 1448. 1735 Byz), but all other manuscripts read *en tō onomati toutō*, 'because of this name' (𝔓72 ℵ A B Ψ 5. 33. etc.), supported by early translations (latt sy co; Cyr). Based on overwhelming external support, it is likely that *onomati* is the more authentic reading.

¹³⁰ Suffering because of 'the name of Christ' (1 Peter 4:14) stems from the gospel tradition (see p. 24 above) and means that Christians face persecution due to their association with Jesus and their opponents' rejection of the gospel message. Given that the two phrases in 1 Peter 4:14 'insulted because of the name of Christ' and 4:16 'suffer as a Christian' are similar, some scholars think that the latter means suffering as a result of living in accord with the gospel. See e.g. Earl Richard, *Reading 1 Peter, Jude, and 2 Peter: A Literary and Theological Commentary*, RNTS (Macon: Smyth & Helwys, 2000), p. 194; Jobes, *1 Peter*, p. 290. However, Williams argues that the name 'Christian' (*christianos*) was a chargeable offence in the judicial court. This is because (1) the phrase was juxtaposed with other criminal offences such as a 'murderer or thief or criminal or . . . troublemaker' (NET; *phoneus ē kleptēs ē kakopoios ē hōs allotriepiskopos*); (2) the name *christianos* was criminalized during the time of Nero, such that

'good works' from both the Judeo-Christian as well as the Greco-Roman tradition.[131] From the text of 1 Peter, 'good works' seems to include (1) behaviours and deeds that would be approved as good by God at the eschatological judgment (cf. 2:12); (2) ethical behaviours deemed as good by Hellenistic and Jewish culture (e.g. love, submission, honour; 2:14–15, 17; 3:2, 4, 8–12); and (3) abstinence from unethical behaviour (2:1, 11).[132]

According to the citation of Psalm 34:12–16 in 1 Peter 3:10–12, good works are mostly depicted as virtuous behaviour. Nonetheless, for the Jews during the Second Temple period, good works began to take on the meaning of fulfilling the law of Moses, which includes virtues, good deeds to help others, as well as faithfulness to God by not participating in idolatry, an understanding that continues into the New Testament.[133] Therefore, non-participation in idolatry as a form of 'good work' and 'godly living' from the Christian (insiders') perspective would be regarded as 'wrongdoing' from the pagan (outsiders') perspective, thus resulting in opposition and persecution.[134]

---

(note 130 *cont.*) even though Christians were not sought out, they could be punished solely based on confessing this name if charges were brought against them; and (3) the second-century practice of conviction based on confessing the name 'Christian' was a continuation from the first century. See Williams, *Persecution in 1 Peter*, pp. 179–236, 275–297. Nonetheless, as Elliott notes, Williams's thesis remains only a possibility because there is no historical evidence to support it as a practice in the first century. See John H. Elliott, review of *Persecution in 1 Peter: Differentiating and Contextualizing Early Christian Suffering by Travis B. Williams*, *BTB* 46.4 (2016), pp. 211–212.

[131] While scriptural citations and allusions show the influence of Jewish traditions, the recipients of 1 Peter comprise both Jews and Gentiles. See e.g. Jobes, *1 Peter*, pp. 23–24; Lewis R. Donelson, *I & II Peter and Jude: A Commentary*, NTL (Louisville: Westminster John Knox, 2010), pp. 9–10. Thus, it is likely that the concept of 'good works' not only reflects Jewish understanding but is also expressed in ways understandable to the recipients in their Greco-Roman context.

[132] In 1 Peter, these 'good works' are described using the adjectives *agathos* and *kalos*, and their various nominal and verbal forms. See Travis B. Williams, *Good Works in 1 Peter: Negotiating Social Conflict and Christian Identity in the Greco-Roman World*, WUNT 337 (Tübingen: Mohr Siebeck, 2014), p. 3.

[133] Ibid., pp. 105–162.

[134] With regard to 'good works' being regarded as 'wrongdoing', external sources, both Christian and non-Christian, from later centuries mention certain pagan charges against Christians of immorality (including incest), cannibalism and harmful magical practices. These might have been misunderstandings of or deliberate vilification of Christian practices of calling each other brothers and sisters, the Lord's Supper and miracles performed by the apostles. Christian apologists such as Justin, Tertullian and Origen defended the Christian faith vigorously. For more details, see Stephen Benko, *Pagan Rome and the Early Christians* (Bloomington: Indiana University Press, 1984). Immorality charges might have had some basis, as reflected in New Testament letters such as 1 Corinthians, 2 Peter and Jude regarding the libertine behaviour of so-called Christians among the Christian community. As it is difficult to ascertain whether these charges originated in the first century, we will not discuss them in detail in this study.

In summary, pagans would certainly reckon the Christian message and change in their lifestyle of worship (denial of traditional gods and rejection of the imperial cult) as subversive – a threat to their traditional values of piety to the gods (*mos maiorum*), honouring of benefactors and the maintenance of the *pax deorum*.

## 2 Threat of economic losses

The second ramification of the Christians' withdrawal from pagan worship was that abandoning the worship of traditional gods led to economic losses for those whose livelihood depended on supplying the needs of cultic practices (for the first ramification, see p. 42 above).[135] For example, craftsmen who made shrines for the various cults, and even farmers and traders who supplied animals and other items for cultic sacrifices. It is no wonder that at Ephesus Demetrius the silversmith and his related trade guild who made shrines for Artemis were determined to oppose Paul (cf. Acts 19:24–27).

On a related note, it is worth mentioning that the owners of the slave girl in Philippi (Acts 16:19) would have suffered from substantial loss of income after Paul cast the spirit of divination from her. From the pagan perspective, the spirit of divination was not malevolent (demonic from the Christian perspective), but a divine being.[136] With the loss of the ability to perform divination, the owners could possibly charge Paul for 'property damage' under Roman law.[137]

Even leaving the synagogue community could cause economic losses to the synagogues. Among those who believed Paul's message at Thessalonica and Berea were many God-fearing Greeks and a few prominent women (Acts 17:4, 12), and the latter were likely patrons of the synagogue, providing benefactions to them.[138]

---

[135] See also Williams, *Persecution in 1 Peter*, p. 256; Harrison, 'Persecution of Christians', p. 296.

[136] Johnston notes that ancient Greeks reckoned that 'the gods found ways to speak to mortals more directly, through the voices of specially chosen women whom the gods temporarily "possessed"', such as the Pythian diviners at Delphi. Sarah I. Johnston, 'Oracles and Divination', in Esther Eidinow and Julia Kindt (eds.), *The Oxford Handbook of Ancient Greek Religion* (Oxford: Oxford University Press, 2015), p. 478. Luke writes that the slave girl had a 'Pythian spirit' (*pneuma pythōna*) in her (Acts 16:16).

[137] Ivoni R. Reimer, *Women in the Acts of the Apostles: A Feminist Liberation Perspective* (Minneapolis: Fortress, 1995), pp. 174–178.

[138] Carolyn Osiek, 'Diakonos and Prostates: Women's Patronage in Early Christianity', *HTS* 61.1/2 (2005), pp. 347–370, 363; Keener, *Acts*, vol. 2, p. 2095; vol. 3, pp. 2542–2543.

It is worthwhile to note that during the early second century (c. AD 110–111),[139] Pliny the Younger wrote that, before his efforts to curb the spread of Christianity, people were scarcely buying sacrificial meats in the market because many had become Christians in Bithynia-Pontus (Pliny, *Letters* 10.96.10). This would certainly have meant loss of income for pagan meat sellers.

From the outsiders' perspective, these economic losses were not loss of 'selfish gains', but of income, threatening the pagans' livelihood and funding of synagogues for the Jews.

### 3 (Alleged) vilification of opponents

In the following we will look into how various parties might possibly perceive themselves as vilified by their opponents, especially from the outsiders' perspective. The secondary reason for pagan opposition was perhaps the abandonment of former immoral ways of life (cf. 1 Peter 4:4) (for the primary reason, see the section above 'Threat to dearly held traditional values'). In the first-century Mediterranean world it was common for people to join voluntary associations and trade guilds as their main platform for socialization.[140] While some activities of these associations and guilds might have involved drunkenness and debauchery, others were better regulated.[141] As religion and daily life were in all aspects highly integrated in those days, these associations and guilds would always involve cultic activities in their gatherings. As such, drunkenness and debauchery became associated with cultic activities.

From the Christians' perspective, these activities had to be avoided because unrestrained desires would lead to immoral behaviour and idolatry. Therefore, 1 Peter 4:3–4 mentions that there were Christians who

---

[139] John G. Cook, *Roman Attitudes Toward the Christians: From Claudius to Hadrian*, WUNT 261 (Tübingen: Mohr Siebeck, 2010), p. 146.

[140] S. G. Wilson, 'Voluntary Associations: An Overview', in John S. Kloppenborg and Stephen G. Wilson (eds.), *Voluntary Associations in the Graeco-Roman World* (London: Routledge, 1996), pp. 14–16; Michael S. Moore, 'Civic and Voluntary Associations in the Greco-Roman World', in Joel B. Green and Lee Martin McDonald (eds.), *The World of the New Testament: Cultural, Social, and Historical Contexts* (Grand Rapids: Baker Academic, 2013), pp. 152–153.

[141] On the excesses of behaviour and the attempts at control, see e.g. Philo, *Against Flaccus* 136; *On Drunkenness* 22–25, 29; the bylaws on the inscription on 'Regulations of the Worshippers of Diana and Antinoüs' from Lanuvium (Campania, Italy; dated AD 136), see Richard S. Ascough, Philip A. Harland and John S. Kloppenborg, *Associations in the Greco-Roman World: A Sourcebook* (Waco: Baylor University Press, 2012), pp. 194–198, esp. 198; also cited in Robert L. Wilken, *The Christians as the Romans Saw Them*, 2nd edn (New Haven: Yale University Press, 2003), pp. 36, 39.

had withdrawn from such former ways of life, described as 'excessive reckless ways' (*hē tēs asōtias anachysis*) and 'wanton idolatry' (*athemitos eidōlolatria*).[142] If these descriptions became known to the pagans as the reason for dissociation, it is understandable that pagans who engaged in these activities would be offended because they were labelled as immoral and their cultic practices as 'wanton'.[143] As Achtemeier notes, 'idolatry' is a concept that was unique to Jews and Christians during the first century, and pagans did not even use terms such as 'detestable idolatry' to describe cultic practices they disapproved of.[144] This would explain the pagan retaliation with 'vilification' (*blasphēmeō*; 1 Peter 4:4). Thus, as mentioned in 1 Peter 4:4, social withdrawal from these former ways of life became a cause of persecution.

In John 8:44–51, we observe a similar reaction from the Jews when Jesus says their father is the devil. Likewise, since John labels Jewish opponents as a 'synagogue of Satan' (Rev. 2:9; 3:9) and portrays imperial authorities as in league with the devil (Rev. 13),[145] both Jewish and pagan opponents would retaliate if they heard these portrayals.

In the Greco-Roman world, rhetorical vilification of one's opponent was a common practice. Some scholars note that although New Testament authors also use this strategy, they are milder compared with many others and there is a level of correlation between the presentation of the opponents and its historicity.[146] My purpose here is not to pass judgment on whether the practice of rhetorical vilification is morally acceptable or whose perspective is correct. Keeping that in mind, we observe that these Christian theological (including ethical and spiritual) perspectives are highly offensive to their opponents. Just as Christians might feel that their opponents had vilified and wronged them (cf. 1 Peter 2:12; 4:4; Rev. 2:9), non-Christian Jews and pagans might also likewise feel that Christians

---

[142] Achtemeier notes that *athemitos* 'means basically contrary to what has been laid down, whether by gods or humans'; e.g. its use in Acts 10:24. It is usually taken to mean 'wanton, disgusting, unseemly' in 1 Peter 4:3; e.g. BDAG, p. 24, 2. As such, from a monotheistic Christian perspective, idolatry is 'unlawful'. See Achtemeier, *1 Peter*, p. 282, n. 77; Mark Dubis, *1 Peter: A Handbook on the Greek Text*, BHGNT (Waco: Baylor University Press, 2010), p. 134.

[143] Achtemeier, *1 Peter*, p. 282.

[144] See also Jobes, *1 Peter*, p. 267.

[145] Similarly, Paul associates his opponents with Satan (2 Cor. 11:12–14) and labels some of them 'dogs' (Phil. 3:2). On the identity of the opponents in the Pauline epistles and in Revelation 2:9 and 3:9, see pp. 28–29 above.

[146] See e.g. Luke T. Johnson, 'The New Testament's Anti-Jewish Slander and the Conventions of Ancient Polemic', *JBL* 108.3 (1989), pp. 419–441; Andreas B. du Toit, 'Vilification as a Pragmatic Device in Early Christian Epistolography', *Bib* 75.3 (1994), pp. 403–412.

had vilified them. Thus, (alleged) vilification of opponents became a cause for persecution.

### 4 Threat of social unrest

The first three reasons stated above would easily have caused Jewish or pagan individuals to gang up on Christians in mob behaviours or to bring charges against them to the local authorities, as in the case of Paul in Iconium (Acts 14:5), Philippi (Acts 16:22) and Jerusalem (Acts 22:24). This may also explain the Roman emperor's edict to expel Jews from Rome in AD 49:[147] 'Since the Jews constantly made disturbances at the instigation of Chrestus, he [the emperor Claudius] expelled them from Rome' (Suetonius, *Life of Claudius* 25.4).[148] From the pattern of Jewish opposition described in Acts, it is likely that in Rome a similar dispute over whether Jesus the Jew was Christ the Messiah caused constant unrest among the Jewish population. The purpose of Claudius' edict was to quell this unrest, which affected all the Jews, whether or not they believed in Jesus as the Christ.

In view of the four reasons above, the outsiders regarded opposing Christians as necessary and justified. Like previous suppression of the Egyptian Isis cult and the Bacchanalian cult for political or moral reasons,[149] the local and regional Roman authorities deemed suppressing the Christian cult as a necessary move to maintain traditional values and order in society. In the first century, the central government (Claudius and Nero) was only indirectly involved in suppressing the Christian cult. For Claudius, the Christian element was indistinguishable from the unrest caused by the Jewish population in Rome, while for Nero the Christians were a scapegoat for the great fire in Rome.

# Summary of theological perspectives

This chapter began with a concise introduction to the historical background of the first century in terms of its social, religious and political

---

[147] For arguments for dating this edict to AD 49, see Engberg, *Impulsore Chresto*, pp. 90–99.

[148] There are three possibilities as to whom 'Chrestus' was: (1) a local Jewish instigator by the name of 'Chrestus'; (2) 'Chrestus' as the messianic claim of a local Jewish instigator; or (3) the claims of some Jews that Jesus was the Christ (Christus). As Engberg (*Impulsore Chresto*, pp. 100–102) notes, even if Suetonius or his source had mistaken 'Christus' as 'Chrestus', it is highly likely that (3) above is the cause of unrest among the Jewish population in Rome. See also Cook, *Roman Attitudes Toward the Christians*, pp. 15–22.

[149] See p. 18 above.

world views, so that we may better understand the reasons for the conflict and persecution early Christians faced. I will now summarize the New Testament authors' theological understanding of who persecuted them and why.

All four Gospels preserved the tradition of Jesus' warning that his disciples would be persecuted due to their association with him. Although the Synoptic Gospels preserved Jesus' prediction that persecution would come even from one's immediate family, this is only reflected in 1 Peter's exhortation to slaves and wives, who were likely facing pressures from their household for their faith. Persecution came from both Jews and pagans who rejected the gospel message.

Other than the author of Revelation, New Testament authors mostly do not depict the Roman authorities as their persecutors. Opposition arose mainly from individuals, who then incited others to join forces with them. With the exception of Herod Agrippa I (Acts 12), Luke depicts pagan local authorities and Roman authorities as mostly executing their duties to keep peace and order when individuals (Jews or pagans) or Jewish local authorities (the Sanhedrin) bring before them their charges against some Christians.[150] There are times when Luke depicts Roman authorities as helping these Christians when the latter were accused. Apart from local authorities in Judea (Jewish religious leaders), other local and regional authorities appear not to have been directly hostile to Christians, until the portrayal of such in Revelation.

From the insiders' perspective, New Testament authors reflect the gospel tradition of suffering for Jesus' name as the fundamental cause of persecution (e.g. Acts 5:41; 9:16; Phil. 1:29; 1 Peter 4:14). Luke's narrative in both his Gospel and Acts clearly highlights that Jesus and Paul (founder and representative proclaimer of the Christian faith respectively) were not guilty of any crime.[151] Together with the narratives of the disciples' and Paul's being accused and being brought before local and regional authorities, Luke portrays this as a fulfilment of Jesus' predictions in Luke 21:12, 17.[152] From the perspective in John's Gospel and Acts, the primary cause of persecution from the Jews was the Christian confession and proclamation of Jesus as the promised Messiah. Luke also presents other aspects

---

150 See also Engberg, *Impulsore Chresto*, p. 89.
151 Cunningham, *Through Many Tribulations*, pp. 242, 281.
152 See also ibid., p. 128.

51

of contention with Jewish opponents that led to persecution: the proclamation of (1) the resurrection of Jesus; (2) the Jewish leaders' responsibility
for the death of Jesus; and (3) Gentile inclusion as God's people apart
from circumcision and Torah observance. Pauline epistles reflect point 3
as the main contention.[153] In sum, while Christians inherited many of
their scriptural interpretations of messianic expectations, eschatology,
apocalypticism and monotheism from the Jews, it was the appropriation
of these scriptural texts to Jesus of Nazareth that caused much contention
and persecution.[154]

Luke perceives other motives of persecution as well: jealousy of the
Jews, economic losses of the pagans and self-serving political motives of
certain rulers. Jealousy and self-serving reasons were motives outsiders
would hardly confess. What the insider perceived as jealousy of the
opponents' success might well have been regarded as zeal for the ancestral
tradition by the outsider, a point Luke acknowledges for the case of Saul.
The outsider would hardly identify with Paul's confession of former
misplaced zeal as ignorance. Similarly, what 1 Peter and 2 Timothy deem
to be 'good works' and 'godly living' might well have been regarded as
wrongdoing, leading to persecution.

While most New Testament authors portray Satan as tempting believers
to be unfaithful to God, and human opponents as belonging to Satan, the
author of Revelation is unique in portraying Satan as the instigator and
reason behind the persecution by the authorities. Satan's revenge for being
defeated in the cosmic battle with God manifests itself as the persecution
of the saints on earth.

For the New Testament authors, the Christians' faithful proclamation
of the gospel message and their godly lifestyle in accord with the gospel
brought about persecution from those who rejected the gospel message.
From the outsiders' perspective, both Jewish and pagan (sometimes
violent) opposition towards Christians was not purely because of the
latter's faith in Jesus, but because of the real or perceived threats Christians brought to society.

In our contemporary terms, the factors leading to conflicts and resulting in persecutions are multilayered and complex: ideological conflicts,

---

[153] This is likely because of the circumstantial nature of the epistles to the Thessalonians,
Galatians, Romans and Philippians. Other Pauline epistles mention suffering persecution, but
rarely contain details regarding the reasons.
[154] See also Hare, *Jewish Persecution of Christians*, pp. 8–18.

misunderstandings, negative ramifications from adopting Christian beliefs and lifestyle. Outsiders perceived these as threats to their dearly held traditional values and economic prosperity, and (alleged) vilifications by Christians. In certain cases, these conflicts escalated into social unrest. What the insider deemed as theological truths (e.g. Jesus as the Messiah and Son of God, rejection of worshipping other gods and the emperor as idolatrous, the evil spiritual forces behind their opponents) was highly offensive to the outsider (e.g. blasphemy of the Jewish God by claiming the human Jesus to be divine, impiety and ingratitude to the pagan gods and the emperor as benefactors, vilification). Both insider and outsider perspectives are critical for us to understand the various ways in which the New Testament Christians responded when facing persecution. Some New Testament authors appear to be aware of certain outsiders' perspectives in their responses, as we will see in chapter 2.

# 2

# What was happening: responses to persecution

Many have the impression that most early Christians resolutely stood firm in their faith when persecuted. Is this an accurate picture? What happened among the early Christians in the New Testament when they faced persecutions? This chapter investigates the forms of persecution these early Christians faced and examines how they responded to persecutions in diverse ways.

## Forms of persecution

It is necessary at this point to revisit our definition of 'persecution', so that we may examine the forms of opposition mentioned in the New Testament that constitute persecution. I will adopt Tieszen's definition,[1] which lists the following elements: (1) unjust action; (2) hostility perpetrated primarily on the basis of religion; (3) resulting in harm (or with the intention to harm); and (4) from the victim's perspective. Persecutions are the means opponents use to curb the propagation and continued practice of the Christian faith. By investigating the forms of persecution, I will also attempt to clarify when early Christians began to face official persecution.

### Tactics and plots

In Acts, Luke chronicles the tactics Jewish and pagan opponents employed against the early Christians. It was common for individuals to stir up others to join forces with them in opposition. This could take two forms: (1) influencing influential people (Acts 6:12; 13:50); or (2) inciting a crowd

---

[1] See pp. 1–3 above.

(Acts 6:12; 14:2, 5, 19; 16:22; 17:5; 19:28–29; 21:27), which could involve a substantial number of people. These opponents would sometimes join forces with their own kind (e.g. other Jews, Acts 18:12; or fellow workers in a related trade, Acts 19:25) or with others. It is ironic that Jewish opponents, who would normally not associate with Gentiles, would join forces with pagans to oppose Christians (e.g. Acts 14:5; 17:5), especially so when early Christian missionaries such as Paul were also Jews.[2] As we will see below, in many of these cases the goal was to press charges against Christians before the ruling authorities to get the former punished or banished.

In Jerusalem, charges against Christians before the Sanhedrin included unauthorized proclamation of Jesus as the Messiah and of his resurrection (Acts 4:7; 5:28; 23:6), blasphemy of God and Moses (Acts 6:11; 21:28b) and defilement or destruction of the temple (Acts 6:13–14; 21:28b). Their purpose was clearly to suppress the Christian movement and punish those who propagated the Christian faith (Acts 4:17–18; 5:28).

In the diaspora, most of the time the goal of the opponents was to expel foreign Christian missionaries from their cities. The legal means of doing so was to press charges against Christians before the local authorities. At times, opponents would escalate and bring their charges to regional authorities. In Corinth, the Jewish opponents brought Paul before Gallio the proconsul (Acts 18:2). The Sanhedrin also brought their charges against Paul before Felix the governor (Acts 24:1–9). Charges before other pagan local or regional authorities included sedition (Acts 16:20; 17:6; 19:26; 24:5), treason (Acts 17:7; cf. 25:8c), proclamations against the (Roman) law (Acts 16:21; 18:13) and against matters relating to the Jewish faith (law, temple, resurrection; Acts 18:13; 24:6; 25:8a; 25:19; 26:7–8).[3]

Other Christians were also implicated in the process. The Jewish opponents at Thessalonica went to the house of Jason, who hosted Paul and Silas. When they did not find them, they dragged Jason and some other believers to the local officials instead (Acts 17:5–6). Similarly, in Ephesus, the crowds seized Paul's travelling companions Gaius and Aristarchus when they could not find him (Acts 19:29). Paul and his

---

[2] See also Keener, who notes that it is ironic for these Jewish opponents to 'join with idolaters to oppose the preacher of monotheism'. Keener, *Acts*, vol. 2, p. 2175.

[3] See also Schnabel, 'Persecution of Christians', p. 547. Contra Schnabel, I have not included defamation of patron gods (Acts 19:26–27) as one of the charges, because these were accusations that had yet to be formally pressed as charges (Acts 19:38–39). See also Darrell L. Bock, *Acts*, BECNT (Grand Rapids: Baker Academic, 2007), p. 610.

companions eventually left the various cities for a variety of reasons, from voluntary (e.g. Acts 14:6, 20; 17:10, 14) to being begged to leave (Acts 16:39), to expulsion (Acts 13:50).

Luke's narrative in Acts exposes certain underhanded means some opponents used to achieve their ends. First, the use of false witnesses. This can be seen during the very early days in Judea, when Hellenistic Jews who opposed Stephen arranged false witnesses in order to press charges against him before the Sanhedrin (Acts 6:11–14). Second, employing a political charge that derived or deviated from the initial contention. For example, the owners of the female slave girl who suffered economic loss charged Paul with 'advocating customs unlawful for us Romans to accept or practise' (Acts 16:19–21).[4] This could be because it was more difficult to charge Paul with 'property damage', since there was no physical injury involved when the Pythian spirit was exorcized. Thus, they deviated from the original cause and charged Paul with a public instead of a private offence.[5] Similarly, the Jewish opponents at Thessalonica charged Paul with 'defying Caesar's decrees, saying that there is another king, one called Jesus' when their initial conflict was portrayed as a dispute over whether Jesus was the Messiah and their motive as jealousy (Acts 17:3, 7). In Corinth, the Jewish opponents jointly derived a charge that Paul was 'persuading the people to worship God in ways contrary to the law' (Acts 18:13). The presentation of the charge is ambiguous here: it could refer to the Jewish law or the Roman law, but it is more likely that the Jewish opponent wanted the proconsul to convict Paul of preaching a new religion that violated the *mos maiorum* of both the Romans and the Jews.[6] Nonetheless, Gallio the proconsul reckoned it as an intra-Jewish dispute about the Jewish law and dismissed their case (Acts 18:15). It is noteworthy that Jewish religious disputes did not constitute criminal offences to the Roman officials (Acts 18:14–15; 25:18–19; 26:30–31), but causing tumults, sedition and treason certainly did.[7] Therefore, it is no wonder that these

---

[4] See also Ben Witherington III, *The Acts of the Apostles: A Socio-Rhetorical Commentary* (Grand Rapids: Eerdmans, 1998), p. 496, who notes that the charge 'masked the real cause of the action'.

[5] Keener, *Acts*, vol. 3, pp. 2470–2471.

[6] Joseph A. Fitzmyer, *The Acts of the Apostles: A New Translation with Introduction and Commentary*, AB 31 (New York: Doubleday, 1998), p. 629; Schnabel, *Acts*, p. 762; Keener, *Acts*, vol. 3, p. 2768; Harrison, 'Persecution of Christians', p. 296.

[7] Winter, *Divine Honours for the Caesars*, pp. 194–195. On sedition and treason as public crime, see Richard A. Bauman, *Crime and Punishment in Ancient Rome* (London: Routledge, 1996), p. 2.

opponents would frame their charges politically as public offences to bring Christians to court.

It is also noteworthy that Luke depicts Jewish opponents as those who plotted against Paul on several occasions, but in vain, and he documents Paul himself testifying to this (Acts 20:19). There were plots against Paul in Greece (Acts 20:3), to mistreat and stone him at Iconium (Acts 14:5), and to kill him at Damascus (Acts 9:23–24) and in Judea (Acts 23:12–23; 25:3). On one occasion they succeeded at Lystra, when Jews from Antioch and Iconium stirred up the crowd to stone Paul (Acts 14:19).

## Official and non-official punishments

John's Gospel depicts Jewish local authorities as those who persecuted the disciples of Jesus with the threat of casting out of the synagogue anyone who confessed Jesus as the Messiah (John 9:22; 12:42; 16:2).[8] Synagogues in and around Jerusalem performed multiple functions: institutional (political and judicial; similar to municipal councils), religious (liturgical and spiritual; similar to cults/temples) and social (similar to voluntary associations).[9] Stambaugh and Balch note that '[a]n important social function of the synagogue was to provide a sense of belonging and to facilitate contacts'.[10] Therefore, being cast out of the synagogue entailed being ostracized by the entire community – family, friends and even perhaps trade associates.[11] In an honour-and-shame society that emphasized community more than the individual, such communal disciplinary action was severe and caused great dishonour (cf. John 12:42–43).

---

[8] For arguments for the historicity of the expulsion during Jesus' time, see Bernier, *Aposynagōgos*; Klink, 'Overrealized Expulsion', pp. 175–84. Nonetheless, it is difficult to ascertain whether such an expulsion was temporary or permanent.

[9] Lee I. Levine, *The Ancient Synagogue: The First Thousand Years*, 2nd edn (New Haven: Yale University Press, 2005), pp. 135–173; Anders Runesson, *The Origins of the Synagogue: A Socio-Historical Study*, CBNTS 37 (Stockholm: Almqvist & Wiksell, 2001), pp. 237–476. In the diaspora, synagogues tended to have mostly religious and social functions because municipal powers were held by city councils.

[10] John E. Stambaugh and David L. Balch, *The New Testament in Its Social Environment*, LEC 2 (Philadelphia: Westminster, 1986), p. 49.

[11] Andreas J. Köstenberger, *John*, BECNT (Grand Rapids: Baker Academic, 2004), p. 288; Marianne Meye Thompson, *John: A Commentary*, NTL (Louisville: Westminster John Knox, 2015), p. 215. Stambaugh and Balch note that archaeological and literary evidence from slightly later centuries has shown that seating in the synagogue was marked by trade (e.g. metalsmiths, cloth makers), such that the people might support one another in the community. Thus, they reckon there might have been similar functions in the first century such that Paul could make contact with fellow tentmakers in Corinth. See Stambaugh and Balch, *New Testament in Its Social Environment*, p. 49.

Luke's Gospel also depicts Jewish local authorities opposing both Jesus and his disciples, but they began formally persecuting the disciples only in the time of the book of Acts. They arrested the apostles and incarcerated them before putting them on trial (Acts 4:3; 5:18). At first, they only threatened the apostles but could not punish them, because the people were praising God for the healing Peter had performed on the paralytic (Acts 4:21). Subsequently, they wanted to put the apostles to death, but Gamaliel dissuaded them and they flogged the apostles instead (Acts 5:33–40). At Stephen's trial, in their fury due to Stephen's accusation that they were like their ancestors who had a history of persecuting God's prophets, they rushed at him, dragged him out of the city and stoned him to death (Acts 7:51–60). After the death of Stephen, systematic persecution of Christians authorized by the Jewish authorities was carried out in Jerusalem (Acts 8:1), executed mainly by Saul, who hunted down Christians from house to house and later extended the hunt from Judea to Damascus. Saul imprisoned them and threatened to put them to death (Acts 8:3; 9:1–2; 22:3–4). Later in the narrative, he testifies how he brought these Christians to synagogues to be punished and forced them to denounce their belief in Jesus (Acts 26:10–11).[12] Luke reports two deaths resulting from persecution, both occurring in Jerusalem: (1) Stephen, whom Jewish opponents stoned to death (Acts 7:59–60); and (2) James, brother of John, whom Herod had executed with the sword (Acts 12:1–2).[13]

For the situation in the diaspora, Luke depicts the physical and verbal violence that individual and group opponents inflicted on Christians. Physical violence included beating (Acts 18:17; 21:30, 32)[14] and stoning (Acts 14:19), which were frequently associated with mob behaviour. Verbal violence mainly involved 'slandering' or other 'abusive language' (*blasphēmeō*; Acts 13:45; 18:6). Paul's own testimonies in his letters (1 Cor. 4:11; 2 Cor. 6:5, 8–9; 11:25) corroborate Luke with regard to these various forms of official and non-official persecutions.

Flogging and stoning were forms of punishment associated with Jewish local authorities. Peterson notes that '[f]logging by the Sanhedrin or

---

[12] In Acts 26:11, Luke has Paul retrospectively refer to denunciation of Jesus as the Messiah to be 'blasphemous'. See Schnabel, *Acts*, p. 1007.

[13] As Herod was a client king of Rome, he could use the official Roman form of execution by sword. See reference in n. 28 below.

[14] On the identity of Sosthenes in Acts 18:17, see ch. 1, n. 77 above. If this Sosthenes was a Christian or was the same person listed in 1 Cor. 1:1, then this beating would have been an unfair and cruel treatment amounting to persecution.

synagogue officials was a serious punishment for those who broke the law' (cf. Acts 22:19; 2 Cor. 11:24).[15] Stoning to death is the form of capital punishment stated in the Mosaic law for a variety of offences, including blasphemy (Lev. 24:14, 16), which explains why Jewish opponents would stone Stephen and Paul. However, stoning was not an official form of Roman punishment. Although Roman law limited the ability of Jewish local authorities to execute criminals (cf. John 18:31), this could not prevent people (Jews or Greeks alike) who disregarded the law from doing so.[16] Thus, stoning was a mob behaviour, perhaps self-justified as legitimate by the Jews, rather than an officially sanctioned punishment by the Romans.[17]

Local authorities were authorized to punish with (public) beating misbehaviour that caused social unrest, sometimes stripping the accused before the beating (Acts 16:22–23; 22:24–25), and incarceration (Acts 16:24) while the person awaited trial.[18] In Thessalonica, the local authorities made Jason and other local believers pay a bond before letting them off. As the host was responsible for the behaviour of his guests, Jason paid this bond on behalf of Paul and Silas to guarantee they would not cause further unrest or would depart from the city.[19]

Other than Acts, Hebrews, 1 Peter and Revelation mention similar forms of verbal and physical violence early Christians faced due to their faith. Hebrews 10:32–34 mentions that the recipients of the letter suffered afflictions in the form of public reproach and affliction, imprisonment and seizure of property. Nonetheless, the author of Hebrews indicates there

---

[15] David Peterson, *The Acts of the Apostles*, PNTC (Grand Rapids: Eerdmans, 2009), p. 227.

[16] Schnabel, *Acts*, p. 391; Keener, *Acts*, vol. 2 p. 1453. For Jewish background on stoning as punishment and Greco-Roman historical sources on stoning as mob behaviour, see Keener, *Acts*, vol. 2, pp. 1453–1455.

[17] Matthews argues that Luke depicted the Jewish local authorities' judicial system as 'base', though seemingly following procedures, but it admitted false witnesses and, during the legal hearing lost control to a mob that murdered Stephen. Shelly Matthews, 'The Need for the Stoning of Stephen', in *Violence in the New Testament* (New York: T&T Clark, 2005), pp. 124–139. However, Schnabel thinks that the Sanhedrin allowed the mob to take over because they viewed Stephen as deserving death by stoning for blasphemy. Schnabel, *Acts*, pp. 390–391.

[18] On imprisonment while awaiting trial, see Bauman, *Crime and Punishment*, p. 11. On meting out punishment to those whom the magistrates deemed as violating public order, see Christian Gizewski, 'Coercitio', in Hubert Cancik and Helmuth Schneider (eds.), *Brill's New Pauly* (Leiden: Brill, 2006), vol. 3, pp. 508–509.

[19] This would explain why the believers sent Paul and Silas away that night (Acts 17:10) and that Paul viewed his departure from Thessalonica as involuntary (cf. 1 Thess. 2:17). See Schnabel, *Acts*, p. 709, n. 20.

had not been deaths resulting from the persecution (Heb. 12:4). 'Public reproach' (*oneidismos*) was a form of shaming the reproached in Greco-Roman antiquity,[20] with the intention of pressurizing the shamed to conform again to the dominant group's values and to deter others from deviating.[21] While imprisonment was a form of official punishment, the text is unclear whether public reproach and seizure of property referred only to official (denouncement before authorities and confiscation) or non-official (reviling in public places and looting) forms of persecution or both.[22] Some among them were still imprisoned and mistreated (Heb. 13:3). As in Acts, official forms of punishment might or might not amount to official persecution. Thus, although Hebrews is clear that Christians faced some kind of persecution – at least non-official– it is unclear whether official persecution was included.

The recipients of 1 Peter were facing verbal abuse and were likely charged before the authorities.[23] They were insulted (1 Peter 4:14) and slandered for wrongdoing (1 Peter 2:12, 15; 3:9, 16; 4:4) and were suffering from 'doing good' (1 Peter 2:20; 3:14). Christian wives could likely be perceived as insubordinate by their non-believing husbands and would have felt fearful in the midst of these tensions (1 Peter 3:1–6).[24] As a whole, these Christians were fearful and threatened (1 Peter 3:14). Their preparedness to give a 'defence' (*apologia*) when asked about their Christian hope might have included either official court hearings or non-official occasions (1 Peter 3:15).[25] However, scholars are divided in their opinion as to whether suffering as a 'Christian' (1 Peter 4:16) meant that the name

---

[20] Craig R. Koester, *Hebrews: A New Translation with Introduction and Commentary*, AB 36 (New York: Doubleday, 2001), p. 459; Luke T. Johnson, *Hebrews: A Commentary*, NTL (Louisville: Westminster John Knox, 2012), p. 269.

[21] David A. deSilva, *Honor, Patronage, Kinship and Purity: Unlocking New Testament Culture* (Downers Grove: InterVarsity Press, 2000), pp. 35–36.

[22] For public reproach, see Acts 16:19–21 for denouncement before authorities and Acts 13:44–45 for reviling in public places. See also Koester, *Hebrews*, p. 460; Johnson, *Hebrews*, pp. 270–271. For confiscation of property as Roman official punishment for public crime, see Lesley Adkins and Roy Adkins, *Handbook to Life in Ancient Rome*, updated edn (New York: Facts on File, 2004), p. 391. Contra Winter (*Divine Honours for the Caesars*, p. 267), who understands all these to be official forms of punishment.

[23] Williams (*Persecution in 1 Peter*, pp. 322–326) also suggests a few conjectured forms of persecution (e.g. economic oppression, social ostracism and spiritual affliction). However, as the text is not explicit on these, I will not include them in our discussion here.

[24] See also John H. Elliott, *1 Peter: A New Translation with Introduction and Commentary*, AB 37B (New York: Doubleday, 2000), p. 574; Jobes, *1 Peter*, p. 203.

[25] Achtemeier, *1 Peter*, p. 231; Williams, *Persecution in 1 Peter*, pp. 309–316. Given the broader historical background and the account in Acts, it seems unnecessary for Elliott to exclude official court hearings. See Elliott, *1 Peter*, p. 627.

'Christian' amounted to a criminal offence, as in the early second century.[26] Thus, 1 Peter is also clear on non-official forms of persecution, but not entirely clear on official forms of persecution.

In Revelation, John describes himself as suffering on the island of Patmos because of his testimony for Christ (Rev. 1:9). He was probably relegated there as an official form of punishment.[27] He also depicts Christians as not only suffering from verbal abuse such as slander (Rev. 2:9) and physical affliction such as imprisonment (Rev. 2:10), but also facing imminent death (Rev. 2:11; cf. 13:15). They were pressured to renounce their faith (Rev. 2:13; 3:8) and Christians such as Antipas had already died for their faith (Rev. 2:13; cf. 6:9–11; 17:6; 18:24; 20:4). While John anticipates other Christians being killed for their faith (Rev. 11:7; 13:10, 15), he also clearly anticipates official forms of persecution in Revelation 13:10 (killed with the sword) and 20:4 (beheading) for refusal to participate in imperial cults (Rev. 13:15). Beheading by sword is one of the official forms of Roman execution for public crimes.[28]

Scholars debate as to whether there was official systematic persecution of Christians during the time Revelation was written.[29] Claims by early church fathers of widespread official persecution decreed by the emperor during the late first to early second century do not have earlier corroborating sources.[30] Nonetheless, it is noteworthy that, in accord with our investigation of the historical background, Revelation 13 does not portray the beast from the sea as demanding worship from the people, but rather the populace as the ones who worship the emperor (Rev. 13:8) and

---

[26] See ch. 1, n. 130 above.

[27] Scholars debate whether John was exiled. For details of arguments, see David E. Aune, *Revelation 1–5*, WBC 52A (Dallas: Word, 1997), pp. 77–80; Koester, *Revelation*, pp. 242–243.

[28] Adkins and Adkins, *Life in Ancient Rome*, p. 391.

[29] Scholars frequently rely on the following to date the writing of Revelation: (1) comments of early church fathers (e.g. Clement of Alexandria, Irenaeus, Eusebius); or (2) attempts to correlate certain details of the visions (e.g. measuring of the temple in Rev. 11:1–2; revival from fatal injury in 13:3; number of the beast in 13:18; heads of the beast in 17:10–11) to specific events between the reign of Nero and Hadrian. For a history of interpretation, see Koester, *Revelation*, pp. 71–79. Nonetheless, all these are not without problems. Koester (*Revelation*, p. 79) rightly notes that 'the imperial cult is only one of the issues Revelation addresses. The book also deals with disputes over the accommodation of Greco-Roman religious practices and complacency due to wealth – issues that could have arisen at various times. Another problem . . . is that Revelation's imagery is evocative. The images of Satan's throne and the beasts do not allow one-to-one correlations with particular figures or structures.' Therefore, Koester (ibid., p. 79) argues that the book was likely written around the last few decades of the first century (AD 80–100), reflecting 'persistent social patterns' rather than 'specific events'.

[30] Harrison, 'Persecution of Christians', pp. 298–299.

the regional or local authorities as those who advocate and enforce imperial cults (Rev. 13:12–15). Therefore, the vision in Revelation 13 may be reflecting an existing or imminent threat that Christians faced towards the end of the first century from regional or local authorities who might sporadically mete out official forms of punishment, such as execution, for non-participation in imperial cults (e.g. Antipas in Rev. 2:13).[31] Given the prophetic nature of apocalyptic literature and John's identifying himself as a prophet (cf. Rev. 1:3; 22:9),[32] even if there was no systematic and large-scale official persecution during his time, he could still have anticipated such a time to come, which indeed happened in a sporadic but intense manner during the second and third centuries and eventually developed into widespread persecution during the time of Emperor Diocletian (AD 303–312).

From the above we observe that, in Acts, Luke portrays systematic and persistent Jewish opposition from individuals and local authorities over a substantial period and across both Judea and the diaspora. There was also sporadic opposition from pagan individuals. The actions they took against Christians were unjust and often underhanded and cruel, with the intention of causing bodily harm to Christians. This opposition was due to practice and proclamation of their Christian faith. According to the definition given earlier, all these clearly constitute persecution.

Pagan local or regional authorities meted out official punishment to Paul and other early Christians because of the unrest the latter caused, rather than directly because of their Christian faith or proclamation. While Luke does not portray pagan authorities as persecuting Christians, he depicts occasions when certain local and regional authorities abused their power: (1) punishing the accused before trial (Acts 16:22; 22:24–25);[33] (2) physical assault of the accused on trial (Acts 23:1–3);[34] and (3) keeping the accused

---

[31] See also Smith, 'Book of Revelation', p. 353. A few scholars suggest that Antipas was publicly executed; see Aune, *Revelation 1–5*, p. 178; Brian K. Blount, *Revelation: A Commentary*, NTL (Louisville: Westminster John Knox, 2009), pp. 56–57. The preposition *para* with the dative bears the sense of close spatial proximity; thus Antipas *apektanthē par' hymin* 'was killed before you' (i.e. 'in your sight').

[32] See also Beale, *Revelation*, pp. 35–36.

[33] While Roman citizens (e.g. Paul) were protected against arbitrary corporal punishment, non-citizens did not have that right. Tristan S. Taylor, 'Social Status, Legal Status and Legal Privilege', in Paul J. du Plessis, Ando Clifford and Tuori Kaius (eds.), *The Oxford Handbook of Roman Law and Society* (Oxford: Oxford University Press, 2016), p. 350.

[34] For various Jewish historical references to Ananias and other high priests regarding their corruption and abuse of power, see Keener, *Acts*, vol. 3, pp. 3268–3270.

unlawfully imprisoned for personal gain (Acts 24:26–27). In this respect, Christians certainly suffered unjust treatment, though these abuses would have happened to others regardless of their religious beliefs and practices.

While it is clear that early Christians faced non-official persecution, the question remains: Was there official persecution? From the perspective of the New Testament authors, the answer is mixed. In the earliest days in John's Gospel and Acts, official persecution came from the Jewish authorities, while Herod (King Agrippa I) was the only Gentile local authority who persecuted early Christians. In Acts, other local authorities were meting out punishments to Christians not because of their beliefs, but rather because of the social unrest they had caused. Thus, Luke does not indicate in Acts that there were official persecutions by pagan authorities. The texts of Hebrews and 1 Peter are not entirely clear on official persecution. Nonetheless, Revelation depicts official forms of punishment meted out to Christians who refused to participate in imperial cults, which, according to our definition, constitutes official persecution.

# Diverse Christian responses

Now we will look at the various responses of Christians as reflected by the New Testament authors and their evaluations of these responses. This differs in some ways from how these authors encourage their audience towards the desired responses. We will focus mainly on the former and defer the latter until chapter 3.

## Resistance and perseverance

Luke portrays a variety of responses to persecution in Acts. First, the apostles understood their suffering for Christ as part and parcel of their portion as his disciples. In the triple tradition, Jesus had said his disciples must 'take up their cross to follow after him' (Mark 8:34 // Matt. 16:24 // Luke 9:23).[35] In the double tradition, those who would not take up their cross to follow him are not 'able' (*dynamai*; Luke 14:27) or 'worthy' (*axios*; Matt. 10:38) to be his disciples. Thus, the apostles rejoiced because 'they had been *counted worthy*' (*katēxiōthēsan*) 'of suffering disgrace' for Jesus'

---

[35] Luke 9:23 is unique in his rendering of taking up the cross 'daily' (*kath' hēmeran*). Cunningham (*Through Many Tribulations*, p. 87) notes this could imply Luke's emphasis that 'suffering persecution is an integral part of discipleship'.

name (Acts 5:41).[36] A number of scholars note the oxymoron here: it is an honour to be dishonoured because of Christ.[37] At Lystra, Iconium and Antioch, Paul and Barnabas told the disciples, 'We must go through many hardships to enter the kingdom of God' (Acts 14:22).

Before his ascension, the resurrected Jesus commissioned his disciples to be his witnesses to the ends of the world after they received the Holy Spirit and were empowered (Acts 1:7; cf. 4:33). Therefore, it comes as no surprise that Luke describes Peter, the disciples, Stephen and Paul as being 'filled with the Holy Spirit' and that they proclaimed Jesus boldly despite persecution (Acts 4:8, 13, 31; 7:5, 8, 55–56; 9:17–22, 28; 13:45–46; 14:3; cf. 5:42). When the disciples heard of these persecutions, they prayed for empowerment and deliverance (5:24–31; 12:5). They also understood these persecutions as fulfilling the Scriptures (e.g. Ps. 2:1–2 in Acts 5:25–28).

Because their experience of the resurrected Jesus was real, the apostles could not disobey God's commission and restrain themselves from testifying about Jesus (Acts 4:20; 5:30–32; cf. 9:1–6, 15–17; 26:15–19). Twice, Peter and the apostles asserted they would obey God rather than 'human beings' – the opposing authorities (Acts 4:19; 5:29). Luke vividly portrays Paul's testimony about the pain he suffered from persecution and his persistence in testifying in spite of it. Paul told the Ephesian elders:

> I served the Lord with great humility and with tears and in the midst of severe testing by the plots of my Jewish opponents . . . I only know that in every city the Holy Spirit warns me that prison and hardships are facing me. However, I consider my life worth nothing to me; my only aim is to finish the race and complete the task the Lord Jesus has given me – the task of testifying to the good news of God's grace.
> (Acts 20:19, 23–24)[38]

---

[36] Although the word 'worthy' (*axios*) is not used in Luke 14:27, it may still be a tradition the disciples were well aware of and is thus reflected in Acts 5:41. It is interesting to note the passive voice here (*katexiōthēsan*), but there is no expressed agent. They could be considered as such by other disciples or, perhaps more importantly, by God.

[37] See e.g. Barrett, *Acts*, vol. 1, p. 300; Bock, *Acts*, p. 252; Schnabel, *Acts*, p. 319.

[38] There is sufficient evidence to suggest that the speeches in Acts, while not verbatim, essentially reflect what the speakers said. For extensive discussion on and argument of this position, see 'Speeches in Acts' in Keener, *Acts*, vol. 1, pp. 258–319.

Through the above, Luke shows that Paul regarded fulfilling God's commission above his own life. This same conviction reappeared when Paul testified before King Agrippa, where he declared that he had not been 'disobedient to the vision from heaven' to testify for Jesus, resulting in and despite persecution (Acts 26:19–21). Paul was not only willing to be bound; he was even willing to die for the Lord (Acts 21:13).

Second, in accord with Jesus' instructions in the gospel traditions (Luke 21:12–13; cf. Mark 13:9 // Matt. 10:18), the apostles seized opportunities to bear witness for Jesus during their trials before local and regional authorities. Peter, the apostles, Stephen and Paul witnessed for Jesus before the Sanhedrin (Acts 4:8–12; 5:29–32; 7:1–53; 23:1–9), while Paul also witnessed before the governors Felix and Festus and King Agrippa (Acts 24:10–21; 25:6–7; 26:1–23). In Luke 21:14–15, Jesus instructed the disciples not to think of how to give a defence against the charges ahead of time, because he himself will give the disciples the 'words and wisdom [*sophia*] that none of your adversaries will be able to resist [*antistēnai*] or contradict'.[39] Developing from this tradition, Luke shows in Acts how this promise is fulfilled in Peter, Stephen and Paul. Members of the Sanhedrin are amazed that Peter can speak with such courage and 'there was nothing they could say' (i.e. 'contradict') because they cannot deny the miracle of the healed paralytic (Acts 4:13–14).

In fact, Peter's defence before the Sanhedrin displays astonishing wisdom. Keener notes Peter's defence displays the rhetorical technique of irony.[40] It is ironical that Peter and John should be charged for a benefaction (healing the paralytic) they have bestowed (Acts 4:9). As Keener points out, 'one's benefaction . . . should weight the burden of proof in favour of the speaker's positive character, and hence one's innocence'.[41] Benefactors should be honoured and failure to do so is unacceptable and shameful in a reciprocal culture.[42] To speak ill of or harm a benefactor is

[39] While Mark and Matthew are similar to each other, they differ from Luke in that the disciples are not to be 'anxious beforehand' (*promerimnaō*; Mark 13:19) or 'anxious' (*merimnaō*; Matt. 10:19) and that the Holy Spirit (Mark 13:11) or the Spirit of the Father (Matt. 10:20) is the one who will speak through the disciples before the tribunal. Both Mark and Matthew also do not have the clause regarding the outcome of the words given. Nonetheless, Luke still portrays the Holy Spirit's empowering Peter and Stephen when they spoke before the tribunal (Acts 4:8; 6:10), such that what happened was not much different from the Markan and Matthean traditions.

[40] Keener, *Acts*, vol. 2, pp. 1145–1148. For references to primary sources, see details therein.

[41] Ibid., p. 1145.

[42] Schnabel, *Acts*, p. 239.

even worse. Thus, Peter quickly shifts the focus to Jesus as the benefactor whom the accusers (the members of the Sanhedrin) have killed (Acts 4:10).[43] This turning of the tables causes them to be at a loss as to what to do and they consequently cannot punish Peter and John (Acts 4:16, 21). How can an 'uneducated' (*agrammatos*) and 'untrained' (*idiōtēs*) speaker such as Peter make such an effective and wise defence using a known rhetorical technique (cf. Acts 4:13a)?[44] No wonder the authorities were astonished (Acts 4:13b), which is precisely the point. It must have been the result of being filled with the Holy Spirit (Acts 4:8), a fulfilment of Jesus' promise in the gospel tradition.

This is also fulfilled in Stephen's trial before the Sanhedrin. His adversaries 'could not stand up against the wisdom [*antistēnai tē sophia*] the Spirit gave him as he spoke' (Acts 6:9–10). In accord with Jesus' teachings and example (cf. Matt. 5:44; Luke 6:28; 23:34),[45] Stephen prays for his persecutors before his death, that God may not hold them accountable for their sin of stoning him (Acts 7:60).[46]

Paul's defence before the tribunals also exhibits wisdom. He asks the Roman commander to give him a chance to defend himself against the charges of the crowd at Jerusalem (Acts 21:39). He chooses to speak in Aramaic (the heart language of Palestinian Jews),[47] so that he can gain a hearing from them, as seen from their response of quietening down to listen to him (Acts 21:40 – 22:2). He shares about how he had previously persecuted the Way, so as to identify with them (Acts 22:3–5). Yet, he also uses this to transition into why he changed from his previous convictions,

---

[43] See also ibid.

[44] On the meaning of *agrammatos* as 'uneducated' and *idiōtēs* as 'untrained', i.e. not professional, see Barrett, *Acts*, vol. 1, p. 233; Bock, *Acts*, p. 195.

[45] A number of important manuscripts ($\mathfrak{P}^{75}$ $\aleph^1$ B D* W Θ) do not have Jesus' prayer in Luke 23:34. However, most scholars find both the internal and external (other manuscript witnesses) evidence strong for its inclusion as original. See e.g. Darrell L. Bock, *Luke*, 2 vols., BECNT (Grand Rapids: Baker, 1994), vol. 2, pp. 1867–1868; François Bovon, *Luke*, tr. James E. Crouch, 3 vols., Hermeneia (Minneapolis: Fortress, 2002), vol. 3, pp. 306–307; David E. Garland, *Luke*, ZECNT (Grand Rapids: Zondervan, 2012), pp. 921–922; John T. Carroll, *Luke: A Commentary*, NTL (Louisville: Westminster John Knox, 2012), p. 466. Scholars who note the various parallels between Jesus and Stephen include Witherington, *Acts*, p. 253; Keener, *Acts*, vol. 2, pp. 1294–1295.

[46] See also Keener (*Acts*, vol. 2, pp. 1461–1462) and Schnabel (*Acts*, pp. 392–393), who see *tautēn tēn hamartian*, 'this sin', as the unjust execution of Stephen.

[47] *Hebrais dialektos*, 'Hebrew dialect', in Acts 21:40 could denote Aramaic or Hebrew. See Schnabel, *Acts*, p. 898. However, it is more likely Paul speaks Aramaic here, which was a more commonly spoken language than Hebrew. See also Barrett, *Acts*, vol. 2, p. 1027; Bock, *Acts*, p. 658.

so that he may bear witness for Jesus before them (Acts 22:6–21). When before the Sanhedrin, he focuses on the doctrinal difference between the Sadducees and Pharisees regarding resurrection, such that the Pharisees side with him (Acts 23:6–9). When before Felix and Festus, Paul defends his innocence and seeks to show that the plaintiffs' accusations are unfounded (Acts 24:10–21; 25:8–12). The Jewish plaintiffs also cannot prove their charges against Paul (Acts 25:7). When Paul is before King Agrippa, he uses Agrippa's familiarity with the Jewish customs and controversies to explain the gospel to him (Acts 26:2–29). Agrippa is obviously aware of Paul's efforts to witness to him (Acts 26:28).

It is noteworthy that Paul's two instances of exercising his Roman citizen rights before the local authorities, each in a slightly different manner, demonstrate his wisdom in response to different circumstances. In the first instance at Philippi, he mentions his Roman citizenship only the day after he is beaten up (Acts 16:37). However, in the second instance at Jerusalem, he immediately mentions his citizenship right before the centurion is about to flog him (Acts 22:25). Keener notes that it was a criminal offence to punish a Roman citizen without a trial. Thus, in the first instance, the magistrates have already abused their power and thus are afraid (Acts 16:38), because they can be removed from office if Paul brings this to the attention of higher-ranking Roman officials.[48] In this way, Paul gains the upper hand to secure the release of Silas and himself.[49] As Keener notes, the 'tables were now turned' – the magistrates try to appease them and beg them to leave (Acts 16:39). Paul and Silas suffered shame from public beating and imprisonment, which reflects badly on their Christian mission. Thus, the local magistrates' admission of their abuse of Roman citizen rights will bring some dignity back to the two missionaries.[50] In the second instance, why did Paul bring up his citizenship rights straightaway? Roman flogging is much more injurious than the local magistrate's beating with rods and can potentially be deadly.[51] It is likely, as Keener notes, that Paul

---

[48] Keener, *Acts*, vol. 3, pp. 2517, 2527–2529.

[49] Ibid., p. 3248.

[50] Ibid., pp. 2526, 2529–2530.

[51] See Fitzmyer (*Acts*, p. 711), who notes that such a Roman whip (known as a *flagrum*) has the capability of not only tearing up flesh, but also of breaking bones. The Roman whip had metal pieces or bones woven into leather straps that could easily tear the flesh of the person whipped, causing crippling or deadly injuries (*Digesta* 48.19.8.3; *Martyrdom of Polycarp* 2.1) (Keener, *Acts*, vol. 3, pp. 3247–3248).

has learned the value of putting hasty officials (who generally act on the assumption that a Jew is not a Roman) in an uncomfortable situation (16:37–39) . . . Paul words his information diplomatically as a question, not challenging the centurion's honour . . . he is more apt to gain favour by dialoguing than by demanding.[52]

Keener's analysis and deductions of the two instances are reasonable, showing Paul's wisdom in exercising his citizen's rights for a fair trial to his advantage.

Third, in accord with the gospel tradition in Matthew 10:23, the disciples fled from the place of persecution to other places, witnessing for Christ wherever they went (Acts 8:2, 4; 12:17). Paul and his companions did the same (Acts 9:23–25, 29–30; 13:50–51; 14:6, 20; 17:10, 14–15). Through Paul's testimony, Luke revealed that Jesus had previously instructed Paul to flee from the persecution in Jerusalem (Acts 22:17–18; cf. 9:26–30). When Paul had to leave a certain city due to their rejection, his practice of shaking off the dust of his feet (Acts 13:51) or his clothes (Acts 18:6) reflected the gospel traditions (Mark 6:11 // Matt. 10:14 // Luke 9:5). From the context of its use, this practice symbolizes that those who reject the gospel message are responsible for the judgment they will consequently receive (Matt. 10:15; cf. Acts 18:6b).[53] Nonetheless, there were times when Paul stayed on despite the persecution; for example, at Corinth and Ephesus (Acts 18:11; 19:10). For the case of staying on in Corinth, it was because the Lord himself in a vision had assured Paul of his protection, as the Lord had 'many people' in that city, implying that many people would come to faith through Paul's continuing ministry there (Acts 18:9–10).[54] It may seem inconsistent that, on the one hand, Paul avoided Macedonia because he knew of a plot against him (Acts 20:3); while, on

---

[52] Keener, *Acts*, vol. 3, pp. 3249–3250.

[53] According to Rogers, the custom of 'shaking off dust from the feet' is to be read against the cultural background of hospitality – inhospitality was regarded as a punishable sin. 'Dusty' feet connote that the host had not provided water for the stranger to wash them, amounting to inhospitality. When the town refuses to receive the gospel messengers, it equates to rejecting their message. Thus, 'shaking dust off the feet' is a protest against inhospitality in terms of the rejection of the gospel message, and the inhospitable hosts are liable to judgment. See T. J. Rogers, 'Shaking the Dust off the Markan Mission Discourse', *JSNT* 27.2 (2004), pp. 169–192. For 'shaking the clothes', there may be an allusion to the custom reflected in Neh. 5:13, which symbolizes the punishment for covenant violation. Thus, the Jews' rejection of the gospel message was akin to such a violation and they would be responsible for incurring God's judgment. See also Bock, *Acts*, pp. 466, 579.

[54] Schnabel, *Acts*, pp. 760–761.

the other hand, he went to Jerusalem despite knowing persecution awaited him there (Acts 21:10–14). Both these instances seem to reflect Paul's conviction that he was supposed to go to Jerusalem (Acts 19:21; 20:3). Thus, in the first instance he avoided Macedonia so as not to jeopardize his trip to Jerusalem. In the second instance he went ahead because he was convicted that he should be in Jerusalem nonetheless. Similarly, when Paul knew of a plot to kill him, he carefully arranged for it to be reported and exposed to the Roman commander (Acts 23:16–22), because he knew it was not time for his martyrdom. This is likely because earlier on Paul saw a vision of Jesus instructing him to testify at Rome (Acts 23:11).

Fourth, similar to what Jesus did in the gospel traditions (Mark 12:9–11 // Matt. 21:42 // Luke 20:17), Luke portrays Peter and Stephen as also using the Scriptures against their Jewish persecutors for rejecting Jesus as the Messiah (Acts 4:11; 7:39–51).[55] In fact, Peter quoted the same Scripture Jesus quoted (cf. Ps. 118:22), to show that God has already prophetically warned against such rejections.[56] Luke also portrays the disciples proving from the Scriptures that Jesus is indeed the promised Messiah (e.g. Acts 2:16–36; 3:12–26; 17:2–6; 26:22–23). Although this is to convince the general audience, it is also in response to the opponents (e.g. Acts 18:28).

The various Christian responses to persecution reflected in Acts show resistance to the pressure to compromise, as well as resilience and perseverance despite persecution. Next, we will look at similar responses as reflected in the Pauline epistles, 1 Peter and Revelation.

In 1 Thessalonians, Paul praises the letter recipients for their perseverance in the faith despite the persecution they are facing. Their perseverance is 'inspired by hope in our Lord Jesus Christ' (1 Thess. 1:3). They are imitating Paul, Silas and Timothy in terms of receiving the gospel message 'with joy given by the Holy Spirit' despite severe persecution (1 Thess. 1:6). The Thessalonian Christians have 'turned to God from idols to serve the living and true God' (1 Thess. 1:9), which will entail their withdrawing from all activities relating to pagan cults and enduring the resultant

---

[55] Paul did so similarly in Acts 28:25–27, citing Isa. 6:9–10 against the Jews at Rome who rejected his message about Jesus. This was in line with the gospel traditions of Jesus' using the same passage in Isaiah for the same purpose (Mark 4:12 // Matt. 13:13–14 // Luke 8:10; cf. John 12:40). However, Luke does not portray the unbelieving Jews in Rome as persecutors of Paul.

[56] See also I. Howard Marshall, 'Acts', in G. K. Beale and D. A. Carson (eds.), *Commentary on the New Testament Use of the Old Testament* (Grand Rapids: Baker Academic, 2007), p. 551.

persecutions.[57] Not only so, but they are actively sharing the gospel message (1 Thess. 1:8).[58] Their positive example served as a model for the believers in other regions, such as Macedonia and Achaia (1 Thess. 1:7). Indeed, Paul later testified to the Corinthians how the Macedonian Christians also had overflowing joy even in the midst of going through a severe trial (2 Cor. 8:1–2).[59] This joy the Pauline churches demonstrated is similar to that of the apostles at Jerusalem (Acts 5:41).

As Paul was concerned that the Thessalonian Christians might be tempted to give up their faith due to persecution, he sent Timothy from Athens to Thessalonica to encourage them to persevere (1 Thess. 3:2–5). Subsequently, Timothy's good report of the Thessalonians' perseverance in faith and love brought much encouragement and assurance to Paul in the midst of his own distress and sufferings from persecution (1 Thess. 3:6–7),[60] such that he even boasted among other churches about the Thessalonians' growth in faith despite persecution (2 Thess. 1:3–5).

More than once, Paul declares that (1) suffering persecution for Christ is ordained and thus inevitable for any believer (Phil. 1:29; 1 Thess. 3:3–4; 2 Tim. 3:12); and (2) he is not ashamed of his suffering for Christ (Phil. 1:20; 2 Tim. 1:12). As such, not only do the recipients of his letters witness Paul's suffering for Christ, but they also participate with him in this suffering (cf. 1 Cor. 1:7; Phil. 1:30; 1 Thess. 1:6).

Paul often spoke of his perseverance in proclaiming the gospel despite facing persecution. He told the Thessalonians of how he and Silas courageously proclaimed the gospel message to them despite the sufferings and insults they had experienced earlier in Philippi (1 Thess. 2:2–6; cf. Acts 16:19–40).[61] Paul reminded Timothy of the persecutions Paul had faced in

---

[57] See p. 42 above and Jeffrey A. D. Weima, *1–2 Thessalonians*, BECNT (Grand Rapids: Baker Academic, 2014), p. 108, who also explains how this behaviour might have led to persecution.

[58] *Ho logos tou kyriou*, 'the Word of the Lord', denotes the gospel message and its related teachings (cf. Acts 8:25; 13:44, 49; 15:36, etc.). It is used interchangeably with *ho logos tou theou*, 'the Word of God', in variant readings of some manuscripts of Acts. See also M. Eugene Boring, *I & II Thessalonians: A Commentary*, NTL (Louisville: Westminster John Knox, 2015), p. 68; Weima, *1–2 Thessalonians*, pp. 105–106; Shogren, *1 and 2 Thessalonians*, pp. 70–71.

[59] Although *thlipsis*, 'trial', may denote a wide range of afflictions, including persecution and other hardships in Christian mission work, it certainly includes persecution (cf. Acts 16:16 – 17:15). See also Thrall, *Second Epistle of the Corinthians*, vol. 2, p. 522; Guthrie, *2 Corinthians*, p. 394.

[60] See also Shogren, *1 and 2 Thessalonians*, p. 140; Boring, *I & II Thessalonians*, p. 122.

[61] Paul's missionary efforts despite facing persecution show his integrity. If he had ulterior motives (e.g. greed), he would not have been willing to suffer persecution. See also Thomas R. Schreiner, *Paul, Apostle of God's Glory in Christ: A Pauline Theology*, 2nd edn (Downers Grove: IVP Academic, 2020), pp. 86–87, who notes Paul's integrity compared with other

Galatia (Pisidian Antioch, Iconium, Lystra) (2 Tim. 3:11). He told the Corinthians of his suffering from persecution in Asia (2 Cor. 1:8a). The suffering was far beyond what he could bear, such that he felt that he was going to die (2 Cor. 1:8b–9). Yet, he understood those excruciating experiences as a way God was teaching him not to depend on himself but on God (2 Cor. 1:9). Indeed, he likens God's power to sustain him to a 'treasure in jars of clay', to show that 'this all-surpassing power is from God and not from us'. 'We are hard pressed on every side, but not crushed; perplexed, but not in despair; persecuted, but not abandoned; struck down, but not destroyed' (2 Cor. 4:7–9). Therefore, he even 'delights' (*eudokeō*) in these sufferings, explaining that God's grace is sufficient for him in his weakness. Only when he is weak is he made strong by God's grace (2 Cor. 12:9–10).

Paul openly expresses his emotions in suffering: '*sorrowful*, yet always *rejoicing*' (2 Cor. 6:10). He relates, 'For when we came into Macedonia, we had no rest, but we were harassed at every turn – conflicts on the outside, *fears within*' (2 Cor. 7:5). Nonetheless, he was comforted by Titus and the good news he brought regarding the Corinthians' deep concern for Paul (2 Cor. 7:6–7).

Lim gives an apt summary of how Paul perceives his suffering in 2 Corinthians, especially with regard to 4:7–10:

> In speaking of the reality of his suffering, Paul is not minimizing the effects of the hardships on him, nor does he suggest that the power of God negates the hardships imposed on him . . . these four antitheses [in 4:8–9] do not serve to highlight Paul's virtuous character, his self-sufficient or his steadfast courage amid adversity, or even his endurance in the midst of hardships. Nor do they merely demonstrate the power of God in rescuing Paul from the hardships. God's power is not divine power revealing itself as weakness and thereby replacing human weakness, but divine empowerment experienced by Paul in his weakness so that he is able to continue his missionary activities and to serve as a living embodiment of the story of Jesus in the manifestation of the resurrection power of God.[62]

---

greedy itinerant preachers who resorted to deceit and flattery in order to take advantage of their audience.

[62] Kar Yong Lim, '*The Sufferings of Christ Are Abundant in Us*' (*2 Corinthians 1:5*): *A Narrative-Dynamics Investigation of Paul's Sufferings in 2 Corinthians*, LNTS 399 (London: T&T Clark, 2009), p. 106.

Paul saw his suffering as an authentication and corroboration of his apostleship as God's servant (cf. 2 Cor. 6:4; 11:23–29).[63] His experience of God's deliverance from the dangers of persecution gives him hope and confidence for future deliverance (2 Cor. 1:10; Phil. 1:19b; 2 Tim. 3:11; 4:17–18). He often requests prayer support for deliverance from such dangers (Rom. 15:31; 2 Cor. 1:11; Phil. 1:19a; 2 Thess. 3:1–2).

Paul also speaks of how he responded to his persecutors: 'When we are cursed, we bless; when we are persecuted, we endure it; when we are slandered, we answer kindly' (1 Cor. 4:12b–13a). This seems to reflect him as a person who 'walked his talk'. He exhorted the Roman Christians to do likewise (Rom. 12:14–21) – obeying Jesus' exhortation according to the gospel traditions to 'love your enemies' (Matt. 5:44; Luke 6:27) and 'bless those who curse you' (Luke 6:28).[64]

Nonetheless, the response above seems to be at odds with other instances. In Acts, Luke depicts Paul's rebuking Elymas the magician with coruscating remarks: 'You are a child of the devil and an enemy of everything that is right! You are full of all kinds of deceit and trickery' (Acts 13:10–11). When Ananias the high priest abuses his power by having Paul assaulted at the trial, Luke depicts Paul's snapping at him saying, 'God will strike you, you whitewashed wall! You sit there to judge me according to the law, yet you yourself violate the law by commanding that I be struck!' Consequently, Paul is rebuked for insulting God's high priest (Acts 23:3–4). Paul replies that he did not realize the person was the high priest, and then quotes Exodus 22:28 to admit he should not have spoken against the man. Nonetheless, some scholars doubt that he did not know, suggesting that Paul was replying ironically, implying that the high priest himself did not obey the Mosaic law.[65] On other occasions in his letters, Paul's emotions seem to run high when he wishes his Galatian opponents to be castrated and calls his Philippian opponents 'dogs', 'evildoers' and 'mutilators of the flesh' (Gal. 5:12; Phil. 3:2).

---

[63] Kelhoffer, *Persecution, Persuasion, and Power*, pp. 30–93. Dunne further proposes that Paul sees suffering persecution for the sake of Christ as an 'alternative identity marker' of the true people of God. John A. Dunne, *Persecution and Participation in Galatians*, WUNT 2.454 (Tübingen: Mohr Siebeck, 2017), pp. 4–7, 193–195.

[64] See p. 115 below for detailed discussion on Rom. 12:14–21 in relation to the gospel tradition.

[65] E.g. Bock, *Acts*, p. 670; Mikeal C. Parsons, *Acts*, Paideia (Grand Rapids: Baker Academic, 2008), p. 315; Richard I. Pervo, *Acts: A Commentary*, Hermeneia (Minneapolis: Fortress, 2009), p. 573; Schnabel, *Acts*, p. 927. Pervo thinks Paul was being 'ingenuous', while others suggest he was being ironical.

Scholars have offered various explanations for Paul's behaviour. Some suggest he is using a common technique of rhetorical vilification of opponents in his letters to make his point.[66] Paul addresses his letters' recipients and is not verbally abusing his opponents directly. Others have suggested Paul's 'eccentric personality'.[67] These various views are not necessarily contradictory, but present multifaceted aspects of possible reasons for Paul's behaviour. On the one hand, it is true that Paul is hot-headed, such that he quarrels with Barnabas over John Mark (Acts 15:37–40) and rebukes Peter publicly (Gal. 2:11–14). Neither should we ignore the use of common rhetorical devices in Paul's letters. On the other hand, it is interesting to note that 2 Timothy 2:24–25 portrays him as a more mellowed person, saying:

> [T]he Lord's servant must not be quarrelsome but must be kind to everyone, able to teach, not resentful. Opponents must be gently instructed, in the hope that God will grant them repentance leading them to a knowledge of the truth.

Or perhaps Paul was like any of us Christians: knowing the standards set by Scripture, succeeding in some instances in abiding by such standards, but failing in other instances due to weakness, with the possibility of transformation and growth into Christlikeness over time. Also, Scripture is known to be honest in portraying the strengths and weaknesses of its characters, without always intending to use all such portrayals as exemplars for emulation.

In Philippians 1:12–14, Paul sees his suffering from persecution as an opportunity to advance the gospel in two ways: (1) to bear witness for Jesus among the guards and all others who knew about his imprisonment; and (2) to be a positive example resulting in other believers also proclaiming the gospel courageously despite persecution.[68] In 2 Timothy 3:9–10

---

[66] E.g. du Toit, 'Vilification as a Pragmatic Device', pp. 403–412; Lauri Thurén, *Derhetorizing Paul: A Dynamic Perspective on Pauline Theology and the Law*, WUNT 124 (Tübingen: Mohr Siebeck, 2000), pp. 66–67; D. Francois Tolmie, *Persuading the Galatians: A Text-Centred Rhetorical Analysis of a Pauline Letter*, WUNT 2.190 (Tübingen: Mohr Siebeck, 2005), pp. 40, 183.

[67] John G. Gager with E. Leigh Gibson, 'Violent Acts and Violent Language in the Apostle Paul', in Shelly Matthews and E. Leigh Gibson (eds.), *Violence in the New Testament* (New York: T&T Clark, 2005), pp. 13–21.

[68] See also Charles B. Cousar, *Philippians and Philemon: A Commentary*, NTL (Louisville: Westminster John Knox, 2013), pp. 33–34. The *praitōrion* (Greek) / *praetorium* (Latin) refers

a similar conviction is depicted: though Paul is in chains, God's word is not chained, such that this motivates Paul to persevere in order that the elect will receive salvation due to his persistent proclamation of the gospel. Thus, Paul saw his suffering as bringing the benefit of salvation and life to those who heard and believed (2 Cor. 1:6; 4:12–13).[69] As such, Paul uses two cultic metaphors to portray his ministry as an offering to God for the benefit of others through his own sacrifice: (1) he is an aroma (of burning incense) of Christ (2 Cor. 2:14); and (2) he is like a drink offering (libation) poured out (Phil. 2:17; 2 Tim. 4:6).[70]

In Romans 5:3–4, Paul describes the good that suffering brings: it produces perseverance, character and hope. Although he does not specify what kind of suffering he is referring to, evidence from the broader context of his discussion points to suffering that can include persecution (cf. Rom. 8:35–36).[71] This hope is inspired by God's love 'poured out into [the] hearts' of the believers by the Holy Spirit (Rom. 5:5). The Holy Spirit intercedes for

---

(note 68 *cont.*) to the official residence of the governor; see BDAG, p. 859. In Phil. 1:13, it refers to the guards working or living in the praetorium. Paul very likely wrote this letter to the Philippians while he was imprisoned, whether in Rome (cf. Acts 28) or in Caesarea (cf. Acts 23:25). See Reumann, *Philippians*, pp. 171–172. A similar situation also occurred in Acts 16:25–34.

[69] See also Lim, *Sufferings of Christ*, p. 43; J. Ayodeji Adewuya, 'The Sacrificial-Missiological Function of Paul's Sufferings in the Context of 2 Corinthians', in Trevor J. Burke and Brian S. Rosner (eds.), *Paul as Missionary: Identity, Activity, Theology, and Practice*, LNTS 420 (London: T&T Clark, 2011), pp. 90–94; Schreiner, *Paul, Apostle of God's Glory*, pp. 83–100. In 2 Corinthians, Paul presents this suffering as broader than that due to persecution, but including that associated with his apostolic ministry, such as danger from bandits and shipwreck, sleepless nights and hunger, poverty, and so on (2 Cor. 6:4–10; 11:23–30). Lim (*Sufferings of Christ*, p. 43) notes that 'Paul interprets his apostolic sufferings as mediatory and beneficial to the Corinthians. On this basis, Paul invites the Corinthians to be part of this narrative of his apostolic ministry of suffering and the story of Jesus.'

[70] Scholars are divided as to whether this aroma refers to the burning of incense at the triumphal procession (so Barrett, Guthrie) or to the Old Testament sacrifice (so Thrall, Harris, Matera). Regardless, in cultic practices both are a form of offering. See C. K. Barrett, *A Commentary on the Second Epistle to the Corinthians*, BNTC (London: Black, 1973), p. 98; Thrall, *Second Epistle of the Corinthians*, vol. 1, p. 198; Frank J. Matera, *II Corinthians: A Commentary*, NTL (Louisville: Westminster John Knox, 2003), pp. 73–74; Murray J. Harris, *The Second Epistle to the Corinthians: A Commentary on the Greek Text*, NIGTC (Grand Rapids: Eerdmans, 2005), p. 248; Guthrie, *2 Corinthians*, pp. 165–170. On libation as sacrifice, see also John Paul Heil, *The Letters of Paul as Rituals of Worship* (Eugene: Cascade, 2011), pp. 151, 175.

[71] Most scholars see the sufferings in Rom. 8 as referring broadly to various types of sufferings. See e.g. Richard N. Longenecker, *The Epistle to the Romans: A Commentary on the Greek Text*, NIGTC (Grand Rapids: Eerdmans, 2016), p. 718; Douglas J. Moo, *The Epistle to the Romans*, 2nd edn, NICNT (Grand Rapids: Eerdmans, 2018), p. 533; Roy E. Ciampa, 'Suffering in Romans 1–8 in Light of Paul's Key Scriptural Intertexts', in Siu Fung Wu (ed.), *Suffering in Paul: Perspectives and Implications* (Eugene: Pickwick, 2019), p. 20.

suffering believers and gives them hope (Rom. 8:23–27). Compared with the greatness of the eschatological hope and glory that will be revealed in believers, Paul regards his present suffering as worthwhile (Rom. 8:18). He is convinced that no suffering (due to persecution or hardships from apostolic ministry) or opposing authorities can separate believers from God's love (Rom. 8:35–39). It is this conviction that motivates him to persevere.

Adewuya rightly notes that Paul responds to persecutions by finding 'inner meaning' to such sufferings, rather than by explaining why Christians suffer persecution. Thus, Paul sees suffering persecution as an inevitable outcome associated with the proclamation of the gospel, as participation in the sufferings of Christ, rather than as a result of his offending his opponents.[72]

A very gentle response to facing persecution is presented in 1 Peter, such that Horrell calls this a 'quiet conformity' and 'polite resistance'.[73] We noted above that the recipients of 1 Peter had adopted a nearly total withdrawal from social activities involving pagan and imperial cults.[74] They had been accused of doing evil – most likely referring to the failure to show honour to the emperor and the gods, and insubordination to those in authority. The text of 1 Peter is very mindful of such an outsider point of view, such that it advocates a strategy of response through 'good deeds' (1 Peter 2:12).[75] Therefore, the motif of submission to those in authority rings out loudly and clearly: (1) citizens are to submit to ruling authorities and honour them (emperors/kings and governors) (1 Peter 2:13–14, 17); (2) slaves are to submit to their master, regardless of whether their master is good or harsh (1 Peter 2:18–19); and (3) wives are to submit to their husbands (1 Peter 3). Submission has the purpose of proving outsider accusations as wrong (1 Peter 2:16) and to win over opposing family members (1 Peter 3:1). Not only do wives need to display a gentle spirit (1 Peter 3:4), but all believers are to demonstrate gentleness and respect when they give a defence of their faith (1 Peter 3:15).

---

[72] Adewuya, 'Paul's Sufferings', p. 98.

[73] David G. Horrell, 'Between Conformity and Resistance: Beyond the Balch–Elliott Debate Towards a Postcolonial Reading of First Peter', in Robert L. Webb and Betsy J. Bauman-Martin (eds.), *Reading First Peter with New Eyes: Methodological Reassessments of the Letter of First Peter*, LNTS 364 (London: T&T Clark, 2007), pp. 133–143.

[74] See pp. 39, 49 above.

[75] Contra Williams (*Persecution in 1 Peter*, p. 255), who argues that good works are primarily the cause, not the remedy for persecution. See also Sean du Toit, 'Negotiating Hostility Through Beneficial Deeds', *TynBul* 70.2 (2019), pp. 221–243, who disagrees with Williams.

As scholars note, submission to those in authority is a social norm of Greco-Roman culture and such 'quiet conformity' is a response to hostility and persecution.[76] However, Carter notes that 1 Peter does not explain *how* to 'honour' the emperor or *how* to submit without compromising one's faith in Jesus.[77] Nonetheless, as Horrell notes, 1 Peter 2:17 makes it clear that one is to fear God and honour the emperor/king, and that would exclude compromising actions such as participation in imperial worship.[78] Therefore, 1 Peter advocates a response to persecution that is a 'quiet conformity' as well as a 'polite resistance', not an assimilation.

In the book of Revelation, some Christians persevered in their faith and did not deny Christ or participate in the pagan or imperial cult even in the face of death (e.g. Rev. 12:11; 20:4). For this, Revelation portrays them as receiving commendation from Christ; for example, some members of the church in Ephesus (Rev. 2:2–3), Smyrna (Rev. 2:9), Pergamum (Rev. 2:13), Thyatira (Rev. 2:19) and Philadelphia (Rev. 3:8, 10).

## Apostasy and assimilation

In the gospel traditions Jesus predicts that some of his followers will fall away when they face persecution. In the parable of the seeds, those that fell on rocky ground and sprang up quickly but withered in the hot sun

---

[76] See e.g. David L. Balch, *Let Wives Be Submissive: The Domestic Code in 1 Peter*, SBLMS 26 (Chico: Scholars Press, 1981), p. 109; Warren Carter, 'Going All the Way?: Honoring the Emperor and Sacrificing Wives and Slaves in 1 Peter 2.13–3.6', in Amy-Jill Levine and Maria Mayo Robbins (eds.), *A Feminist Companion to the Catholic Epistles and Hebrews*, FCNTECW 8 (London: T&T Clark International, 2004), pp. 14–33; Horrell, 'Between Conformity and Resistance', pp. 134–135. Balch (*Let Wives Be Submissive*, p. 105) notes that the author of 1 Peter 'stress[es] the importance of Christians seeking peace and harmony in their household relationships and with society'.

[77] Carter, 'Going All the Way?', p. 14. While Carter is correct in this observation, he goes too far in suggesting that 1 Peter advocates participation in pagan and imperial cults and feasts at home and in associations as legitimate, as long as the participants have an inner commitment to Christ as Lord in their hearts (cf. 1 Peter 3:15). Carter argues that it is impossible not to participate and yet regain the pagan opponents' approval. See Carter, 'Going All the Way?', pp. 29–30. However, Carter has neglected Peter's eschatological perspective – it is at the day of judgment that believers will be vindicated regarding these accusations through good works (1 Peter 2:12; 4:5, 16–19). See also Sean du Toit, who disagrees with Carter, 'Practising Idolatry in 1 Peter', *JSNT* 43.3 (2021), pp. 411–430.

[78] Horrell, 'Between Conformity and Resistance', p. 135. Horrell gives four reasons why Carter's suggestion (see n. 77 above) is unlikely (cf. 1 Peter 2:13–17): (1) ruling authorities are framed as 'human' institutions; (2) this would thus implicitly deny the emperor as divine; (3) Christians are not supposed to abuse their freedom for evil purposes; and (4) emperors are to be honoured like all other people, and thus not worshipped. Therefore, we need to note that, although many pagans may not distinguish between honours offered to the gods and the emperor based on ontology (see p. 15 above), Christians certainly make such a distinction.

are likened to those who initially receive the word with joy but quickly fall away when they face persecution (Mark 4:16–17 // Matt. 13:20–21; cf. Luke 8:13). The wording in Mark 4:17 and Matthew 13:21 is nearly identical, and Luke 8:13 bears a similar meaning but seems to be more generic, without identifying the 'testing/temptation' as 'persecution' or directly relating it as a consequence of the word (see Table 2.1).

**Table 2.1 Textual comparison of Mark 4:17, Matthew 13:21 and Luke 8:13 (my trs.)**

| Mark 4:17 | Matthew 13:21 | Luke 8:13 |
| --- | --- | --- |
| 'when tribulation or persecution happens as a consequence of the Word, *they fall away*' | 'when tribulation or persecution happens as a consequence of the Word, *[such a person] falls away*' | 'in time of testing, they give up' |

In the Olivet discourse, Matthew further notes Jesus' predicting that, during times of persecution, many will 'fall away' (*skandalizō*), and will betray and hate one another (Matt. 24:10).[79] *Skandalizō* (Matt. 13:21; 24:10; Mark 4:17) conveys the idea that persecution will lead some disciples into the sin of giving up their faith,[80] while Luke's use of *aphistēmi* ('give up'; Luke 8:13) also connotes abandonment of the faith.[81]

Certainly, the temptation to give up their faith can be strong for some believers, as reflected by the warnings against apostasy in Hebrews (2:1–4; 3:7 – 4:13; 5:11 – 6:12; 10:19–39; 12:14–29).[82] No matter what their former background might be, whether Jewish (including Gentile God-fearers) or pagan, they may be tempted to revert to their former way of life.[83] The

---

[79] Most scholars understand this betrayal to be from within the church. See Gundry, *Matthew*, p. 479; R. T. France, *The Gospel of Matthew*, NICNT (Grand Rapids: Eerdmans, 2007), p. 906; David L. Turner, *Matthew*, BECNT (Grand Rapids: Baker Academic, 2008), p. 574; Grant R. Osborne, *Matthew*, ZECNT (Grand Rapids: Zondervan, 2010), p. 875.

[80] BDAG, p. 926, 1b; France, *Matthew*, p. 906; Osborne, *Matthew*, p. 875.

[81] BDAG, p. 157, 1a; Bock, *Luke*, vol. 1, p. 735.

[82] There were certainly Christians who apostatized under the pressure of persecution. During the early second century, some among the accused said they 'stopped being Christians' some years before (Pliny, *Epistles* 10.96.6). See also Karen L. King, 'Rethinking the Diversity of Ancient Christianity: Responding to Suffering and Persecution', in Eduard Iricinschi, Lance Jenott, Nicola Denzey Lewis and Philippa Townsend (eds.), *Beyond the Gnostic Gospels: Studies Building on the Work of Elaine Pagels*, STAC 82 (Tübingen: Mohr Siebeck, 2013), p. 64.

[83] Scholars differ in their opinion as to whether the recipients of Hebrews were Jewish Christians or a mixture of both Jewish and Gentile Christians. For the former view, see e.g. Thomas R. Schreiner, *Commentary on Hebrews*, BTCP (Nashville: B&H, 2015), pp. 6–10; Ian K. Smith, 'The Letter to the Hebrews', in Mark Harding and Alanna Nobbs (eds.), *Into All the World:*

author of Hebrews perceives apostasy as a grave danger and thus writes to his audience to encourage them to persevere in faith. I will discuss how he does this in greater detail in chapter 3. While the threat of apostasy is real, the author of Hebrews expresses his confidence that his recipients have not and will not apostatize (Heb. 6:9–10; 10:39).

On the other hand, other Christians responded to opposition and persecution not by apostasy, but by cultural assimilation. This applies to both Jewish and pagan oppositions. With regard to pagan opposition, Koester aptly summarizes the issue at stake:

> Assimilation has to do with *the extent to which* Jesus' followers could accommodate the practices of non-Christians while remaining true to their own faith. Reasons for accommodation included the desire to maintain good social and business relationships with people outside the Christian community ... Religious festivals were public events that included sacrifices, banquets, and distributions of meat ... The Jewish refusal to share sacrifices and meals with others was considered antisocial and even offensive (Philostratus, *Vita Apollonii* 5.33.4), and Christians who refused to participate would be seen negatively as well ... Private meals held by families or associations could include rites honouring a deity ... Members of trade and professional associations often shared meals, and at these events honours were given to various gods and deified emperors. Christians might want to participate in private meals to maintain good relationships with family, friends, and business associates, yet doing so could give the impression that they honoured gods in whom they did not believe. But refusing to join in such meals was also a problem, since it risked offending people, which could make life socially and financially difficult.[84]

According to Koester's explanation above, the attempt to assimilate in itself does not imply that Christians become untrue to their own faith. It

---

(note 83 *cont.*) *Emergent Christianity in Its Jewish and Greco-Roman Context* (Grand Rapids: Eerdmans, 2017), pp. 184–207. For the latter view, see e.g. Koester, *Hebrews*, pp. 64–79; Gareth L. Cockerill, *The Epistle to the Hebrews*, NICNT (Grand Rapids: Eerdmans, 2012), pp. 19–23. Although Johnson (*Hebrews*, pp. 36–38) identifies the Jewish cult as possibly a 'new attraction' (for former pagans) or a 'return' (for former Jews), he reminds us that the text itself does not give any hint of the ethnicity of its recipients.

[84] Koester, *Revelation*, p. 99; emphasis mine.

is the *extent* to which one assimilates that matters and is thus controversial among Christians. The issue becomes 'How much can Christians assimilate before becoming unfaithful to Jesus?' As seen in the section above, some Christians responded by withdrawal from all social activities associated with cult practices. Nonetheless, other Christians did not hold the same view, such as those among the churches of Corinth (1 Cor. 8 – 10), Pergamum (Rev. 2:14–15) and Thyatira (Rev. 2:20), who advocated that it is permissible for Christians to participate in these social meals and eat food sacrificed to idols.

The book of Revelation advocates a strong stance against compromising under persecution. As Koester notes, the churches in the province of Asia faced three major problems: 'conflict with outsiders, assimilation, and complacency'.[85] Conflict with outsiders pertains to both Jewish and pagan opposition, which I discussed in chapter 1. Assimilation is the attempt to adopt existing social practices acceptable to the opponents in order to avoid conflicts. Complacency arises from the seduction of acquiring wealth through unethical means. Avoiding conflicts and seduction of wealth (including avoiding economic losses due to persecution; cf. Rev. 13:17) often involved participation in social (private and public) meals associated with pagan and imperial cults, which is against the teachings of the gospel. Thus, all three led to unfaithfulness to Christ should the believer compromise by giving up the faith or by engaging in pagan cultic activities or unethical behaviour.[86]

For Revelation, assimilation by participating in pagan and imperial cultic activities is unfaithfulness to Christ and not being true to their faith. Those who compromise (i.e. the 'non-conquerors') by participating in the imperial cult, either by giving up their faith or while still claiming to be Christians, will have as their portion the lake of eternal burning sulphur (Rev. 14:10; 19:20). Those who gave up their Christian faith would return to their former pagan ways, because there were no 'free-thinkers' or 'non-religious people' in those days.

Apparently, some Corinthian Christians justified their eating of food sacrificed to idols by claiming to have the knowledge that since there is

---

85 Ibid., pp. 96–103.

86 As Oropeza notes, 'The main purpose of the book [Revelation] is to combat assimilation and apostasy,' although faithful followers of Christ who are suffering persecution may also receive comfort from its message. B. J. Oropeza, *Churches Under Siege of Persecution and Assimilation: The General Epistles and Revelation*, ANTC 3 (Eugene: Cascade, 2012), p. 180.

only one true God and pagan gods are not gods (1 Cor. 8:1, 4–6), there is no problem in eating such food.[87] They perhaps also asserted that 'all things are lawful' for them to do (1 Cor. 10:23, NRSV). Although the context of 1 Corinthians is more likely social pressure than persecution, other Christians who faced persecution could also hold such similar justifications.

In response, Paul refuted this argument by citing Scriptures that (1) participation in feasts involving sacrificial food amounts to idolatry (1 Cor. 10:1–18; cf. Exod. 32:6); and (2) idolatry is associated with the worship of demons (1 Cor. 10:19–23; cf. Deut. 32:17).[88] While Paul is clearly aligned to the mandate given by the Jerusalem council with regard to abstaining from food sacrificed to idols (Acts 15:29), he also instructs the Corinthians regarding other ethical (e.g. considerations for the weaker believers; 1 Cor. 8:7–13) and practical issues (e.g. what to do at the market and at private meals where food sacrificed to idols was sold or served; 1 Cor. 10:23–33). For Paul, as long as the believer does not know the idolatrous origin of the food (from the market as well as in private meals) and does not cause anyone to stumble in doing so, it is all right to eat it (1 Cor. 10:25–32). For Paul, participating *knowingly* in pagan and imperial cultic activities is unacceptable, but eating food offered to idols *unknowingly* is acceptable. The former is to be resisted while the latter is a form of assimilation Paul regards as not going against the Christian faith.

Unlike Paul, Revelation does not have such pastoral concerns in view but categorically forbids eating idol food.[89] While Revelation portrays

---

[87] See e.g. David E. Garland, *1 Corinthians*, BECNT (Grand Rapids: Baker Academic, 2003), p. 368; Gordon D. Fee, *The First Epistle to the Corinthians*, rev. edn, NICNT (Grand Rapids: Eerdmans, 2014), p. 396. For a proposed list of the Corinthians' opinions quoted by Paul and his corresponding rebuttal, see John Fotopoulos, 'Arguments Concerning Food Offered to Idols: Corinthian Quotations and Pauline Refutations in a Rhetorical Partitio (1 Corinthians 8:1–9)', *CBQ* 67.4 (2005), pp. 618–630.

[88] While it is undeniable that Christians at Corinth faced pressures to participate in imperial festive celebrations, Paul seems to address participation in pagan cultic meals in general (which includes imperial cults). Therefore, it seems too narrow for Winter to restrict 1 Cor. 8 – 10 to participation in imperial cult celebrations and *daimoniōn* in 1 Cor. 10:20 to refer to the genii of the emperor. See Winter, *Divine Honours for the Caesars*, pp. 215–225. In fact, Paul's quotation of Deut. 32:17 LXX in 1 Cor. 10:20 shows that his understanding of pagan gods as 'demons' is in line with the Jewish understanding of his time (Ps. 106:37; Isa. LXX 65:3; 65:11; Bar. 4.7). See also Garland, *1 Corinthians*, p. 480; Richard L.-S. Phua, *Idolatry and Authority: A Study of 1 Corinthians 8:1–11:1 in the Light of the Jewish Diaspora*, LNTS 299 (London: T&T Clark, 2005), pp. 137–146.

[89] See also Koester (*Revelation*, p. 100), who notes three categories of responses: (1) those who categorically forbid eating in all circumstances (e.g. Acts 15:20, 29; Revelation); (2) those who think that it is all right for most circumstances (e.g. some in Corinth, Pergamum,

Christ as rebuking and calling those who compromise to repent (e.g. Rev. 2:14–16a), Christ also pronounces judgments on unrepentant advocates and church members (Rev. 2:16b, 21–23). Clearly, both Paul and John are against such attempts at cultural assimilation to avoid persecution or financial losses arising from offending others.

With regard to Jewish opposition, some Christians (likely both Jewish and Gentile) even tried to avoid persecution by advocating that Gentile Christians should be circumcised and obey the Torah. While this view might have originated from certain Jewish Christians who held that full proselytization was the only way for Gentiles to be included as the people of God (cf. Acts 15:1; see also p. 23 above), the 'agitators' (*hoi anastatounte*) among the Galatian churches (Gal. 5:12) advocated this view with the motive of avoiding persecution (Gal. 6:12).

Scholars are divided on who these 'agitators' might have been and what kind of persecution they were trying to avoid. Although their 'cover story' may be zeal for the law (cf. Acts 21:20–21), Paul accuses them of not keeping the law themselves (Gal. 6:13) and exposes their motive: they wish to have a 'good standing' (*euprosōpēsai*) and thus 'are forcing' (*anankazousin*) the Gentile Christians to be circumcised 'only for the purpose of' (*monon hina*) avoiding persecution (Gal. 6:12). For our purpose here, it suffices to say that the identity of the agitators does not affect our understanding of their motive for avoiding persecution.[90]

What kind of persecution were they trying to avoid? From Paul's argument in Galatians 2:16 – 6:10, the dispute centres around the means by which one becomes included in the people of God (by Torah obedience or by faith in Christ)[91] and how the Torah may be fulfilled. Therefore, it is most likely that, by assimilating to Jewish customs, they were trying to avoid persecution from Jews who did not believe in Jesus.[92]

---

Thyatira); and (3) those who think that, with very few exceptions, it is not all right for most circumstances (e.g. Paul). This does not mean that John and Paul contradict each other, though we may say that Revelation portrays a stricter view than Paul does.

[90] For various views on who these opponents ('agitators') were, see ch. 1, n. 66 above.

[91] Although the phrase *hē pistis Iēsou Christou* (e.g. Gal. 2:16; 3:22) may mean 'faith in Christ' or 'faithfulness of Christ', I think the former is more likely. For details of my argument, see Chee-Chiew Lee, *The Blessing of Abraham, the Spirit, and Justification in Galatians: Their Relationship and Significance for Understanding Paul's Theology* (Eugene: Pickwick, 2013), p. 20.

[92] See e.g. James D. G. Dunn, *The Epistle to the Galatians*, BNTC (Peabody: Hendrickson, 1993), pp. 336–337; Schreiner, *Galatians*, p. 377; Moo, *Galatians*, p. 393; David A. deSilva, *The Letter to the Galatians*, NICNT (Grand Rapids: Eerdmans, 2018), p. 505.

More recently, a few scholars have argued that the 'agitators' here were trying to avoid persecution from local authorities (pagan opponents) (1) through gaining the status of *religio licita* for the whole Christian community by being included in the Jewish community; thus being able to avoid participation in the pagan form of the imperial cult and to meet legally every week;[93] or (2) through their dissociation from uncircumcised Gentile Christians among them who did not participate in imperial cults.[94] While I do not dismiss the pressure Gentile Christians faced from non-participation in pagan and imperial cults, it is difficult to explain why Paul does not mention this in his letter to the Galatians if this is the main issue he responds to.[95]

For Paul, the requirement of circumcision defeats the purpose and work of the cross of Christ (Gal. 2:21; 5:2, 4) and amounts to another gospel, which is not a gospel at all (Gal. 1:6–7). For Paul, it is not acceptable to compromise through cultural assimilation in order to avoid persecution. It is also noteworthy that Paul appeals to the Old Testament extensively in Galatians (see esp. Gal. 3 – 4). This is almost certainly his response to his Jewish opponents who see his gospel message as a threat to their traditionally held values of circumcision, Torah obedience and segregation from the uncleanness of Gentiles.[96] It is his effort to prove that the gospel he proclaims is in accord with what God promised in the Old Testament – their commonly held authoritative tradition.

## Accommodation and adaptation

Peter's denial of Jesus three times is a well-known gospel tradition that appears in all four Gospels (Mark 14:66–70 // Matt. 26:69–75 // Luke 22:56–62 // John 18:15–18, 25–27). The Markan and Matthean traditions note that Jesus predicts all his disciples will fall away when he is arrested (Mark 14:27 // Matt. 26:31). Peter, however, is so sure that even if others

---

[93] See p. 21 above.

[94] Hardin, *Galatians and the Imperial Cult*, pp. 85–155; A. V. Prokhorov, 'Taking the Jews out of the Equation: Galatians 6.12–17 as a Summons to Cease Evading Persecution', *JSNT* 36.2 (2013), pp. 172–188; Winter, *Divine Honours for the Caesars*, pp. 226–249. For point 1, see Winter; for point 2, see Hardin.

[95] See also Te-Li Lau, review of 'Galatians and the Imperial Cult: A Critical Analysis of the First-Century Social Context of Paul's Letter', *BBR* 20.1 (2010), pp. 130–131. For a fair critique of Winter and Hardin on this issue, see deSilva, *Galatians*, pp. 368–375.

[96] See p. 41 above.

fall away, he will not (Mark 14:29 // Matt. 26:33). He declares that even if he dies, he will not deny Jesus, and *all* the disciples say likewise (Mark 14:31 // Matt. 26:35). Yet with all that confidence and determination, they *all* flee when Jesus is arrested (Mark 14:50 // Matt. 26:56b), fulfilling the prediction. The Lukan tradition records only Peter's pledge that he is willing to go to prison and even to die for Jesus (Luke 22:33), but does not mention the other disciples' pledge or their eventual flight.

The Synoptic Gospels note that Peter wept bitterly after his denial, but John's Gospel does not. Instead, John's Gospel has a separate episode depicting Jesus' reinstatement of Peter by asking him three times, 'Do you love me?' (John 21:15–17).[97] The Synoptic Gospels depict a remorseful Peter and we can safely assume that he and the other disciples who fled all repented. The Lukan tradition mentions Jesus' praying that Peter's faith will not fail and that he will strengthen others after his repentance (Luke 22:32). John's Gospel depicts the grace Jesus extends to Peter to accommodate his weaknesses, affirming his repentance and predicting that Peter will die as a martyr (John 21:18–19).

In the Markan and Lukan traditions, the standards Jesus sets are high: if anyone is ashamed of him and his words, the Son of Man will be ashamed of him when he comes again in glory (Mark 8:38 // Luke 9:26). The double tradition preserves a similar high standard: whoever denies Jesus before people, Jesus will deny them before the Father; whoever acknowledges Jesus, he will likewise acknowledge (Matt. 10:32–33; Luke 12:8–9). Peter is certainly not the only believer who repeatedly denied Jesus under the pressure of persecution. While all four Gospels depict denial of Jesus as a weakness and an undesired response, they also accommodate disciples who were weak but repentant.

The double tradition and John's Gospel preserve Jesus' exhortation on not being afraid of persecution (Matt. 10:26–31 // Luke 12:4–7; cf. John 14:27). However, John's Gospel is unique in addressing the fear of persecution from opposing Jewish authorities (John 7:13; 9:22; 19:38; 20:19)[98]

---

[97] A number of scholars see this episode as related to Peter's denial of Jesus in John 18. See e.g. D. A. Carson, *The Gospel According to John*, PNTC (Grand Rapids: Eerdmans, 1991), p. 675; George R. Beasley-Murray, *John*, rev. edn, WBC 36 (Dallas: Word, 1999), pp. 404–405; Köstenberger, *John*, p. 595; Edward W. Klink III, *John*, ZECNT 4 (Grand Rapids: Zondervan, 2016), p. 911.

[98] The phrase *ho phobos/phobeō tōn Ioudaiōn*, 'the fear of the Jews', appears four times in John's Gospel. For our purpose here, 'the Jews' in this phrase refers to the Jewish leaders who oppose Jesus as the Messiah. Other occurrences in John's Gospel may refer to (1) the

by portraying how a number of characters respond to this fear: the blind man and his parents, the Jewish rulers who believed in Jesus, Joseph of Arimathea, Nicodemus and the disciples. As mentioned previously, the opposing Jewish leaders had threatened to cast out anyone who confessed that Jesus was the Christ (John 9:22; 12:42; cf. 16:2).[99] Bennema aptly reminds us, 'This fear of "the Jews" should not be underestimated, since the consequences for professing openly that Jesus was the Messiah were severe. Jesus even warns his followers that they could be killed (16:2).'[100] I have shown elsewhere how John's Gospel uses dualistic language to depict responses to facing persecution in order to bring out moral and theological implications.[101] In what follows, I will examine these in the same manner.

Scholars have noted the contrast between the blind man and his parents in their response to the Pharisees.[102] When questioned about how their son received his sight, they claim 'they know' their son was indeed born blind, but 'they do not know' how he received his sight (John 9:20–21). Nonetheless, John reveals that they do know how their son received his sight, but hide this because they are 'afraid of the Jewish leaders' (John 9:22–23). They do not dare to speak about Jesus in public, for fear of being associated with him or his messianic claims. In doing so, although they avoid the risk of being cast out of the synagogue, they 'aligned themselves with the side of lies – darkness and sin' (cf. John 8:44).[103] In contrast to his parents, the blind man makes a public confession that Jesus is from God in spite of the Pharisees' insults and intimidation (John 9:24–33). As a result, although he is cast out (most likely from the synagogue) before

---

(note 98 *cont.*) inhabitants of Judea; or (2) an ethnic entity. For detailed discussions, see D. Francois Tolmie, 'The Ἰουδαῖοι in the Fourth Gospel: A Narratological Perspective', in Gilbert van Belle, Jan G. van der Watt and Petrus Maritz (eds.), *Theology and Christology in the Fourth Gospel*, BETL 184 (Leuven: Leuven University Press, 2005), pp. 377–399; Urban C. von Wahlde, 'Narrative Criticism of the Religious Authorities as a Group Character in the Gospel of John: Some Problems', *NTS* 63.2 (2017), pp. 222–245.

[99] See p. 57 above on the social implications of being 'cast out of the synagogue'.

[100] Cornelis Bennema, *Encountering Jesus: Character Studies in the Gospel of John*, 2nd edn (Minneapolis: Fortress, 2014), p. 342.

[101] Chee-Chiew Lee, 'A Theology of Facing Persecution in the Gospel of John', *TynBul* 70.2 (2019), pp. 189–204. Most of the materials in the above are adapted from this article.

[102] Andy M. Reimer, 'The Man Born Blind: True Disciple of Jesus', in Steven A. Hunt, D. F. Tolmie and Ruben Zimmermann (eds.), *Character Studies in the Fourth Gospel: Narrative Approaches to Seventy Figures in John*, WUNT 314 (Tübingen: Mohr Siebeck, 2013), p. 437; Bennema, *Encountering Jesus*, p. 255.

[103] Lee, 'Facing Persecution', p. 190; see also Raymond E. Brown, *The Gospel According to John*, 2 vols., AB 29 (Garden City: Doubleday, 1966), vol. 1, p. 365.

them (John 9:34),[104] he 'aligned himself with the side of truth – light and salvation'.[105]

Later in the narrative, 'many even among the leaders believed in him. But because of the Pharisees they would not openly acknowledge their faith for fear they would be put out of the synagogue' (John 12:42). John reveals that this is because they love their own honour more than God's (John 12:43).[106] Two Jewish leaders are named in John's Gospel: (1) Joseph of Arimathea; and (2) Nicodemus. Do both of them love their own honour more than God's? How does John evaluate them?

John gives very little information about Joseph, other than stating that he is 'a disciple of Jesus, but secretly because he feared the Jewish leaders' (John 19:38). Unless familiar with the Synoptic Gospels, the audience/readers would not know that Joseph is a Jewish leader (Matt. 27:57; Mark 15:43; Luke 23:50–51).[107] Some interpreters think John depicts Joseph's 'fear' and 'secrecy' as negative, but Joseph's request for Jesus' body from Pilate shows his courage and redresses this negative characterization.[108] Although 'fear of the Jewish leaders' seems to connect Joseph to the blind man's parents and the Jewish leaders who believe in Jesus, John does not give any negative comments regarding Joseph. Similarly, when the disciples meet behind closed doors due to this same fear, John also does not comment on them negatively (John 20:19). As Michaels notes, even Jesus acted secretly before 'his hour' to be arrested (7:1–10;

---

[104] Klink, *John*, p. 449. Although the text does not indicate directly that the blind man was cast out of the synagogue, it is very likely this happened, as such legal proceedings usually took place in the synagogue.

[105] Lee, 'Facing Persecution', pp. 190–191. Jesus proclaims that whoever follows him will have 'the light of life' (John 8:12). The blind man sees this true light and believes in Jesus (9:35–38). See also Bennema, *Encountering Jesus*, pp. 247–248.

[106] On the shame associated with being ostracized, see p. 57 above. The genitives here (*tōn anthrōpōn and tou theou)* more likely denote source ('belonging to') while *doxa* here more likely refers to 'honour' due to one's status (BDAG, p. 257, 3). That is, they prefer to guard their own honour rather than God's. By doing so, God will be dishonoured when his people deny him. Alternatively, the phrase *he doxa tou theou* may also mean 'praise from God' with the genitive denoting source ('coming from') and *doxa* referring to approval from God. See Jouette M. Bassler, 'Mixed Signals: Nicodemus in the Fourth Gospel', *JBL* 108.4 (1989), p. 641.

[107] It is difficult to be sure whether John's audience knew the Synoptic Gospels, although they might have known the other gospel traditions regarding Joseph of Arimathea. See Wendy S. North, 'John for Readers of Mark?: A Response to Richard Bauckham's Proposal', *JSNT* 25.4 (2003), p. 466; Edward W. Klink III, *The Sheep of the Fold: The Audience and Origin of the Gospel of John*, SNTSMS 141 (Cambridge: Cambridge University Press, 2007), pp. 180–182. The point here is that we need not assume John expects his audience to know.

[108] Carson, *Gospel According to John*, p. 629; Beasley-Murray, *John*, p. 358; Köstenberger, *John*, pp. 554–555; Bennema, *Encountering Jesus*, pp. 343–344; Klink, *John*, pp. 817–818.

8:59; 11:54–57; 12:36).[109] Therefore, John does not portray fear of the Jewish leaders as negative in itself, but only when moral integrity is compromised.

Some interpreters also note that the request for Jesus' body was not as risky as some might think, because the Jewish leaders earlier requested that Jesus' body be brought down from the cross before the Sabbath began (John 19:31). Joseph could have been perceived as a representative of the Jewish leaders.[110] However, if the Jewish leaders were to discover his act of burying Jesus in a tomb rather than in a common grave for criminals, his identity as Jesus' disciple would have been exposed. Thus, if Joseph had loved his 'own honour more than God's', he would not have taken this risk.

Unlike the little information on Joseph of Arimathea, John introduces Nicodemus as a Pharisee and a Jewish leader right at the beginning (John 3:1). Nonetheless, there is no mention throughout the narrative whether Nicodemus has believed or whether he is a disciple of Jesus. When Nicodemus first came to see Jesus, he did so at night, perhaps to avoid being seen as associated with Jesus, especially given Jesus' earlier conflict with the Jewish leaders at the temple (John 2:13–25). There may be some sort of secrecy involved here too. When the Jewish leaders opposed Jesus at the Feast of the Tabernacles, Nicodemus reminded them that they should not condemn Jesus without first having a hearing. Consequently, the Pharisees sneered at him (John 7:45–52). Furthermore, Nicodemus took the risk of being associated with Jesus when he and Joseph of Arimathea buried Jesus (John 19:39–42). If Nicodemus loved his own honour more than God's, he would not have spoken up for Jesus or taken the risk.

Although John depicted the blind man as a positive character, but his parents and the Jewish leaders who believed but feared to confess publicly as negative characters, his characterization of Joseph of Arimathea and Nicodemus appears to be deliberately ambiguous.[111] He does not comment on Joseph, Nicodemus or the disciples meeting behind closed doors

---

[109] J. Ramsey Michaels, *The Gospel of John*, NICNT (Grand Rapids: Eerdmans, 2010), p. 979.

[110] William J. Lyons, 'Joseph of Arimathea: One of "the Jews," but with a Fearful Secret!', in Steven A. Hunt, D. F. Tolmie and Ruben Zimmermann (eds.), *Character Studies in the Fourth Gospel: Narrative Approaches to Seventy Figures in John*, WUNT 314 (Tübingen: Mohr Siebeck, 2013), p. 652; Bennema, *Encountering Jesus*, p. 344.

[111] Lee, 'Facing Persecution', p. 198.

positively or negatively. As Koester notes, this may be John's way of portraying the 'complexities of life'.[112] Therefore, John does not always indicate public confession of faith in Jesus as the desired response to persecution. This may be John's way of accommodating instances of secrecy while not directly approving of them.

In chapter 1, we noted that Jews and pagans alike honoured the Roman emperor by offering prayers and sacrifices to their God/gods for the well-being of the emperor and the empire. I also mentioned earlier that 1 Peter instructed believers to submit to ruling authorities and to honour the emperor without prescribing how to go about doing so.[113]

It is noteworthy that Romans 13:1–7 follows right after Paul's exhortation on how to face persecution (Rom. 12:14–21) and thus can be understood as one of the aspects of doing 'good' (*agathos*; Rom. 12:21; 13:3) in response to hostility.[114] In this respect, Romans 13:1–7 is very similar to 1 Peter in exhorting believers to submit to authorities and to be ready to do 'good works' as a response to persecution.[115] Romans 13:1–7 not only mentions submission to authorities as obligatory on the basis of their being God's agent for executing justice, but Paul also makes this the reason for paying taxes and respecting rulers (Rom. 13:6–7).[116] This is a strong echo of Jesus' saying 'Give back to Caesar what is Caesar's and to God what is God's' (Mark 12:17 // Matt. 22:21// Luke 20:25).[117] As Paul juxtaposes paying taxes and respecting, and describes them as 'debts' owed to the authorities (Rom. 13:7), paying taxes can be seen as a way of showing honour to the authorities. Towner suggests that, in view of Claudius' earlier expulsion edict involving unrest among the Jews (likely due to their dispute about Christ), Paul's teaching in this passage regarding paying taxes and doing good could be an attempt to employ existing social

---

112 Craig R. Koester, 'Theological Complexity and the Characterization of Nicodemus in John's Gospel', in Christopher W. Skinner (ed.), *Characters and Characterization in the Gospel of John*, LNTS 461 (London: Bloomsbury T&T Clark, 2013), p. 169.

113 See p. 75 above.

114 For scholars who see a connection between Rom. 12:14–21 and Rom. 13:1–8, see James D. G. Dunn, *The Theology of Paul the Apostle* (Grand Rapids: Eerdmans, 1998), pp. 674–680; Harrison, *Paul and the Imperial Authorities*, p. 309; Frank Thielman, *Romans*, ZECNT (Grand Rapids: Zondervan, 2018), p. 601.

115 Although Titus 3:1–2 is similar to Rom. 13:1–7 and 1 Peter in its teaching to submit to authorities and do good works, its immediate literary context does not address persecution.

116 See *dio* in Rom. 13:5 and *dia touto* in Rom. 13:6, both meaning 'for this reason'.

117 See also Joseph A. Fitzmyer, *Romans: A New Translation with Introduction and Commentary*, AB 33 (New York: Doubleday, 1993), p. 670; Moo, *Romans*, p. 822.

conventions, so as to maintain social stability and earn a good reputation for the church.[118]

I discussed earlier that 1 Peter advocates good works as a response to persecution, as well as what 'good works' entailed in Greco-Roman and Judeo-Christian understanding.[119] At this point, it is necessary for us to revisit this issue. Du Toit points out that 'doing what is beneficial to others is prevalent in the ancient world and is considered a virtue'.[120] A few scholars suggest that civic benefaction can be part of what Romans 13:3–4 and 1 Peter 2:14–15 refer to as 'good works', because these two passages mention the authorities commending good works, and civic benefactors were usually commended publicly.[121] Others doubt this reference as many Christians would not have had the financial capability to perform civic benefactions.[122] However, du Toit notes that benefactions could include a wide range of deeds performed for the benefit of others, by individuals (e.g. paying off the debt for someone) or by groups (e.g. donations by associations for civic purposes).[123] Therefore, while both texts seem to include broader forms of 'good works', there is no need to restrict such good works to civic benefactions.[124] According to 1 Peter, such (publicly acknowledged) good works proved that Christians could benefit and not harm society.

In 1 Timothy 2:1–2 believers are exhorted that 'petitions, prayers, intercession and thanksgiving be made for *all people – for kings and all those in authority,* that we may live peaceful and quiet lives in all godliness and holiness'. This is very similar to the contemporaneous Jewish tradition of praying for and honouring the emperor as a form of imperial cult that we

---

[118] Philip H. Towner, 'Romans 13:1–7 and Paul's Missiological Perspective: A Call to Political Quietism or Transformation?', in Sven K. Soderlund and N. T. Wright (eds.), *Romans and the People of God* (Grand Rapids: Eerdmans, 1999), pp. 160–169. Towner adds that such stability would also make it conducive for the Roman church to support his mission to Spain.

[119] See p. 75 above.

[120] Du Toit, 'Negotiating Hostility', p. 223.

[121] See e.g. Bruce W. Winter, *Seek the Welfare of the City: Christians as Benefactors and Citizens,* FCCGRW (Grand Rapids: Eerdmans, 1994), pp. 25–40; Towner, 'Romans 13:1–7', pp. 165–166. As defined by Williams, 'civic benefactions (or euergetism) in the Greco-Roman world was a type of gift-exchange in which a member of the local or provincial elite used his (or her) private wealth or power to benefit a city, its citizenry, or a group of citizens, and in return, received reciprocal recognition of the contribution as a benefaction.' Williams, *Good Works in 1 Peter,* p. 69.

[122] See e.g. Achtemeier, *1 Peter,* p. 184, n. 64; Williams, *Good Works in 1 Peter,* pp. 68–104.

[123] For examples from primary sources, see du Toit, 'Negotiating Hostility', pp. 222–225.

[124] See e.g. Moo, *Romans,* p. 817, n. 313; Jobes, *1 Peter,* pp. 175–176.

saw previously.[125] It is also in line with the Jewish tradition of praying for the welfare of their foreign ruler and the state (cf. Jer. 29:7; Bar. 1.11; 1 Macc. 7:33). Nonetheless, 1 Timothy 2:5 clearly states that 'there is one God and one mediator between God and mankind, the man Christ Jesus', in contrast to the pagan concept of the Roman emperor as the *pontifex maximus* – high priest and mediator between the gods and the people.[126]

From the above, we observe how the Pauline epistles and 1 Peter advocate responses to persecution by adapting current practices, such as honouring the emperor through paying taxes, offering prayers and thanksgiving to God for the emperor, and performing good works (bestowing individual or civic benefactions) to fulfil their social and civic responsibilities as good citizens without compromising faithfulness to Christ. These responses are attempts to demonstrate that Christians are not a threat to the well-being of society, despite being perceived as such by outsiders.[127]

# Summary of theological perspectives

The forms of persecution we observe from the New Testament texts reflect both official and non-official persecution. During the earliest days, with the exception of Herod Agrippa I, all official persecution came from Jewish authorities in Judea against the disciples of Jesus. While both Jewish and pagan non-official persecution existed from the earliest days in the diaspora, it was not until nearly the end of the first century that official pagan persecution began to be more obvious. Acts and the Pauline epistles reflect the former, while Revelation mostly reflects the latter, with Hebrews and 1 Peter possibly reflecting both. It is also important to note that official forms of punishment must not be too quickly identified as official persecution, because the former may reflect only pagan officials exercising their authority in addressing social unrest and charges brought against Christians by individual Jewish or pagan opponents.

---

[125] See pp. 21–22 above and I. Howard Marshall and Philip H. Towner, *A Critical and Exegetical Commentary on the Pastoral Epistles*, ICC (London: T&T Clark International, 2004), p. 422. 'Jewish tradition' refers to beliefs and customs of the Jews – largely shaped by their understanding of their Scriptures – that have been passed on over the generations. Jewish writings, inscriptions and artefacts would reflect their contemporaneous Jewish traditions.

[126] See p. 16 above.

[127] See pp. 41–50 above.

Luke's crafting of the narrative in Acts is remarkable, from which we may infer his theology of facing persecution.[128] While Luke portrays Jewish and pagan opponents using similar tactics against the early Christians (e.g. inciting the crowd, bringing political charges to the authorities in the guise of initial religious or economic conflicts), he depicts some Jewish opponents using underhand methods such as false witnesses and murderous plots. Nonetheless, Luke also honestly and fairly depicts other Jewish opponents who did not persecute the disciples (e.g. Roman Jews in Acts 28).

As a whole, Luke paints a very positive picture of early Christian responses to persecution. The disciples and their leaders (Peter, Stephen and Paul) responded to persecution in a manner consistent with Jesus' teachings on how his disciples are to face persecution. (1) They considered suffering for Christ as integral to discipleship and thus faced persecution with joy, courage and perseverance by the Holy Spirit's empowerment. Stephen prayed for his persecutors as taught by Jesus. (2) The leaders seized the opportunities to witness for Christ whenever they stood on trial before the authorities, demonstrating remarkable wisdom as promised by Christ through the work of the Holy Spirit. (3) Although they fled from persecution, they continued to proclaim the gospel wherever they went. (4) They appealed to the Scriptures not only to prove that Jesus was the promised Messiah, but also to show that rejection of Jesus and God's consequent judgment are foretold in the Scriptures. Luke also portrays Paul's responding to the dangers of persecution in a variety of ways (e.g. to escape or to stay on), depending on the circumstances and conviction he received directly from the Lord. Nonetheless, from our contemporary perspective, Paul can be rather offensive in his verbal response to some opponents as seen in Acts. However, Luke does not comment negatively on Paul's behaviour. These portrayals in Acts represent Luke's theology, illustrating (1) his notion of exemplary and desired responses to persecution; and (2) his purpose in showing that the disciples were able to live according to Jesus' teachings in the gospel traditions on how they should face persecution.

---

[128] By suggesting that Luke crafted his narrative for the rhetorical purpose of persuading his recipients to stand firm in their faith while facing persecution, I do not mean that Luke has in any way fabricated any part of his narrative. Rather, I affirm the historicity of Acts while acknowledging that all accounts of historical events are naturally subjective and reflect the perspective of the narrator, even if they demonstrate objectivity and accuracy.

This positive picture is also reflected and corroborated in the Pauline epistles (with regard to Paul himself and the churches he wrote to: Thessalonians, Philippians), in 1 Peter (believers faced persecution when they abandoned their previous lifestyle), in Hebrews (certain believers lost their property and were imprisoned) and in Revelation (certain faithful saints who persevered in witnessing and suffering even in the face of death, depicted both in the letters to the seven churches and in the visions). Paul, in particular, is always ready to share his emotions openly – joy, fear and pain in his sufferings from persecution. Perseverance in Paul is motivated by his conviction of God's calling him and by his experience of God's faithfulness, empowerment and deliverance. Paul sees his suffering for Christ as worthwhile because (1) it brings the gospel and salvation to those who hear him; (2) it is an example and motivation for other disciples to do the same; (3) it produces character and hope; and (4) it is an honour for him to participate in Christ's suffering. These values motivate his perseverance.

By comparison, the other New Testament writings, unlike in Acts, do not always paint positive pictures of faithfulness when enduring persecution. Fear of persecution and its consequences (e.g. loss of honour and economic benefits, and at times even threat of death) causes Christians to respond in various ways: secrecy, denial, cultural assimilation or apostasy. The author of Hebrews portrays the threat of apostasy his audience face, though he does not indicate that any of them apostatized. In view of Jesus' parable of the seeds sown on rocky ground, it should not be surprising that there were indeed cases of apostasy,[129] even if the New Testament authors rarely mention them. Such approaches in Acts and Hebrews likely have rhetorical purposes, and we will look into this in chapter 3. In this respect, other New Testament authors seem to be more down to earth in reflecting diverse Christian responses. Pauline epistles (such as Galatians and 1 Corinthians) and Revelation reflect that some people in their recipients' community had already compromised their faithfulness to Christ by cultural assimilation – adopting existing Jewish or pagan customs as part of their Christian life (e.g. knowingly eating food sacrificed to idols, accepting circumcision and Torah observance). They had done so to avoid conflict, economic disadvantage and persecution, which Paul and John deem as opposing the truth of the gospel.

---

[129] See n. 82 above.

All four Gospels depict as a negative example Peter's denial of Jesus for fear of persecution. Nonetheless, their narratives accommodate disciples who were weak but repentant. John's Gospel further portrays the fear of persecution as a problem Jesus' disciples faced. While John clearly portrays a positive example to be emulated (the blind man) and negative examples to be avoided (his parents and the Jewish leaders who believed but dared not confess), he also portrays other characters ambiguously (Joseph of Arimathea and Nicodemus) without any indication of his approval or disapproval. This is perhaps John's way of accommodation, not wishing to classify every case of secrecy neatly into dualistic categories (right/wrong, good/bad), unless moral integrity is compromised.

Other than demonstrating resistance to compromise and perseverance while facing persecution, Pauline epistles (Rom. 13:1–7; 1 Tim. 2:1–2) and 1 Peter 2:13 – 3:7 also propose adaptations to certain existing cultural practices (submission, good works, prayers for ruling authorities) in response, but without compromising faithfulness to Christ. Together with the use of Jewish Scriptures to prove authenticity of Jesus as the promised Messiah, these adaptations are likely apologetic moves to show the outsiders that Christians are not a threat to society. The use of the Jewish Scriptures attempts to show Jewish opponents that Christian beliefs are not contrary to but rather a fulfilment of the Scriptures. Adaptations to existing cultural practices are attempts to show that Christians are good and respectful citizens who are not subversive (cf. outsiders' perceived threat to traditionally held values, threat to social unrest, alleged vilification of opponents). These responses we have observed are not comprehensive in responding to the outsiders' perspectives, but demonstrate attempts to do so in some ways. As this is a descriptive study of the New Testament authors' theological perspective, we will not be assessing how effective these responses were.

My summary above clearly shows that believers in the New Testament have diverse responses to persecution. Even in similar situations, Paul is depicted as employing different strategies, depending on the circumstances (e.g. whether to flee from persecution, when to exercise Roman citizen rights). In Acts, the defence speeches of Peter and Stephen before the Sanhedrin were provocative, given their counter-accusation against their accusers. They did not seem to have the intention of pacifying the tribunal. On the contrary, Paul's defence before the Roman tribunals mostly lack such counter-accusations. While Acts 4 and 7 depict Peter and

Stephen employing non-conciliatory approaches by counter-accusing their opponents when they stand trial, 1 Peter 3:15–16 and 2 Timothy 2:25–26 seem to advocate a milder and gentler approach.

Even New Testament authors themselves can have differing opinions on the same issue (e.g. facing the fear of persecution, eating food offered to idols). While John is similar to Mark 8:38 and Luke 9:26 in his evaluation of some Jewish leaders who dare not publicly confess their faith in Jesus for fear of shame (John 12:42–43), he seems deliberately ambiguous with his evaluation regarding two of these Jewish leaders – Joseph of Arimathea and Nicodemus. Paul (1 Cor. 8; 10), Acts 15:20 and Revelation 2:14, 20 are all against eating food offered to idols, but only Paul (1 Cor. 10:23–33) makes a provision for eating unknowingly. New Testament authors hold on to the same base line – faithfulness to Christ – but their opinions and responses are not always identical. Nevertheless, their differing opinions do not contradict each other, but reflect diverse perspectives on the same issue.

# 3

# How to stand firm to the end: persuading and empowering perseverance

It is common for modern people to think that emotions are irrational and the use of emotions is manipulative. How does this compare with first-century Greco-Roman culture? In this chapter, by tracing how the New Testament authors persuade their audience to persevere in faith despite facing persecution, we will not only examine their use of logical reasoning, but will also study how emotions and the use of emotions play an important role in their persuasion.

## Cultural background: the art of persuasion

Most of us would agree that New Testament authors use literary and oral conventions of their day to communicate their teachings; for example, letter writing, biography, speeches, poetry and apocalyptic writings. Many Christians throughout history would also profess that God uses human authors in their context to reveal his truths. Therefore, we will examine the literary and cultural milieu of the New Testament authors in terms of their conventions of persuasion.

### Rhetorical conventions

Many of us are familiar with the use of exhortations, exemplars to emulate and reasoning (*logos*) as forms of persuasion in the New Testament. These are some of the common persuasion techniques in Greco-Roman rhetoric.[1]

---

[1] See e.g. Abraham J. Malherbe, *Moral Exhortation: A Greco-Roman Sourcebook*, LEC 4 (Philadelphia: Westminster, 1986), pp. 121–134; Mario M. DiCicco, *Paul's Use of Ethos, Pathos,*

They are also commonly used across many cultures, including our own. Communication in first-century Greco-Roman culture was mostly aural, even letters and other literary works were read aloud to the audience.[2] Therefore, persuasion techniques used in speeches were also often employed in writings, achieving similar effects when read aloud.[3]

In Greco-Roman rhetoric, the orator typically uses three kinds of proof to support his main point:[4] (1) *ethos*; proving to the audience the orator and his message are credible; (2) *logos*; proving with logical argumentation to convince the audience; and (3) *pathos*; stirring up certain emotions of the audience to direct them towards the course of action the orator has intended.[5] Paul's defence of the authenticity of his apostleship and message (Gal. 1:1, 11–12) is a typical example of building *ethos*.[6] Other than appealing to *logos*, the author of Hebrews uses *pathos* frequently – stirring up emotions such as fear, confidence, empathy, honour and shame,[7] which we will see below.

Although the apostle Paul apparently claims he does not use 'eloquence' (*hyperochē logou*) or 'persuasive words of wisdom' (*peithoi sophias logoi*)[8]

---

and Logos in 2 Corinthians 10–13, MBPS 31 (Lewiston: Mellen Biblical Press, 1995), pp. 188–259; Bryan R. Dyer, *Suffering in the Face of Death: The Epistle to the Hebrews and Its Context of Situation*, LNTS 568 (London: Bloomsbury, 2017), pp. 132–174.

[2] The practice of individual silent visual reading was rare, even for those who were literate. Their practice was to read aloud. See Pieter J. J. Botha, 'The Verbal Art of the Pauline Letters: Rhetoric, Performance and Presence', in Stanley E. Porter and Thomas H. Olbricht (eds.), *Rhetoric and the New Testament: Essays from the 1992 Heidelberg Conference*, JSNTSup 90 (Sheffield: Sheffield Academic Press, 1993), p. 414; Ben Witherington III, *New Testament Rhetoric: An Introductory Guide to the Art of Persuasion in and of the New Testament* (Eugene: Cascade, 2009), pp. 1–3.

[3] Cf. Witherington, *New Testament Rhetoric*, p. 20. More recently, Parsons and Martin have shown that Greek tertiary education, perhaps even in secondary education, used *progymnasmata* (preliminary exercises for speech composition) for training in writing and this could plausibly explain how New Testament writers or their amanuenses were able to incorporate rhetorical devices in their writings. Mikeal C. Parsons and Michael W. Martin, *Ancient Rhetoric and the New Testament: The Influence of Elementary Greek Composition* (Waco: Baylor University Press, 2018), pp. 1–9, 275–281.

[4] Witherington, *New Testament Rhetoric*, pp. 15–16; Chee-Chiew Lee, 'The Use of Scriptures and the Rhetoric of Fear in Hebrews', *BBR* 31.2 (2021), p. 192. The process mentioned above is known as *inventio*.

[5] On *ethos*, see e.g. Aristotle, *Rhetoric* 2.1.3, 2.1.5; *Rhetorica ad Herennium* 1.7. On various forms of arguments employed in *logos*, see e.g. *Rhetoric to Alexander* 1429–1430. On *pathos*, see e.g. Aristotle, *Rhetoric* 2.2–2.11; Quintilian, *Institutio oratoria* 6.1.7–6.1.11.

[6] DeSilva, *Galatians*, p. 139.

[7] See also H. Gorman, 'Persuading Through *Pathos*: Appeals to the Emotions in Hebrews', *ResQ* 54.2 (2012), pp. 77–90.

[8] There is a textual variant here with several readings, which may be classified mainly into two groups of witnesses: (1) those with the adjective *anthrōpinos*, 'human', modifying *sophia*, 'wisdom' (e.g. ℵ² A C 1 42 131); and (2) those without the adjective (e.g. 𝔓⁴⁶ ℵ* B D 33). Earlier manuscripts support point 2.

in his preaching (1 Cor. 2:1, 4) and that he is not trained as a professional rhetorician (2 Cor. 11:6),[9] scholars do not doubt that there are identifiable rhetorical devices in Paul's letters.[10] Rather, it is more likely that (1) in 1 Corinthians 2:1–4, Paul wishes to emphasize God's power at work through the Spirit over sole human effort; and (2) in 2 Corinthians 11:5–6, he is not less knowledgeable compared with the other 'super-apostles', even if he does not speak as eloquently as them.[11]

Besides the Pauline epistles and Hebrews, other New Testament writings also exhibit the use of rhetorical techniques.[12] I will explain below how and why these New Testament authors incorporate various techniques in their use of persuasion. One technique common across all of them is the use of the Jewish Scriptures. Like their Jewish contemporaries, they believed these Scriptures were divinely inspired and were thus authoritative (cf. 2 Tim. 3:16; 2 Peter 1:21).[13] Like their Greco-Roman contemporaries, Jewish and Christian authors employed authoritative tradition as a rhetorical device.[14] It is important to note that not only are they persuading their audience to persevere despite persecution, but they are fully convinced that God can empower his people to persevere (e.g. John 17:11–12; 2 Thess. 2:16–17; Heb. 7:25; 1 Peter 5:10; Rev. 7:3).

---

[9] 2 Cor. 11:6 is a first-class conditional sentence, in which the protasis 'even if I am untrained in speaking' is assumed for argument's sake to be true. It does not necessarily equate with the facts. Thus, we should not deduce from the protasis that Paul was not trained in rhetoric. On the nuance of the first-class conditional sentence, see Daniel B. Wallace, *Greek Grammar Beyond the Basics: An Exegetical Syntax of the New Testament* (Grand Rapids: Zondervan, 1996), pp. 690–694.

[10] See e.g. Thrall, *Second Epistle of the Corinthians*, pp. 677–678; Guthrie, *2 Corinthians*, pp. 517–518.

[11] Matera, *II Corinthians*, p. 248.

[12] New Testament authors do not all have the same level of education and it was common to engage an amanuensis, who might have had varying levels of literary skills. The author of Hebrews is exceptionally skilled in rhetoric, while other authors are less skilled. As rhetoric was taught in secondary education, it is likely Paul could have received some elementary training in Tarsus. Furthermore, in the Mediterranean cities speeches were often given in the public square (*agora*) where citizens commonly gathered to listen. Thus, the New Testament authors or their amanuenses might also have picked up some commonly used rhetorical techniques through these opportunities. Cf. Witherington, *New Testament Rhetoric*, p. 11.

[13] E. Earle Ellis, *The Old Testament in Early Christianity: Canon and Interpretation in the Light of Modern Research* (Eugene: Wipf & Stock, 2003), pp. 3–5.

[14] Dennis L. Stamps, 'The Use of the OT in the NT as a Rhetorical Device: A Methodological Proposal', in *Hearing the Old Testament in the New Testament*, MNTS (Grand Rapids: Eerdmans, 2006), pp. 9–37; Christopher D. Stanley, 'The Rhetoric of Quotations: An Essay on Method', in Craig A. Evans and James A. Sanders (eds.), *Early Christian Interpretation of the Scriptures of Israel: Investigations and Proposals*, JSNTSup 148 (Sheffield: Sheffield Academic Press, 1997), pp. 54–56.

## Honour and shame

Another prominent feature of Greco-Roman culture to note is 'honour and shame'. In that culture, people greatly desired honour and were very averse to shame (dishonour). Honour and shame were thus a powerful force regulating social behaviour. DeSilva gives an excellent account of how '[h]onoring and shaming became the dominant means of enforcing all those values that were not legislated and of reinforcing those values that were covered by written laws', and I will attempt to summarize this below.[15]

First, I mentioned earlier that public shaming (e.g. reviling, beating, exclusion from community, seizure of property, imprisonment) was used by the dominant culture (e.g. Jewish and Gentile opponents) as a means of pressurizing deviants (usually the minority; e.g. Christians) to conform to the dominant group's values (e.g. circumcision is the means by which one is included as God's people; participation in pagan cults is crucial to maintain the *pax deorum*) and to deter others (e.g. on-lookers) from deviating.[16] Christians who could not withstand the shame would compromise, as we saw in the previous chapter. So, what could have led other Christians to endure the shame and persevere in their faith?

Second, minority cultures attempt to redefine what constitutes honour and shame for them. As deSilva notes, this strategy can be seen in Jewish, Gentile and Christian writings.[17] I mentioned an oxymoron earlier: 'it is an honour to be dishonoured because of Christ'.[18] This is an example of redefining what the majority culture deemed as 'dishonourable' (being flogged by local authorities; cf. Acts 5:40–41) as an 'honour' (suffering for Christ) for the minority culture. Another way of expressing this is that it is a matter of being convinced whether it is more important to receive honour from God or from people.[19]

---

[15] DeSilva, *Honor, Patronage, Kinship and Purity*, pp. 36, 35–42.

[16] See p. 60 above. On this mechanism of social behaviour, see also Timothy MacBride, 'Aliens and Strangers: Minority Group Rhetoric in the Later New Testament Writings', in Mark Harding and Alanna Nobbs (eds.), *Into All the World: Emergent Christianity in Its Jewish and Greco-Roman Context* (Grand Rapids: Eerdmans, 2017), p. 303.

[17] For primary sources, see p. 40, n. 17 in deSilva, *Honor, Patronage, Kinship and Purity*, pp. 39–40.

[18] See p. 64 above.

[19] See also Te-Li Lau, *Defending Shame: Its Formative Power in Paul's Letters* (Grand Rapids: Baker Academic, 2020), p. 172.

While the New Testament authors are similar to their cultural milieu in their use of these two strategies of pressurizing and redefining,[20] they are also different in some ways. Recently, Lau has also done an important study on Paul's use of shame in his letters. Lau notes that Paul is similar to his contemporaneous Greco-Roman moralists in (1) understanding shame to be an emotion people experience when they realize their behaviour violates their moral norms (i.e. sin results in shame); and (2) using shame as a 'pedagogical tool' to discourage dishonouring behaviour (redefined according to Christian theology and perspective) and to motivate repentance.[21] Consequently, Lau concludes that Paul's 'shaming rhetoric is not destructive but redemptive, not disintegrative but re-integrative'.[22] Nonetheless, Lau has also shown that Paul is different from his contemporaries in his conviction that such shaming techniques are not effective without the 'transformative and empowering work' of the Holy Spirit.[23] In what follows, I will examine how the New Testament authors incorporate honour and shame as part of their rhetorical strategy to persuade their audience towards persevering in the Christian faith.

# Persuasions to persevere

Sayings and stories of Jesus were passed on in some form of oral and written gospel traditions before they were preserved in the Four Gospels. In this section, we will examine how various New Testament authors develop and apply certain gospel traditions in their teaching to persuade Jesus' followers to persevere in their faith despite persecution. As we examined earlier how the four evangelists use characterization to teach their audience about facing persecution,[24] I will not repeat them here.

## Mark

Mark begins addressing the topic of the disciples facing persecution with the parable of the seeds falling on four types of soil (Mark 4:1–20). As mentioned previously, unlike Luke, who is more general in his description, Mark links the seed falling on rocky ground and withering when

---

[20] MacBride, 'Aliens and Strangers', p. 305.
[21] Lau, *Defending Shame*, pp. 151–166.
[22] Ibid., p. 172.
[23] Ibid., pp. 167–172.
[24] See 'Summary of theological perspectives' in ch. 2 above.

scorched by the sun to those who fall away due to persecution (Mark 4:5–6, 16–17; cf. Luke 8:13).[25] This marks his first warning that some disciples will apostatize due to persecution.

Scholars have noted Mark's use of the literary device of a triad and a corresponding cyclical pattern in Jesus' three predictions of his passion, death and resurrection (only distinctives are listed in Table 3.1).[26]

**Table 3.1 Cyclical narrative pattern in Mark 8:31 – 10:45**

| *Predictions of his passion, death and resurrection* | | |
| --- | --- | --- |
| *First prediction:* Suffer and be rejected (8:31). | *Second prediction:* Delivered to men (9:30–32). | *Third prediction:* Delivered to local and regional authorities, suffer humiliation (10:32–34). |
| *The disciples' erroneous reaction* | | |
| Peter rebukes Jesus (8:32). | Disciples argue about who is the greatest (quest for glory) (9:33–34). | James and John ask to sit on Jesus' right and left (quest for glory) (10:35–37). |
| *Jesus' corrective teaching* | | |
| The cost of discipleship in terms of shame and glory (8:34–38). | True greatness comes in the form of humility and servanthood (9:35–37). | James and John will go through Jesus' baptism and drink his cup. True greatness is conferred by God and comes in the form of servanthood, as exemplified by Jesus (10:38–45). |

What we need to note here is how the theological message brought across through this literary device relates to facing persecution. We observe that each cycle is an amplification of the previous one. In the first

---

[25] See ch. 2, p. 77 above.

[26] On the use of triad, see Mark L. Strauss, *Mark*, ZECNT (Grand Rapids: Zondervan, 2014), p. 48. On the cyclical pattern, see R. T. France, *The Gospel of Mark: A Commentary on the Greek Text*, NIGTC (Grand Rapids: Eerdmans, 2002), p. 320; Robert H. Stein, *Mark*, BECNT (Grand Rapids: Baker Academic, 2008), p. 386; Strauss, *Mark*, p. 403. Although Matthew and Luke also record Jesus' three predictions of his passion, the Markan pattern is absent from them.

cycle (Mark 8:34–38), Jesus solemnly declares that following him inevitably entails suffering ('taking up the cross') and this is clearly associated with suffering for Jesus and the gospel (i.e. persecution), even to the point of death ('saving and losing one's life'). If the disciples are afraid to suffer shame (i.e. are ashamed of Jesus and his word), they may seem to have saved their own lives by denying Jesus.[27] However, at the glorious eschatological coming of Jesus, he will be ashamed of them and thus they will lose their lives.

In the second and third cycles, the disciples are on a quest for honour: wanting to be the greatest (Mark 9:33–34) and to occupy honourable seats beside the messianic King (Mark 10:35–37).[28] In both cycles, Jesus makes it clear that true greatness is manifested in humility and servanthood. In the third cycle, this concept is amplified with the example of Jesus himself (Mark 10:45). Jesus uses the metaphors of 'cup' and 'baptism' to portray his sufferings (cf. Mark 14:36; Luke 12:50; John 18:11).[29] James and John will be partaking in Jesus' sufferings by sharing his cup and participating in his baptism (Mark 10:39). In contrast, Jesus is not in the position to grant James and John places of honour (Mark 10:40).

The theological message emerges clearly through these three cycles. First, as disciples, their portion will only be suffering shame for Christ and his gospel, not honour due to positions of authority. Second, those who try to avoid the shame of suffering for Christ now will eventually suffer shame at the eschaton. Which matters more? To be shamed by persecutors temporally or to be shamed by the glorious Jesus at the final judgment? Here we see the regulatory function of shame and honour (glory) at work to motivate perseverance and faithfulness to Christ.

Finally, in the Olivet discourse (Mark 13:9–13) Jesus once again warns his disciples of suffering hatred and persecutions due to his name. Persecutors will press charges against the disciples before local and regional authorities and the latter will suffer punishment. Even so, disciples must bear witness before the tribunal and must first proclaim the gospel to the nations.[30] Nonetheless, Mark portrays Jesus as assuring the disciples of

---

[27] On being ashamed of Jesus and his word as denying Jesus, see also Stein, *Mark*, p. 410.

[28] See also Strauss, *Mark*, p. 454.

[29] France, *Mark*, p. 416; Strauss, *Mark*, p. 455.

[30] Some scholars understand *prōtos*, 'first', to refer to the preaching of the gospel to the nations before the destruction of the temple. See e.g. France, *Mark*, p. 516; Stein, *Mark*, p. 600;

the Spirit's wisdom to guide them. Persecutions will arise from one's own family members, even to the extent of being put to death by them. Nevertheless, the one who perseveres to the end shall be saved.

In his Gospel, Mark persuades his audience to persevere by presenting Jesus' teachings in the following manner: (1) Warnings of persecution are given ahead of time: people who decide to follow Jesus should know what they are in for. (2) Desired responses to persecution are stated: not being ashamed of suffering for Jesus, continuing to witness for Jesus despite opposition and persevering to the end. (3) Promises by Jesus function as assurance: the presence and wisdom of the Spirit counter anxiety, and the sure hope of salvation motivates towards perseverance.

# Matthew

Matthew's Gospel has five major discourses interspersed between related narratives.[31] In a few of these discourses, Matthew addresses the issue of facing persecution in a way that matches the topic of the discourse.

The first discourse (Matt. 5:1 – 7:29) focuses on Jesus as the fulfilment of the law (Matt. 5:17–19) – he is the authoritative interpreter of the law and its practice (Matt. 5:21 – 7:29). In accord with Jewish tradition, the disciples' obedience to the law is righteousness (Matt. 5:20; 6:1; cf. Deut. 6:25).[32] Therefore, it comes as no surprise that Jesus declares that those who are persecuted because of righteousness are 'blessed' (*makarios*)

---

Strauss, *Mark*, p. 575. However, it may be better to understand 'first' in its immediate context to refer to the proclamation of the gospel to the nations as prior to the disciples' witness before kings and governors for the following reasons. First, this is a Markan insertion into the pericope of witnessing before tribunals (cf. Matt. 10:17–20 // Luke 12:11–12), which likely indicates his intention to relate this to the immediate context. Second, the narrative in Acts corroborates this: Paul's witness before the tribunals is a consequence of persecution due to his missionary work to both Jews and Gentiles.

[31] France, *Matthew*, p. 8; Turner, *Matthew*, p. 9. Marked at the end by the same phrase *kai egeneto hote etelesen ho Iēsous*, 'when Jesus had finished' (7:28; 11:1; 13:53; 19:1; 26:1), these five discourses are (1) Jesus and the fulfilment of the law (Matt. 5:1 – 7:29); (2) missions and their opposition (Matt. 10:5 – 11:1); (3) parables of the kingdom (Matt. 13:1–52); (4) relationships among disciples (Matt. 18:1–35); and (5) the coming judgment (Matt. 24:3 – 25:46).

[32] For examples of associating righteousness with obedience to the law in the Second Temple literature, see Steven M. Bryan, *Jesus and Israel's Traditions of Judgement and Restoration*, SNTSMS 117 (Cambridge: Cambridge University Press, 2002), pp. 57–68. Righteousness here is not just 'good conduct' (so Gundry; Turner) but more specifically 'obedience to the law'. Gundry, *Matthew*, p. 73; Turner, *Matthew*, p. 143. The disciples' obedience to the law must exceed that of the scribes and Pharisees (Matt. 5:20) in a way that reflects the succeeding passages on Jesus' interpretation of the law and its applications (Matt. 5:21–48). These are over and above their traditional understanding, as marked by the repeated phrase 'you have heard that it was said . . . But I say to you'.

(Matt. 5:10). This *makarios* is the last of the eight (Matt. 5:3–10) and is a Matthean introduction to the next *makarios* – the blessedness of suffering persecution for Jesus as found in the double tradition (Matt. 5:11–12 // Luke 6:22–23).[33] Matthew marks both the *makarioi* with the verb *diōkō* (persecute) to emphasize his focus on persecution.[34] Although the content is very similar to the Lukan saying (italicized), it differs from the latter (see Table 3.2).

**Table 3.2 Textual comparison of Matthew 5:11–12 and Luke 6:22–23**

| Matthew 5:11–12 | Luke 6:22–23 |
| --- | --- |
| *Blessed are you when people insult you*, persecute you and falsely say all kinds of *evil* against you *because of* me. *Rejoice* and be glad, because *great is your reward in heaven*, for in the same way they persecuted *the prophets* who were before you. | *Blessed are you when people* hate you, when they exclude you and *insult you* and reject your name as *evil*, *because of* the Son of Man. *Rejoice* in that day and leap for joy, because *great is your reward in heaven*. For that is how their ancestors treated *the prophets*. |

The disciples will face persecution for obeying the law (and other portions of Scripture) as interpreted by Jesus, which at times radically differs from contemporaneous interpretations acceptable to the Jewish leaders.[35] These interpretations most likely are not restricted to those in this discourse, but include others such as Jesus' interpretations of himself as the Lord of the Sabbath (Matt. 11:28 – 12:21) and as the rejected Messiah

---

[33] The first eight *makarioi* in Matt. 5:3–10 use the third-person plural (with 'theirs is the kingdom of God' as an inclusio; my tr.), while Matt. 5:11–12 uses the second-person plural.

[34] See also Gundry, *Matthew*, pp. 73–74.

[35] On the one hand, I agree with Hare that 'those who are persecuted because of their righteous behaviour are in reality being persecuted because of their relationship with Jesus, who is the source and cause of their distinctive way of life'. On the other hand, I disagree with Hare that it is 'improbable' that this righteousness is related to Torah-obedience or Jesus' dispute over 'the correct interpretation of Torah'. See Hare, *Jewish Persecution of Christians*, p. 132. In fact, Hare's argument (p. 137) that the Christians' high claims regarding Jesus could have caused persecutions from the Jews favours the argument that these claims arose from interpretations of the Torah (e.g. Jesus is the Lord of the Sabbath) and the messianic psalms. Nonetheless, Matt. 5:21–48 is not about 'wrong' traditional interpretations, but about fulfilling the law in a way beyond that taught by the scribes and Pharisees (Matt. 5:20).

(Matt. 21:42; cf. Ps. 118:22–23, see also Matt. 26:62–66).[36] Disciples who are persecuted because of their faith in Jesus are blessed, because they belong to the kingdom of God and great is their reward in heaven (Matt. 5:10, 12). That they suffer such persecution confirms their standing as kingdom citizens, and their reward most likely refers to their inheritance of the kingdom.[37]

Although Jesus' teaching on non-retaliation (Matt. 5:38–42) does not directly refer to how disciples should respond to their persecutors, it may be applied to such a situation.[38] As Turner notes, 'Not only is the disciple to avoid evil by nonretaliatory reaction when oppressed by a more powerful person; the disciple is also to promote good by a generous, benevolent response to those who are less powerful.'[39] For the next saying on love for enemies (Matt. 5:43–48), however, Matthew marks it with the verb *diōkō* (persecute), relating it to how disciples should face persecution – by praying for their persecutors (cf. Luke 6:27–28). This saying in Luke is more general and can be applied to enemies of all kinds, not just those who oppose the disciples because of their faith in Jesus. The saying is more condensed in Matthew compared with Luke (similarity italicized in Table 3.3 on page 104).

The rationale behind this is that they should reflect the same nature ('sons of') as their heavenly Father, who is perfect and who does good to both good and evil people; thus, they should do more than what the unbelievers ('Gentiles') would do (Matt. 5:45–48).[40]

---

[36] On Jesus' understanding of the Sabbath and its relationship to the Isaianic quotation in Matt. 12:15–21, see Chee-Chiew Lee, 'Scripture as God's Word', in Roland Chia (ed.), *Dei Verbum: The Bible in Church and Society* (Singapore: Sower, 2020), pp. 8–11. On messianic interpretations of Ps. 118 during the Second Temple period, see Craig L. Blomberg, 'Matthew', in G. K. Beale and D. A. Carson (eds.), *Commentary on the New Testament Use of the Old Testament* (Grand Rapids: Baker Academic, 2007), p. 74.

[37] On corroboration of the disciples' standing, see Kelhoffer, *Persecution, Persuasion, and Power*, pp. 237–238; on rewards as inheritance of the kingdom, see Col. 3:24; Osborne, *Matthew*, p. 170.

[38] Both Gundry and Turner see the sayings of salt and light (Matt. 5:13–16) as related to persecution. Gundry, *Matthew*, p. 75; Turner, *Matthew*, p. 154. Gundry sees the disciples' witness as the reason for persecution, while Turner understands it as the disciples' witness during persecution. However, I have not included these sayings here because the text itself does not clearly mark these sayings as related to persecution, though they may be applied to such a context.

[39] Turner, *Matthew*, p. 175.

[40] On the children (*huioi*, 'sons'; Matt. 5:45) of God reflecting the nature of God's character, see France, *Matthew*, p. 226; Osborne, *Matthew*, p. 213. *Ethnikoi*, 'Gentiles' (Matt. 5:47), here refers to people outside the community of the disciples; see France, *Matthew*, p. 227.

**Table 3.3 Textual comparison of Matthew 5:44–45 and Luke 6:27–28**

| Matthew 5:44–45 | Luke 6:27–28 |
| --- | --- |
| But *I tell you, love your enemies and pray for those who* persecute *you*. | But *to you* who are listening *I say: love your enemies*, do good to those who hate you, bless those who curse you, *pray for those who* ill-treat *you*. |

In accord with the early Christians' practice of proving Jesus as the promised Messiah from Scripture,[41] the central theme of Matthew's Gospel is to show that Jesus is the fulfilment of the Scriptures (Law, Prophets and Writings).[42] Thus, this first discourse could be an apologetic move to show that Jesus (and thus Christianity) is not against the law, but he is the fulfilment of the law. This is not just for Jewish opponents, but is also to convince the disciples that they are suffering for a right and worthy cause.

The second discourse focuses on mission and its opposition. Much of the material in this discourse is reflected in the double and triple traditions, including that in Mark 13:9–13, which I will not repeat here,[43] except to highlight how Matthew is *distinct* in presenting this material (see italicized words in the following). First, as Hare notes, Matthew 10:5–15 differs from Mark 6:7–13 and Luke 9:1–6 *by associating persecution with the rejection of the gospel message* (Matt. 10:6–33).[44] Second, the persecutors are as dangerous as wolves, *but the disciples are to be wise and gentle in response* (Matt. 10:16; cf. Luke 10:3).[45] Third, the disciples will bear witness for Jesus before both the rulers and *the Gentiles* at the tribunal (Matt. 10:18; cf. Mark 13:9–10). Fourth, should the disciples be persecuted in a city, *they are to flee to another* (Matt. 10:34). Fifth, since the disciples are not greater than but would be like their master, *they will thus face persecution, just like Jesus* (Matt. 10:24–25; cf. Luke 6:40).[46]

---

[41] See p. 69 above on Acts.

[42] France, *Matthew*, pp. 10–14; Osborne, *Matthew*, pp. 31–32, 38–40.

[43] See pp. 100–101 above.

[44] Hare, *Jewish Persecution of Christians*, pp. 98–100. As noted previously (see p. 3 above), rejection of the gospel or opposition to the missionaries' message does not necessarily entail persecution, unless it involves unjust treatment.

[45] In Luke 10:3, the metaphor of sheep among wolves seems to depict more the danger of missions, while in Matthew's context (Matt. 10:17–23), the wolves clearly refer to the persecutors. Also, the metaphors of serpents and doves are Matthean, not Lukan.

[46] Unlike Matthew, Luke 6:40 does not apply this saying to the context of persecution.

Sixth, the disciples should not fear the persecutors and (Matt. 10:26–28) for three reasons: (1) *All secrets will be made known* (Matt. 10:26b). This could mean that (a) what the persecutors have done by harming them in secret will be exposed; or (b) the disciples should publicly proclaim what Jesus has said to them privately.[47] (2) One should fear God more because he can destroy both body and soul, compared with the persecutors who can destroy only the body (Matt. 10:28). (3) God, who looks after the less valuable sparrows, will all the more look after them (Matt. 10:29–31). The third reason displays the use of the rhetorical technique *a minore ad maius* (from the lesser to the greater or, in Hebrew, *qal wāḥômer*). While reason 1 is uniquely Matthean, reasons 2 and 3 are in common with Luke 12:4–5.

Seventh, since the disciples have been assured as to why they should not fear (Matt. 10:26–31), *Matthew draws the inference* (*oun*, 'therefore'; Matt. 10:32) that the disciples should not be afraid to acknowledge Jesus before people and he motivates the audience to do so by stating the consequences: 'Whoever acknowledges me before others, I will also acknowledge before my Father in heaven. But whoever disowns me before others, I will disown before my Father in heaven' (Matt. 10:32–33).[48]

Eighth, by using a few other sayings reflected in the double tradition Matthew *once again emphasizes that persecution will arise from one's family*:[49] (1) Jesus brings division and tension, rather than peace, among

---

[47] Neither Mark 4:22 nor Luke 12:2 associates this saying on 'hidden secrets will be exposed' with persecution (cf. Matt. 10:26). Furthermore, for the subsequent saying on 'whatever said in the dark will be proclaimed on the rooftops', Matthew makes Jesus the person who says things in the dark and the disciples the people who should publicly proclaim, compared with Luke, who frames it as things the audience say in secret will be made known publicly (cf. Matt. 10:27; Luke 12:3). On both possible meanings stated above, see Turner, *Matthew*, p. 278; Osborne, *Matthew*, pp. 396–397.

[48] This series of sayings on not fearing the persecutors and the consequences of acknowledging and denying Jesus occurs in the double tradition (Matt. 10:26–33 // Luke 12:2–9). Conceptually, although the consequence of denying Jesus (Matt. 10:32–33 // Luke 12:8–9) is similar to the consequence of being ashamed of Jesus and his words (Mark 8:38 // Luke 9:26), the two sayings occur in different contexts: see this note for the former and n. 49 below for the latter.

[49] The sayings on 'taking up the cross' and 'the paradox of finding/losing one's life' occur in two forms: one in the triple tradition and the other in the double tradition. The triple tradition (Mark 8:34 – 9:1 // Matt. 16:24–28 // Luke 9:23–27) locates these sayings after Jesus' first prediction of his passion, but Matt. 16:27 differs from Mark 8:38 and Luke 9:26 by omitting the saying on being ashamed of Jesus and his words and replacing it with a more generic form of judgment according to what one has done. The double tradition (Matt. 10:37–39 // Luke 14:26–27) locates these sayings in the context of Jesus' demand for his disciples to love him more than they do their family members. '[A] man's enemies will be the members of his own household' (10:36) is uniquely Matthean. Unlike Matt. 10:37–39, the sayings in Luke 14:26–27 and 17:33 are not associated with persecution.

family members (Matt. 10:34–39; cf. 10:21; Luke 12:51–53); (2) Jesus' disciples need to be willing to suffer ('take up their cross') and to love him more than their family members (Matt. 10:37–38; cf. Luke 14:26–27) and (3) the paradox of finding one's life by losing it and vice versa (Matt. 10:39; cf. Luke 17:33).

Finally, Matthew uses sayings on hospitality and its reward to wrap up this discourse: those who (1) receive God's messengers (Jesus, prophets, the righteous; Matt. 10:40–41) and (2) give water to insignificant people ('little ones') will be rewarded. While these may not be related directly to facing persecution, they may have implications for supporting those who face persecution. The reward for the hospitality extended to a disciple who is insignificant (Matt. 10:42) may be somewhat related to the parable of the sheep and the goats (the true and false disciples), where Jesus equates hospitality that has been given to or withheld from the needy with the same treatment towards him (Matt. 25:31–46).[50] The reference to imprisonment is likely related to persecution and this would motivate the disciples to support those in need, including those who suffer persecution.[51]

Matthew consolidates most of Jesus' teachings on persecution into this second discourse, which includes (1) predictions of how disciples will be persecuted and by whom; (2) how they should respond; and (3) assurances and promises of Jesus when facing persecution. In the third discourse, Matthew includes as one of the parables of the kingdom the parable of the seed sown on rocky soil, which refers to those who apostatize when they face persecution. However, compared with Mark, he does not make additional comments.

Before the fifth discourse are seven woes to the scribes and Pharisees (Matt. 23:13–36), in which the last woe condemns them for rejecting and murdering messengers (prophets, wise men and scribes) sent by Jesus, just as their ancestors did to the former prophets (Matt. 23:29–36 // Luke 11:47–51). This is a reference to and prediction of the unbelieving Jewish leaders persecuting Jesus' disciples, though the emphasis seems to be on those who proclaim Jesus' kingdom message.[52] The manner of their

---

[50] See also France, *Matthew*, p. 965; Gundry, *Matthew*, p. 514. 'One of these little ones' (*hena tōn mikrōn toutōn*) in Matt. 10:42 is semantically similar to 'one of the least of these' (*heni toutōn tōn elachistōn*) in Matt. 25:40, 45.

[51] We see how the author of Hebrews develops this gospel tradition on p. 125 below.

[52] According to Hare (*Jewish Persecution of Christians*, pp. 106, 113, 125), Matthew portrays Jewish persecution as primarily against the Christian missionaries rather than the general Christian population. While Hare is correct that Matthew's emphasis is on the persecution

persecution of Jesus' messengers (kill, crucify, flog in synagogues, persecute from city to city) alludes to the second discourse on missions (Matt. 10:17–18, 23) and the fifth discourse (Matt. 24:9). Because of their shedding of the blood of the righteous (Matt. 23:35; cf. 5:10), they will face God's judgment and be condemned to hell (Matt. 23:33). This condemnation to hell is uniquely Matthean. For the disciples who are suffering persecution, the assurance of God's judgment on their persecutors serves as an encouragement, because God will avenge and vindicate his righteous people (i.e. those who obey the law as interpreted by Jesus).

Finally, in the fifth discourse on the coming judgment, Matthew once again portrays Jesus' reiterating that disciples will be persecuted, hated by all the nations (Gentiles) and will even be put to death (Matt. 24:9; cf. 10:21). Once again, Jesus warns that many will fall away from their faith (Matt. 24:10a; cf. 13:21),[53] while some within the community of disciples will betray and hate one another due to the pressure of persecution (Matt. 24:10b; cf. 10:22).

Observations from Matthew's redaction of his sources show his focus on addressing his audience on the persecution they face from their Jewish opponents.[54] Although a number of Jesus' sayings in the Markan and/or Lukan traditions do not refer directly to persecution, he applies them analogously to the context of facing persecution. He not only states Jesus' teachings on how the disciples should face persecution, but often provides the rationale for doing so (appealing to *logos*). One of the literary features of Matthew is the contrast between true and false disciples.[55] As Gundry notes, true disciples are those who endure persecution, while false disciples are those who deny their association with Jesus to avoid persecution and will even betray their fellow disciples to the persecutors.[56] This literary feature of contrasting characteristics and consequences of true and false disciples cautions Matthew's audience to discern for themselves which party they belong to.

---

from Jewish opponents suffered by Christian missionaries (cf. Matt. 13:16–19; 23:34), we should note that passages such as Matt. 5:10–12, 10:34–39, and 24:9–10 can also refer to Christians more generally.

[53] In the context of these verses (Matt. 13:21; 24:11), *skandalizō* means to deny one's faith in Jesus (cf. Matt. 26:31, 33). See BDAG, p. 926, 1b.

[54] See also Gundry, *Matthew*, pp. 5–10; Hare, *Jewish Persecution of Christians*, pp. 125–129.

[55] E.g. Matt. 7:21–23; 13:1–9, 18–23, 18–30, 36–43; 22:11–14; 24:45–51; 25:1–46.

[56] Gundry, *Matthew*, p. 6.

# Luke–Acts

In Luke's Gospel, nearly all the presentations of Jesus' teachings on persecution are found in the triple and double traditions. Those in the triple tradition include (1) the parable of the seed falling on rocky ground (Luke 8:13); (2) taking up the cross to follow Jesus and the consequence of being ashamed of Jesus (Luke 9:23–27); (3) being charged before local and regional authorities as an opportunity to bear witness, and the promise of wisdom by the Holy Spirit (Luke 21:12–15; cf. 12:11–12); and (4) persecution from one's community and being hated by all (Luke 21:16–17). However, Luke adds the word 'daily' to 'take up their cross' (Luke 9:23; cf. Mark 8:34 // Matt. 16:24), stressing the continuing nature of self-denial even if it entails death. In contrast, this saying in Mark and Matthew could refer more specifically to a one-time commitment in response to an imminent threat of death due to persecution.[57]

Those in the double tradition include (1) two *makarioi* on the blessedness of facing persecution and on rejoicing (Luke 6:22–23); (2) love for enemies and non-retaliation (Luke 6:27–36); (3) fearing God more than the persecutors, because the former has authority to cast a person into hell while the latter can kill only the body (Luke 12:4–5); (4) God who looks after sparrows will all the more look after the persecuted disciples (Luke 12:6–7); and (5) the consequences of acknowledging or denying Jesus before persecutors (Luke 12:8–9).

The context where these sayings occur is usually similar to Mark for the triple tradition and to Matthew for the double tradition. Thus, where the context is similar, they function in ways similar to those in Mark and Matthew to encourage perseverance.

Nonetheless, Luke embeds a few unique materials among these traditions: the persecution from one's community is expanded from the immediate family to include relatives and friends (Luke 21:16) and the promise of 'not a hair of your head will perish' (Luke 21:18). Also, as noted above,[58] first, a number of sayings in Luke are framed more generally compared with Matthew (e.g. love of enemies, seeds on rocky ground),

---

[57] Richard B. Vinson, *Luke*, SHBC (Macon: Smyth & Helwys, 2008), p. 285; Garland, *Luke*, p. 390; James R. Edwards, *The Gospel According to Luke*, PNTC (Grand Rapids: Eerdmans, 2015), p. 276.

[58] See the sections on 'Matthew' and 'Mark' before this section on 'Luke-Acts'.

though they are broad enough to apply to facing persecution.[59] Second, although Luke's Gospel has no significant distinctives in presenting Jesus' teachings on persecution compared with Mark and Matthew,[60] the narrative in Acts portrays the disciples as being able to face persecution in a manner consistent with Jesus' teachings and is thus an exemplar of the desired responses to persecution. Besides this positive characterization of the disciples in Acts,[61] Luke seeks to encourage his audience to persevere in faith despite persecution by showing how the disciples experienced Jesus' promises of deliverance in the gospel traditions (Luke 21:19; cf. Matt. 10:29–31; Luke 12:6–7) in the narrative of Acts: (1) the apostles' miraculous escape from prison (Acts 5:19; 12:6–17; 16:25–26); and (2) plots against Paul being thwarted (Acts 9:23–25; 14:5–6; 20:3; 23:12–23). Thus, Luke seeks to encourage his audience to persevere in faith by showing how Jesus' teachings on facing persecution and his promises of deliverance are actualized in the exemplary responses and experiences of the early disciples by the Spirit's empowerment.

# John

In the previous chapter, we saw how John addresses the fear of persecution in his Gospel through characterization, his positive or negative evaluations of some characters as well as his ambiguous portrayal of a few of these

---

[59] This does not imply that Luke's audience was facing lesser persecution than Mark's or Matthew's. Rather, it seems to be Luke's tendency to present those sayings more broadly to encompass other kinds of mistreatment.

[60] Cunningham (*Through Many Tribulations*, pp. 295–327) summarizes the theology of persecution in Luke–Acts as six 'functions': (1) persecution is part of the plan of God; (2) persecution is the rejection of God's agents by those who are supposedly God's people; (3) the persecuted people of God stand in continuity with God's prophets; (4) persecution is an integral consequence of following Jesus; (5) persecution is the occasion of the Christian's perseverance; and (6) persecution is the occasion of divine triumph. While I concur mostly with Cunningham's summary, I would like to note the following. First, these six points are in many ways common among the Synoptic Gospels, although Luke more fully develops point 3 in Luke–Acts compared with Matthew. Second, using Cunningham's own words (p. 297), I propose that point 1 be rephrased as 'persecution "always occurs within God's providence"', because 'part of the plan of God' may give an impression that such unjust treatment by persecutors originated from God, rather than as a result of sin. Third, I would also rephrase point 2 as 'persecution is due to the rejection of God's agents'. As mentioned earlier, rejection does not necessarily entail persecution. Furthermore, while 'those who are supposedly God's people' (i.e. unbelieving Jews) are featured in Luke–Acts as persecutors of the disciples, they are not the only group of persecutors in Acts: there were also pagan persecutors.

[61] Even when Luke mentions Mark's 'deserting' Paul and Barnabas in Pamphylia (Acts 15:38), he does not specify the reason for the desertion. Therefore, it is not clear whether Mark deserted them owing to suffering from persecution. This supports my view that Luke depicts only positive responses to persecution in Acts.

characters. In this section, we will focus on how John uses dualistic language and the discourses of Jesus in John's Gospel to address this fear of persecution.[62]

Other than John 12:24–26, most of Jesus' teaching on facing persecution is found in the Farewell discourse (John 13 – 17; cf. 15:18–23; 16:1–4a, 32–33; 17:11–18). At first glance, Jesus' sayings in John 12:24–26 do not seem directly related to persecution:

> Very truly I tell you, unless a grain of wheat falls to the ground and dies, it remains only a single seed. But if it dies, it produces many seeds. Anyone who loves their life will lose it, while anyone who hates their life in this world will keep it for eternal life. Whoever serves me must follow me; and where I am, my servant also will be. My Father will honour the one who serves me.

Nonetheless, a number of literary connections between John 12:23–28, 33–34 and John 21:18–19 associate the former with persecution (see Table 3.4 on page 111).[63]

Furthermore, 'love' and 'honour/glory' connect John 12:25–26 with 12:42–43.[64] By not confessing Jesus as Christ due to valuing 'one's honour more than God's glory' or valuing 'honour from people more than from God' is likely an illustration of 'loving one's life'. In contrast, 'those who hate their lives by confessing Christ and bearing the shame of condemnation and excommunication will actually receive eternal life and honour from God'.[65] From John's description regarding the kind of death Jesus and Peter would face (John 12:23, 27–28, 33; 21:18–19), martyrdom is glorifying to God.

Similar sayings in the Synoptic Gospels are less polarized than in John (cf. Mark 8:35 // Matt. 16:25 // Luke 9:24). Thus, John's use of the dualistic word pairs 'love–hate' and 'life–death' (John 12:25–26) seems deliberate

---

[62] This section is largely drawn from my article 'Facing Persecution', pp. 189–204. Nonetheless, I will summarize only the salient points in this section.

[63] Ibid., pp. 192–193; see also Gilbert van Belle (ed.), 'Peter as Martyr in the Fourth Gospel', in *Martyrdom and Persecution in Late Antique Christianity: Festschrift Boudewijn Dehandschutter* (Leuven: Uitgeverij Peeters, 2010), pp. 281–309, esp. p. 287; Köstenberger, *John*, p. 380.

[64] See ch. 2, n. 106 above for exegetical details on the Greek syntax of John 12:43. There is also a semantic overlap between *timaō*, 'honour', and *doxa*, 'glory'; see L&N, §§87.4, 87.8.

[65] Lee, 'Facing Persecution', p. 193.

**Table 3.4 Literary connections between John 12:23–28, 33–34 and 21:18–19**

| | |
|---|---|
| 'Whoever serves me must follow me' (12:26a). | Jesus commissions Peter to serve him by pastoring his sheep (21:15–17) and commands Peter to follow him (21:19). |
| 'where I am, my servant also will be' (12:26b). | Jesus died at the hands of those who opposed him. Likewise, Peter will also be martyred (21:18). |
| Jesus' death was glorifying to God (12:23, 27–28). | Peter's death will also glorify God (21:19). |
| 'He [Jesus] said this to show the kind of death he was going to die' (12:33–34). | 'Jesus said this to indicate the kind of death by which Peter would glorify God' (21:18–19). |

and maximizes the distance between the opposite terms,[66] thereby intensifying the paradox that eternal life is obtained through death. The metaphor of the seed dying to produce more fruitful life subsequently (John 12:24) serves to illustrate this concept. We also see John's attempt to redefine what is regarded as shame (suffer persecution for Jesus) by the dominant culture to be true honour in God's sight.

John depicts Jesus' delineating the disciples sharply from the rest of humanity in 15:19: 'If you *belonged to the world*, it would *love* you as its own. As it is, you *do not belong to the world*, but I have chosen you out of the world. That is why the world *hates* you.' Such a dualistic expression makes it impossible for anyone to sit on the fence or to be identified with both sides:[67] it is not possible to belong to Jesus and yet be loved by the world. This forces the audience to make a choice and to evaluate for themselves which side they are on.

Another such dualistic expression is in John 16:33: '*in me* you may have *peace. In this world* you will have *trouble*.' This forms a stark contrast and is an assurance that one can still receive peace from Jesus despite suffering tribulation inflicted by the world. Jesus admonishes his disciples to take

---

[66] James L. Resseguie, 'A Narrative-Critical Approach to the Fourth Gospel', in Christopher W. Skinner (ed.), *Characters and Characterization in the Gospel of John*, LNTS 461 (London: Bloomsbury T&T Clark, 2013), p. 6.

[67] Lee, 'Facing Persecution', p. 200.

courage, because his victory over the world is 'the basis of the disciples' courage and experience of peace' (John 16:33).[68] This is the only instance in John's Gospel where Jesus instructs his disciples on how to face persecution – with courage! This is not surprising, given John's consistent portrayal of the disciples' fear of persecution from the Jewish authorities as an important motif in the narrative.

In John 17:11–19, Jesus prays for his disciples concerning the persecution they will face. We observe a number of parallel features in this prayer (see Table 3.5).

**Table 3.5  Parallel features of Jesus' prayer in John 17:11–19**

| 'in the world' (17:11–13) | 'of/out of the world'[69] (17:14–16) | 'into the world' (17:17–19) |
| --- | --- | --- |
| While the Son entreats the Father to keep them in his name, the Son has also kept them in the Father's name. Like Jesus and his Father, the disciples are to be 'one'. | The Son entreats the Father to keep them from the evil one, rather than take them out of the world. Like Jesus, the disciples are not of the world. | While the Son entreats the Father to sanctify the disciples, the Son has also sanctified them by sanctifying himself. Like the Father sends Jesus into the world, Jesus sends the disciples into the world. |

There is a strong emphasis on divine providence and union with Christ here. It is both the Father and the Son who (1) keep the disciples in the Father's name from falling away (17:11–12); and (2) sanctify the disciples with the Father's word (17:17, 19), so that they may testify for Jesus in the world (17:20; cf. 15:27). As Thompson explains, 'To be kept "in your name" means to be protected and guarded as those who belong to the Father and so identified, or marked, by the Father's name.'[70] For Jesus, the solution to help disciples face persecution is not to relieve them by taking them out of the world, but rather to have the Father protect them from the evil

---

[68] Ibid., p. 201.

[69] In this section, the same prepositional phrase *ek tou kosmou* has to be rendered differently in English to reflect its nuance: (1) the disciples are 'not of the world'; and (2) Jesus entreats his Father not to take the disciples 'out of the world'.

[70] Thompson, *John*, p. 352.

one.[71] In this prayer, John emphasizes that it is not what the disciples can do to keep themselves from falling away when facing persecution, but rather divine providence – as Jesus said, '[A]part from me you can do nothing' (John 15:5b). This concept functions as an assurance of divine empowerment to persevere in the face of persecution.

Three times Jesus forewarns his disciples of imminent persecution with the phrase 'All this I have told you' followed by the purpose of the warning: (1) so that they will not fall away (John 16:1); (2) so that they will recall what he said (John 16:4); and (3) so that they may have peace (John 16:33). The forms (excommunication from the synagogue and killing) and reason (persecutors think they are serving God by doing so) of persecution in John 16:2–3 are framed by 1 and 2 as an *inclusio* (John 16:1, 4),[72] while the prediction of the disciples deserting Jesus when he is arrested (John 16:32) precedes 3.

How do the forewarnings achieve these purposes? Although the immediate context does not elaborate on this, we may infer from the larger context that the Holy Spirit will help the disciples to recall what Jesus said (John 14:26). They will thereby realize what Jesus predicted about the persecutions is true and thus have courage to believe his promises will also be true, promises such as (1) they will receive everlasting life through dying for Jesus (John 12:24–26); (2) Jesus has conquered the world and thus they can experience peace from him despite persecution (John 16:33); and (3) God will preserve them so that they may not fall away (John 17:11–12).

While the Synoptic Gospels clearly associate testifying for Jesus during trial when facing persecution (Mark 13:9 // Matt. 10:18 // Luke 21:12–13), John's Gospel is less direct – the disciples are to testify for Jesus (John 15:26–27; 19:35; 21:24), whether or not they are facing persecution (John 4:39–42; 9:10–33).

For John, responding to the fear of persecution by compromising one's moral integrity is unacceptable. The way to overcome fear of

---

[71] Although *ek tou ponērou* (John 17:5) may mean 'that which is evil' or 'the evil one', it more likely means the latter here, because John depicts Satan as 'the prince of this world' (12:31; 14:30; 16:11). See also Andrew T. Lincoln, *The Gospel According to Saint John*, BNTC 4 (Peabody: Hendrickson, 2005), p. 437; Klink, *John*, p. 721.

[72] Craig S. Keener, *The Gospel of John: A Commentary*, 2 vols. (Peabody: Hendrickson, 2003), vol. 2, p. 1025; Lincoln, *Gospel According to Saint John*, p. 413; Klink, *John*, p. 672.

persecution is not to deny the reality of fear, but to face fear with courage that is grounded on Jesus' victory and God's providence.[73]

## Pauline epistles

Paul uses exhortations, himself as exemplar and logical reasoning predominantly to encourage his audience to persevere in faith when facing persecution. A number of his exhortations are similar to the gospel traditions, such as (1) forewarning of persecution and God's providence (e.g. Luke 12:6–7; John 16:1–4); (2) rejoicing in persecution (Matt. 5:12; Luke 6:23), not being afraid (e.g. Matt. 10:26–31; Luke 12:4) and experiencing peace (e.g. John 14:27; 16:33); (3) non-retaliation and loving one's enemies (Matt. 5:43–44; Luke 6:27–28); and (4) eschatological shame and honour (e.g. Mark 8:38).

First, when Paul began to proclaim the gospel at Thessalonica he forewarned them of imminent persecutions (1 Thess. 3:4).[74] Like the Gospels, Paul does not hesitate to let believers know that those who follow Jesus are destined for persecution (Phil. 1:29; 1 Thess. 3:3; 2 Tim. 3:12; cf. John 15:18–20). In 2 Timothy 4:15, he even named the opponent (Alexander the metalworker), so that Timothy might be wary of him and the harm he might inflict.

Second, he exhorts the believers to rejoice and pray (Rom. 12:12; Phil. 2:18–19; 4:4–6; 1 Thess. 5:16–17). Although the immediate context of Philippians 4:4 and 1 Thessalonians 5:16 does not mention persecution, the larger context of both letters addresses the persecution the letter recipients had been suffering (Phil. 1:29–30; 1 Thess. 2:14). In his letter to the Philippians, Paul exhorts them not to be afraid of their opponents (Phil. 1:28) and further encourages them that their prayer will result in experiencing God's transcendent peace (Phil. 4:7). Paul seems to view the believers' enduring suffering as a corroboration of their true standing in Christ. It is an evidence from God of (1) their salvation (Phil. 1:28); and (2) their identity as the elect of God (2 Thess. 1:4–6).[75] This encourages the believers to persevere in their present suffering for their faith with joy.

Third, Paul stresses the importance of non-retaliation and good deeds in response to hostility (Rom. 12:17–21; 1 Thess. 5:15). His exhortation

---

[73] Lee, 'Facing Persecution', p. 204.

[74] The 'we' in 1 Thess. 3:4 is most likely inclusive of Paul, Titus and the Thessalonians. See Shogren, *1 and 2 Thessalonians*, p. 137; Weima, *1–2 Thessalonians*, p. 214.

[75] Kelhoffer, *Persecution, Persuasion, and Power*, pp. 92–93.

to 'bless those who persecute you' (Rom. 12:14) is clearly reminiscent of Matthew 5:44 and Luke 6:27.[76] Nonetheless, he develops the basis of returning good for evil in a different direction compared with Jesus' saying in the double tradition. The latter stresses the example of the heavenly Father (Matt. 5:45–48; Luke 6:35–36), while Paul explains the basis with two scriptural quotations: (1) God's people do not take revenge, because God is the one who will avenge them (Deut. 32:35).[77] This theological understanding is common in Jewish tradition (e.g. Prov. 20:22; T. Gad 6.7).[78] (2) Doing good to one's enemies has the same effect as 'heaping coal on [their] head' (Prov. 25:21–22). The meaning of this metaphor is not entirely clear, but it suffices to say that Paul is presenting acts of kindness here as an alternative to retaliation.[79] Although we are unclear whether Paul is depicting a positive outcome of kindness in Romans 12:17–21, he clearly exhorts Titus to 'show integrity, seriousness and soundness of speech that cannot be condemned' in his teaching, so the opponent 'may be ashamed because they have nothing bad to say about us' (Titus 2:7–8).[80] As Mounce notes, this does not imply that the opponents would be convinced of the Christian's goodness, but rather they would not have 'justifiable charges' against them.[81]

---

[76] Rom. 12:14a: 'Bless those who persecute you' seems to be a conflation of Matt. 5:44, 'love your enemies and pray for those who persecute you', and Luke 6:28, 'bless those who curse you, pray for those who ill-treat you'. See also Fitzmyer, *Romans*, p. 655; Moo, *Romans*, p. 667.

[77] Paul's quotation here (*emoi ekdikēsis, egō antapodōsō*, 'vengeance is mine, I will repay') is nearer the MT (*lî nāqom wĕšillēm*, 'to me is vengeance and recompense') than the LXX (*en hēmera ekdikēseōs antapodōsō*, 'on the day of vengeance, I will repay'; my tr. The LXX has a strong sense of eschatological judgment, while the MT does not necessarily convey such an eschatological emphasis. See also Mark Seifrid, 'Romans', in G. K. Beale and D. A. Carson (eds.), *Commentary on the New Testament Use of the Old Testament* (Grand Rapids: Baker Academic, 2007), p. 680; Fitzmyer, *Romans*, p. 657.

[78] Gordon M. Zerbe, *Non-Retaliation in Early Jewish and New Testament Texts: Ethical Themes in Social Contexts*, BAC (London: Bloomsbury Academic, 2015), p. 167; Thielman, *Romans*, p. 595.

[79] Thielman, *Romans*, p. 596; James D. G. Dunn, *Romans 9–16*, WBC 38B (Dallas: Word, 1988), pp. 750–751. See therein the various meanings (positive or negative connotations) scholars have proposed. Scholars reckon negative connotations (e.g. that cause opponents to suffer guilt or experience God's judgment) are unlikely in this context, because they would be contrary to Paul's emphasis on non-retaliation. Positive connotations (e.g. leading the opponents to repentance) are possible, but contemporaneous cultural evidence of such metaphorical meaning is weak.

[80] The identity of the opponents in Titus is unclear. They could include those within or outside the church (1:9–16). See Mounce, *Pastoral Epistles*, p. 414. The 'opponent' is singular in Titus 2:8, but the singular is most likely a general rather than a specific reference. See Jon Laansma, 'Titus', in Philip W. Comfort (ed.), *1–2 Timothy, Titus, Hebrews*, CBC (Carol Stream: Tyndale House, 2009), p. 257.

[81] Mounce, *Pastoral Epistles*, p. 414; see also Collins, *1 & 2 Timothy and Titus*, p. 345.

Fourth, after describing how he persevered despite suffering persecution (2 Tim. 2:8–10), Paul quotes this 'trustworthy' saying, which reflects the apocalyptic eschatology of the early church and the understanding of honour and shame associated with it:

> If we died with him,
>     we will also live with him;
> if we endure,
>     we will also reign with him.
> If we disown him,
>     he will also disown us;
> if we are faithless,
>     he remains faithful,
>     for he cannot disown himself.
> (2 Tim. 2:11–13)

Paul most likely quotes this hymn as a motivation for both himself and Timothy: if they now endure persecution and die with Christ (regarded as shameful by the dominant culture), eventually they will live and reign with him (regarded as honour from God and his people); if they disown him now to avoid shame (attempt to preserve their honour), Jesus shall disown them and they will eventually be shamed (which results in loss of honour). Paul's encouragement to the Thessalonians also reflects another aspect of apocalyptic eschatology: God will vindicate the righteous (1) by counting them worthy and relieving them from oppression, and (2) by punishing their persecutors (2 Thess. 1:5–9; cf. Phil. 1:28). Their perseverance shall glorify God and they will also be glorified (i.e. receive honour) by God (2 Thess. 1:10–12).

I mentioned earlier that some believers in Corinth might have compromised by cultural assimilation, justifying their practice of eating idol food in order to avoid conflict.[82] Paul warns the Corinthians that such behaviour will incur God's judgment, as scriptural history has shown, and they are living at the end of the ages (1 Cor. 10:11).[83] Eschatological reward and judgment are two sides of the same coin, providing God's people the

---

[82] See pp. 79–80 above.
[83] See also Paul Gardner, *1 Corinthians*, ZECNT (Grand Rapids: Zondervan, 2018), p. 437; Anthony C. Thiselton, *The First Epistle to the Corinthians*, NIGTC (Grand Rapids: Eerdmans, 2000), p. 744.

motivation to remain faithful to him, even if it entails difficulties. Thus, Paul warns the Corinthians of complacency and reminds them of God's faithful providence. God will provide a way to overcome the temptation to compromise – one should not claim that it is too difficult to resist (1 Cor. 10:12–13). Paul also recognizes, however, that some believers may be weak when suffering for their faith; so he exhorts the Thessalonians to 'encourage the disheartened, help the weak, [and] be patient with everyone' (1 Thess. 5:14). In fact, Paul does just that by sending Timothy to the suffering Thessalonians (1 Thess. 3:2–5) and the wavering Corinthians (1 Cor. 4:17; 16:10) to encourage them.

In order to encourage the believers to persevere and in line with his belief in God's faithful providence, Paul tells them of his intercessory prayers for them: (1) that they might be sanctified by God and kept blameless at the eschatological judgment (1 Cor. 1:8; 1 Thess. 5:23); (2) that the loving and gracious God would encourage and strengthen them in every 'good deed and word' (2 Thess. 2:16–17);[84] and (3) that God would protect them from the evil one (2 Thess. 3:3).[85] Reciprocally, Paul requests the believers to pray for him likewise and shares his experience of God's deliverance as a testimony of God's faithful providence (2 Cor. 1:8–11; cf. 2 Tim. 3:10–11).

Paul also redefines honour and shame for believers of Christ. Suffering for Christ is an honour, not a shame (Rom. 5:3; 2 Tim. 1:12). As such, he invites Timothy and other believers to imitate and join him in suffering for Christ (2 Cor. 1:6–7; 1 Thess. 1:6; 2 Tim. 1:8; 2:3; cf. 1 Cor. 4:16), so that, like him, they may experience God's comfort, which will produce 'patient endurance' in them (2 Cor. 1:6). While the opponents seek to shame the believers by persecuting them, Paul seeks to honour the suffering believers by praising them for enduring the shame. Therefore, he praises the Thessalonians for enduring persecution (2 Thess. 1:3–5) and expresses his confidence in the Philippians' courage to stand firm continually despite facing persecution (Phil. 1:27–28).[86] In Romans 5:3–5 (cf. Rom. 8:28), Paul

---

[84] The idiom 'deed [*ergon*] and word [*logos*]' primarily refers to what a person does and says when interacting with others (cf. Luke 24:19; Acts 7:22; Rom. 15:18; Col. 3:17) (Shogren, *1 and 2 Thessalonians*, p. 307). For the Thessalonians, it would include standing firm in their faith and holding fast to the teachings they received (2 Thess. 2:15).

[85] Grammatically, *apo tou ponērou* could mean either 'from the evil one' or 'from evil' (Fee, *Corinthians*, p. 319; Shogren, *1 and 2 Thessalonians*, pp. 314–316). In view of the eschatological overtones of 2 Thessalonians, I have rendered the phrase as the former.

[86] See also Weima, *1–2 Thessalonians*, pp. 75–76, who notes Paul's use of praise as a form of persuasion: it not only establishes his relationship with the letter recipients in terms of *ethos*, but is also an 'implicit challenge for the letter recipients to live up to the praise'.

urges the believers to see their sufferings for Christ as glorious, and points out the benefits of such suffering for character building.[87] Believers with such hope of eschatological glory will not be put to shame because of God's love, which the Holy Spirit puts into the believers' hearts (Rom. 5:2, 5). Paul regards the believers' present suffering as incomparable with the eschatological glory (Rom. 8:18). When believers feel weak in their sufferings, both the Holy Spirit and Christ Jesus intercede for them (Rom. 8:26, 34), so that believers are empowered to be more than conquerors when suffering persecution and none of the opposing forces will ever be able to separate them from God's love (Rom. 8:31–39). Through this, Paul assures the believers of God's providential care in their sufferings. These exhortations not only appeal to *logos*, but also to *pathos* (e.g. praising to elicit the sense of honour) and *ethos* (e.g. Paul's own suffering for Christ as a corroboration of his apostleship, which establishes credibility, and his love for the letter recipients, which establishes goodwill).[88]

# Hebrews

Many scholars have written about the appeal to *logos* that the author of Hebrews ('the author' from here onwards) employs in persuading his audience, who most likely had a Jewish background, to persevere in their faith in Jesus despite facing persecution.[89] The author does little to build his own *ethos*, but rather establishes the authority of his message based on God's final revelation in his Son, who bears the same divine nature as the Father (Heb. 1:1–3a). Nonetheless, the author frequently appeals to *pathos* in his letter, especially in arousing the emotions of fear and empathy. In this section, we will examine how the author incorporates *pathos* and

---

[87] For details on the 'suffering' in Rom. 5:1–5 as referring to suffering from persecution, see p. 74 above.

[88] For detailed discussions on Paul's appeal to *logos*, *pathos* and *ethos*, see Troy W. Martin, 'Invention and Arrangement in Recent Pauline Rhetorical Studies: A Survey of the Practices and the Problems', and Duane F. Watson, 'The Role of Style in the Pauline Epistles: From Ornamentation to Argumentative Strategies', in *Paul and Rhetoric* (London: T&T Clark, 2010), pp. 103–110, 134–135; Thomas H. Olbricht and Jerry L. Sumney (eds.), *Paul and Pathos*, SBLSymS 16 (Atlanta: SBL, 2001).

[89] It is important to note that believers with a 'Jewish background' not only include ethnic Jews but also Gentiles who were proselytes or God-fearers. Cockerill goes further to include Gentiles who became acculturated into the Jewish religious traditions after their conversion to Christ owing to their interactions with ethnic Jewish believers. As Cockerill notes, ethnicity is not the focus in Hebrews, since the author does not mention Jews or Gentiles, or distinguish between them. See Cockerill, *Epistle to the Hebrews*, p. 20, and ch. 2, n. 83 above.

*logos* in his persuasion and what effect these could have on his audience.[90] Scriptural allusions and citations also abound as proofs in the appeal to both *pathos* and *logos*. Hebrews is also well known for the use of exemplars from Scriptures, who serve as 'a great cloud of witnesses' of how faithful people of God throughout the ages persevered despite not being able to see the object of their faith (Heb. 11:1 – 12:3).

As we have noted previously, persecuted Christians were brought before the authorities, either due to their opponents pressing charges against them or due to the unrest caused by the opposition. The audience had experienced public humiliation, imprisonment and loss of personal property, which could be due to looting by the mob or as a form of punishment by the authorities (Heb. 10:33–34).[91] They could be facing a real threat of death, even if there had not yet been any cases of martyrdom (cf. Heb. 2:15; 12:4).[92] Therefore, in what follows I will examine how the author addresses their fear of authorities, death and economic losses. We will also look at how the author encourages his audience after warning them and how he appeals to empathy as a means of motivating the audience to support one another to persevere in faith.

## Addressing the fear of authorities

While the author acknowledges the sufferings and humiliation the audience have endured for their faith (Heb. 10:32–33), he reminds them of a greater authority they need to fear – God, who will judge covenant violators who disregard the salvation accomplished by his Son Jesus. Regarding the former, reminding the audience of their achievement in enduring suffering for Christ is an appeal to *pathos* and can have the following rhetorical effects: to elicit a sense of confidence that they can succeed again and a sense of fear of losing their honour should they fail to continue to endure.[93]

Regarding the latter, the author appeals to *logos* by employing the common rhetorical argument of 'from lesser to greater',[94] which he uses

---

[90] The materials in this section are mainly adapted from my articles 'The Rhetoric of Empathy in Hebrews', *NovT* 62.2 (2020), pp. 201–218; 'Use of Scriptures', pp. 191–210. A detailed description of the rhetoric of Hebrews would fill a commentary and is thus beyond the scope of this book. Therefore, I will be able to summarize only a few key approaches in this section.

[91] See pp. 59–60 above.

[92] Dyer, *Suffering in the Face of Death*, pp. 77–130.

[93] David A. deSilva, *Perseverance in Gratitude: A Socio-Rhetorical Commentary on the Epistle 'to the Hebrews'* (Grand Rapids: Eerdmans, 2000), p. 356.

[94] Oropeza, *Churches Under Siege*, pp. 52, 56. Cf. Heb. 10:27–31; 12:18–29.

repeatedly in Hebrews: (1) if disobedience to the message of the angels leads to punishment, how much more the message of the Son, who is greater than the angels (Heb. 2:1–3); (2) if violation of the former covenant (sinning and rejecting Yahweh) results in God's vengeance, how much more the violation of the new covenant (sinning and rejecting Jesus) that is superior to the former (Heb. 10:26–31; cf. Deut. 32:36); and (3) if those who reject the God who warned them from the earthly Mount Sinai cannot escape God's vengeance, how much less likely to escape are those who reject the God who warned them from the heavenly Mount Zion (Heb. 12:22–25).

Besides this, the author also uses Moses and his parents as exemplars of those who had faith and were not afraid of the authorities. By faith, Moses' parents did not fear Pharaoh's edict to kill all male newborns, but kept Moses alive (Heb. 11:23). By faith, Moses was not afraid of Pharaoh and left Egypt because he saw the invisible God (Heb. 11:27).[95]

Other than *logos*, the author also appeals to *pathos* by describing (1) the fearsome God and his dreadful, fiery judgment (Heb. 10:26, 30–31; 12:18–21, 29); (2) God's word as a sharp sword that can penetrate into the thoughts and attitudes, so that all ulterior motives will be exposed at judgment (Heb. 4:12–13); and (3) that there is no 'second chance' for those who wilfully reject God's gift of his Son (Heb. 6:4–8; 10:26–27; 12:16–17).[96] It is 'impossible' for these wilful people to be brought back to repentance, since they have experienced God's benefaction but responded ungratefully by rejecting the gift of his Son and thereby dishonouring him (Heb. 6:4–8).[97] There is 'no sacrifice left' for those who keep on sinning

---

[95] Although the author of Hebrews portrays Moses as fearless, Exod. 2:14–15 mentions that Moses, because of fear, fled after killing an Egyptian. However, as Gray notes, the author could likely be referring to Moses' disregard of the wealth and honour that resulted from his familial relationship with Pharaoh in Heb. 11:25–26, rather than the incident of killing the Egyptian. Patrick Gray, *Godly Fear: The Epistle to the Hebrews and Greco-Roman Critiques of Superstition*, SBLAcBib 16 (Atlanta: Society of Biblical Literature, 2003), pp. 171–175.

[96] As this chapter focuses on persuasion, it is not within my scope to discuss here whether the author of Hebrews implies that believers can lose their salvation in Christ. For various views on this see e.g. Herbert W. Bateman (ed.), *Four Views on the Warning Passages in Hebrews* (Grand Rapids: Kregel, 2007); Oropeza, *Churches Under Siege*, pp. 37–41; Smith, 'Hebrews', pp. 191–200.

[97] In the ancient patron–client and honour–shame culture, receivers of gifts were obliged to reciprocate with acts of gratitude. Failure to do so amounted to 'injustice' and 'sacrilege', bringing dishonour to the giver and shame to the receiver. For details, see deSilva, *Perseverance in Gratitude*, pp. 223–224.

deliberately by '[trampling] the Son of God underfoot, [treating] as an unholy thing the blood of the covenant that sanctified them, and [insulting] the Spirit of grace' (Heb. 10:26, 29).[98] Esau serves as a negative example of 'no second chance' because he could not reverse the consequences of rejecting his God-given birth right, even when he subsequently deeply regretted it (Heb. 12:16–17). These examples are meant to warn and elicit a sense of fear in the recipients of Hebrews in order to steer them towards faithfulness to God.[99]

## Addressing the fear of death and suffering

While there is a universal fear of death in general, there is evidence that the author of Hebrews is especially addressing the audience's fear of death as a threat arising from persecution. In Jewish tradition, the devil brought death to the first humans by tempting them to disbelieve and disobey God's word (Gen. 3:1–7; Wis. 2.23–24; cf. Rev. 12:9). Due to their fear of death, people are constantly tempted to disbelieve and disobey God, despite his promise of deliverance and victory. This is the case for both the wilderness generation and Hebrews' audience.

The author uses Psalm 95:7b–11 as his scriptural proof that those who disbelieve God's ability to deliver them from their enemies will forfeit God's promise of entering his rest (Heb. 3:7 – 4:11). Psalm 95:7b–11 alludes to Numbers 13 – 14, where the wilderness generation were afraid to die (Num. 14:2–3, 9) and refused to believe that God was able to fulfil his promise of conquering their Canaanite enemies and bringing them into the Promised Land. I have shown elsewhere that (1) this 'rest' in Psalm 95:11 refers to rest from enemies (Deut. 12:10; 25:19; Josh. 23:1) – 'the peace that results from victory over the enemies in battle'; and (2) the 'rest' in Hebrews 4:9–11 refers to Jesus' victory over the devil through his sacrificial death, thereby breaking the devil's power over death (cf. Heb. 1:13; 2:8–9, 14–15; 10:13).[100] Similarly, the audience are facing the temptation of giving up their faith because of fear of persecution and the associated threat of death. If they give up, they will be like the wilderness generation who

---

[98] For details on the Old Testament scriptural background for Heb. 10:26–29 and how the exemplar of Esau connects to Heb. 6:4–6 and 10:35, see Lee, 'Use of Scriptures', pp. 198–203.

[99] Oropeza, *Churches Under Siege*, p. 53.

[100] Lee, 'Use of Scriptures', pp. 195–198; 'Rest and Victory in Revelation 14:13', *JSNT* 41.3 (2019), pp. 348–349, esp. n. 12; Chi-Yee Chan, 'The Interpretation of the "Rest" Tradition in the Epistle to the Hebrews', ThM thesis, Singapore Bible College, 2016 (in Chinese).

(1) disbelieved God's promise of victory over death and deliverance from enemies (i.e. the persecutors); and (2) disobeyed God's command to enter his rest. Thus, the author warns his audience against disbelief and exhorts them to obey God and 'make every effort to enter that rest' (Heb. 3:12; 4:11). They must not fear death, but rather should fear forfeiting the promised rest (Heb. 4:1; *phobēthōmen*, 'let us fear').

How then can the audience overcome this temptation? The answer is, by approaching God for help, because he is gracious and believers can have the confidence of finding his mercy and grace to overcome temptation whenever they need to (Heb. 4:16). What is the basis of such confidence? The author repeatedly emphasizes Jesus' ability to empathize with the believers' fear of death and the temptation to disobey God. Jesus became fully human, so that he may fully experience human weakness and suffering when tempted in every way (Heb. 2:10–18). Despite being tempted, Jesus did not sin and is thus able to help those who are similarly tempted (Heb. 4:15).

The author depicts Jesus' temptation and suffering very graphically: with *strong cries and tears* Jesus pleaded with his Father 'who could save him from death' when facing imminent suffering on the cross (Heb. 5:7). This reflects Jesus' struggle with the fear of death and the temptation to avoid suffering the intense humiliation and pain of crucifixion. Yet, he obeyed and submitted to God's will and thereby 'became the source of eternal salvation for all who obey him' (Heb. 5:9). When offering sacrifices for sin on behalf of God's people, every high priest is aware of his own weakness to sin, such that he is able 'to deal gently with those who are ignorant and are going astray' (Heb. 5:1–2). Similarly, Jesus is a merciful and faithful high priest who can fully empathize with their fear of death and suffering when facing persecution (Heb. 2:17; 4:15). Therefore, believers who have been weak and tempted to sin can approach God and Jesus for help with confidence and without fear, because Jesus will deal gently with them and not meet them with outbursts of anger.[101] It is only by God's help that the audience can persevere in their faith despite facing persecution. Thus, by emphasizing Jesus' empathy and gentleness, the author attempts to instil a sense of confidence in the audience and motivate them to seek God's help.

---

[101] Lee, 'Rhetoric of Empathy', p. 211, n. 50. I noted that in Heb. 5:2, *metriopatheō* (to be gentle) 'has the sense of moderating one's feelings, in contrast to outbursts of emotions (e.g., anger, grief) or indifference'. See BDAG, p. 643.

Besides the above, the author presents Jesus as the pre-eminent one above the cloud of witnesses. Jesus is the ultimate among the exemplars, who disregarded the most degrading shame by enduring the cross and hostility from sinners, but eventually became elevated as the most honoured of all – seated at the right hand of God. Struggling believers are to look to Jesus because he is the founder of their faith and the one who can bring their faith to perfection (*archēgon kai teleiōtēn*, 'founder and perfector'; Heb. 12:2). By doing so, they will not become weary and lose heart (Heb. 12:1–3). In first-century culture, it was appropriate to reciprocate the benefaction received from Jesus with a willingness to suffer for him.[102] Thus, nearing the end of the letter, the author exhorts his audience to suffer for Jesus by 'bearing the disgrace he bore' as their appropriate response (Heb. 13:13).

## Addressing the fear of economic losses

In the past, the audience had joyfully accepted the loss of property when persecuted (Heb. 10:34). The author attributes their joy to their hope of receiving 'better and lasting possessions' (Heb. 10:34). Since the audience have confidence to enter God's presence by Jesus' blood (Heb. 10:19), the author exhorts them not to 'throw away' their confidence, because if they persevere, they will eventually receive the promised reward (Heb. 10:35). He then cites Isaiah 26:20 and Habakkuk 2:3–4 as his scriptural proof. The context of these two passages speaks of God's coming vengeance, punishing the oppressors of his people and those who are unfaithful, while rewarding his people who endured faithfully.[103] Similarly, the audience are to wait for God's eschatological judgment (Heb. 10:37; cf. Isa. 26:10) and 'live by faith', because God rejects the one who 'shrinks back' (Heb. 10:38; cf. Hab. 2:3–4 LXX).[104]

---

[102] DeSilva, *Perseverance in Gratitude*, p. 501.

[103] See also John N. Oswalt, *The Book of Isaiah: Chapters 1–39*, NICOT (Grand Rapids: Eerdmans, 1986), pp. 469, 489; Gary V. Smith, *Isaiah 1–39*, NAC 15A (Nashville: B&H, 2007), pp. 440–441; Ralph L. Smith, *Micah–Malachi*, WBC 32 (Waco: Word, 1984), pp. 96–97; George H. Guthrie, 'Hebrews', in G. K. Beale and D. A. Carson (eds.), *Commentary on the New Testament Use of the Old Testament* (Grand Rapids: Baker Academic, 2007), p. 982.

[104] For details on how the author adapts and appropriates Isa. 26:20 and Hab. 2:3–4, see e.g. Guthrie, 'Hebrews', pp. 981–984; Johnson, *Hebrews*, p. 273; Cockerill, *Epistle to the Hebrews*, pp. 492–493, 507–512. As Mackie notes, 'the eschaton's fearsome and imminent approach disallows any manner of retreat from the community'. Scott D. Mackie, *Eschatology and Exhortation in the Epistle to the Hebrews*, WUNT 2.223 (Tübingen: Mohr Siebeck, 2007), p. 231.

Next comes the well-known list of faithful people throughout the ages who put their hope in God despite not being able to see the object of their faith (Heb. 11:1–40). Some of them had endured hardships and oppression even to death, and the author remarked that 'the world was not worthy of them' (Heb. 11:38). Some of them 'did not receive the things promised' but 'welcomed them from a distance' and longed for the heavenly 'city' God had prepared for them (Heb. 11:13–16). Likewise, the author later reminds his audience to look forward to 'the city that is to come' (Heb. 13:14).

The author employs these exemplars to encourage the audience to emulate their faith and endurance. He depicts Moses as one who 'regarded disgrace for the sake of Christ as of greater value than the treasures of Egypt, because he was looking ahead to his reward' (Heb. 11:26). This reflects a careful characterization in response to the economic losses arising from persecution, because this 'reward' (*misthapodosia*) Moses was looking forward to is the same reward the audience previously looked forward to with confidence (Heb. 10:35).[105] As Koester notes, the author may be employing 'the greater to the lesser argument' here: if Moses could give up such a great amount of wealth and honour for Christ, the audience should also be able to endure the loss of property, which is so much less compared with Moses.[106]

Near the end of the letter, the author exhorts his audience to keep themselves 'free from the love of money and be content with what you have' (Heb. 13:5a). Although this could be a broad reference, it could also relate to the fear of economic losses due to persecution. The author then cites Deuteronomy 31:6 and Psalm 118:6–7 as the basis for this exhortation. God will not leave or forsake them, even when they are in financial need (Heb. 13:5b; cf. Deut. 31:6). Thus, they may have confidence that since the Lord is their helper, they will not be afraid of what people can do to (e.g. persecute) them (Heb. 13:6; Ps. 118:6–7).

## Empathy as catalyst for community perseverance

Greco-Roman rhetoricians and Jewish writers were known to arouse their audience's feelings of empathy towards those in need so as to motivate the

---

[105] See also Harold W. Attridge, *The Epistle to the Hebrews: A Commentary on the Epistle to the Hebrews*, Hermeneia (Philadelphia: Fortress, 1989), p. 342, n. 63.

[106] Koester, *Hebrews*, p. 509.

audience to offer help.[107] This is in line with the findings of modern psychology that affective empathy usually precedes altruistic behaviour.[108] Likewise, the author appeals to *pathos* by arousing his audience's empathy for those who are suffering for their faith, in order to motivate help and thus create community support. He also employs exemplars of empathy for the audience to emulate. We have seen above that the author empha- sizes the ability of Jesus to empathize with the audience and to help them, so as to encourage them not to be afraid to approach Jesus for help when weak and tempted to give up. Besides Jesus, the author also depicts Moses as an exemplar of empathy: he willingly associated himself with God's people and suffered mistreatment with them, rather than be known as the son of Pharaoh's daughter (Heb. 11:24–25). Though not mentioned directly in the text of Hebrews, the audience would likely have known the exodus story of how Moses helped his people when he saw them being mistreated (Exod. 2 – 14).

First, the author reminds his audience of how they had previously empathized with those who were mistreated and imprisoned for their faith (Heb. 10:33–34). I mentioned above how such reminders could motivate the audience to do the same again. Second, near the end of the letter, he exhorts his audience to empathize with those who are persecuted for their faith: 'Continue to remember those in prison *as if you were together with them in prison*, and those who are ill-treated *as if you your- selves were suffering*' (Heb. 13:3). It is no coincidence that prior to this, the author exhorts his audience to love one another like siblings (*philadelphia*, 'brotherly love') and to extend hospitality (Heb. 13:1–2).[109] This is because helping them would entail love and hospitality: visiting them, providing food and clothing for them, and even seeking their release from prison. Doing so would involve risk of shame for associating with them and sacri- fice of material possessions for them. In this regard, recalling Moses' example would encourage them to do likewise.[110]

---

[107] Lee, 'Rhetoric of Empathy', pp. 205–209.

[108] Ibid., pp. 217–218.

[109] The Mediterranean culture of hospitality (*philoxenia*) typically involves hosting strangers (thus reflected in the NIV, NLT, ESV) and establishing a 'guest-friendship' with the stranger. See Joshua W. Jipp, *Divine Visitations and Hospitality to Strangers in Luke–Acts: An Interpretation of the Malta Episode in Acts 28:1–10*, NovTSup 153 (Leiden: Brill, 2013), p. 72. Nonetheless, its reference in Rom. 12:13 and 1 Peter 4:9 includes hospitality extended to fellow believers, regardless of whether they already knew one another.

[110] Cockerill, *Epistle to the Hebrews*, p. 502, esp. n. 26; Koester, *Hebrews*, p. 460.

While the practice of hospitality is common in the Greco-Roman world, this emphasis on supporting those suffering for their faith bears similarities to the tradition reflected in Matthew 25:31–46, where Jesus regarded hospitality performed for the needy (feeding, clothing and visiting those in prison) as performed for him and duly rewarded it.[111] This common tradition could explain the author exhorting them (1) to 'consider how [they] may spur one another on towards love and good deeds, not giving up meeting together . . . but encouraging one another' and associating their former perseverance and acts of empathy with eschatological reward (Heb. 10:24–25, 33–36); and (2) to practise hospitality because of the possibility of entertaining angels unknowingly (Heb. 13:2; cf. Gen. 18; Judg. 6:11–22; 13:1–22).

## Other means of encouragement

In this section, we will look into other approaches the author of Hebrews takes in his attempt to encourage perseverance: (1) identifying with the audience; (2) shame and confidence as balance; and (3) suffering as discipline. We will also consider if there is anti-imperial rhetoric in Hebrews.

The author of Hebrews uses the first-person plural pronoun ('we/our/us') frequently as a way of identifying himself with his audience when he warns them (e.g. 2:1, 3; 3:6, 14; 4:11, 13; 12:1, 25). Scholars have noted that this is a way of 'building rapport' and 'showing solidarity' that he himself is not spared from the danger of apostasy.[112] This inclusive attitude will help to gain a hearing from his audience.

Although the author warns the audience of the dire consequences of apostasy, he then switches to expressing his confidence in them. After shaming the audience for being immature in their faith (Heb. 5:11–14) and warning that there is no second chance for those who deliberately reject God's Son after experiencing the benefactions of God (Heb. 6:4–8), the author nonetheless expresses confidence in his audience, because of their deeds and love in serving fellow believers (Heb. 6:9–10). When drawing the analogy of the unfaithful Israelites (1) who did not believe the good news and thus did not enter into God's promised rest; and (2) who did

---

[111] See also William L. Lane, *Hebrews 9–13*, WBC 47B (Nashville: Thomas Nelson, 1991), p. 511.

[112] Oropeza, *Churches Under Siege*, p. 13.

not live by faith and shrank back, the author uses the inclusive 'we' to express his confidence that he and his audience are not like the Israelites who disbelieved or shrank back and were thus destroyed (Heb. 4:2–3; 10:38–39). By doing so, the author balances both negative and positive approaches, such that his audience will not be unduly upset or discouraged. This approach was another rhetorical practice at that time.[113]

It is interesting to note that the author depicts enduring suffering as a form of God's discipline (Heb. 12:5–11). In view of the metaphor of the athlete in this context (cf. Heb. 12:1, 11–12), discipline here is likely non-punitive (i.e. believers are not suffering persecution due to their sin) and develops endurance.[114] Suffering persecution is a corroboration of their standing as legitimate children of God (Heb. 12:8; cf. Prov. 3:11–12) and it is character forming – though unpleasant, it produces 'righteousness and peace' (Heb. 12:10–11).[115] The idea of suffering hardship as discipline from God can also be found in both Greco-Roman and Jewish traditions.[116] While the author of Hebrews is unique among the New Testament authors regarding this depiction of discipline, the idea of suffering persecution as a corroboration of a Christian's standing and as character forming is common across the New Testament.

In chapter 1, we noted that the early Christians ascribed titles to Jesus that were also used of the Roman emperor, such as the Son of God or the Great High Priest, such that misunderstandings of treason and conflicts could easily arise.[117] Both these titles are very important in Hebrews, and the author develops the implications of Jesus as the Son of God and the Great High Priest at length. The question is whether the author is explaining these solely in terms of the Jewish tradition. Or is he harbouring anti-imperial rhetoric in explaining who the Son of God and the Great High Priest truly are? Admittedly, we will not be able to ascertain fully

---

[113] *Rhetorica ad Herennium* 4.37.49. See also Gorman, 'Persuading Through *Pathos*', pp. 82–84; Oropeza, *Churches Under Siege*, p. 56.

[114] DeSilva, *Perseverance in Gratitude*, pp. 447–448; Koester, *Hebrews*, p. 526.

[115] The author cites Prov. 3:11–12 here as proof of legitimacy as God's children, though transforming the punitive discipline in the context of Proverbs to a non-punitive one. See deSilva, *Perseverance in Gratitude*, pp. 448–449; N. Clayton Croy, *Endurance in Suffering: Hebrews 12:1–13 in Its Rhetorical, Religious, and Philosophical Context*, SNTSMS 98 (Cambridge: Cambridge University Press, 1998), pp. 217–218.

[116] For details of these Greco-Roman and Jewish sources, see Croy, *Endurance in Suffering*, pp. 83–161; Matthew Thiessen, 'Hebrews 12.5–13, the Wilderness Period, and Israel's Discipline', *NTS* 55.3 (2009), pp. 369–373. DeSilva (*Perseverance in Gratitude*, p. 449) notes that Hebrews also closely reflects the concept in Seneca, *De providentia*, 1.6, 2.5, 4.11–12.

[117] See p. 16 above.

the intentions of the author, though we can attempt to do so by our interpretation of his text. However, we must also fully acknowledge our
inevitable presuppositions and subjectivity in the process. It seems to me
that there are no obvious indications that the author is doing such a comparison. On the contrary, his exposition is clearly steeped in covenantal
language found in Jewish tradition. His audience or later readers who are
sensitive to imperial language could possibly think of such a comparison,
but we cannot be sure if the author has such intentions. Based on the
evidence from the text of Hebrews, it is unlikely that the author is primarily engaging in apologetic moves in defence of Jesus' identity as the
Son of God and the Great High Priest against the Roman imperial
backdrop as a means to persuade his audience to persevere in its faith.[118]
This differs from Revelation (see below), where its figurative language
clearly refers to a critique of imperial Rome.

# 1 Peter

1 Peter employs a strong eschatological perspective in encouraging its
readers to persevere in their faith. Like other New Testament authors, he
uses Scripture as proof, exemplars for emulation and develops sayings of
Jesus in the gospel tradition. In modern sociological terms, in order for a
marginalized group to survive, social cohesion by building up the group's
common experiences is important. According to Talbert's analysis, the
approach 1 Peter takes creates social cohesion for the Christians from
their common experience of salvation and suffering in Christ.[119]

Peter assures the readers they are the elect of God (1 Peter 1:1; 2:9–10)
who have been granted salvation and given an eternal inheritance through
faith in Jesus (1 Peter 1:3–4, 9). They can be assured of this because of
God's providence: (1) the Spirit sanctifies them so they may be obedient
to Christ (1 Peter 1:2);[120] (2) God's power guards their salvation until the

---

[118] Jason A. Whitlark, *Resisting Empire: Rethinking the Purpose of the Letter to 'the Hebrews'*,
LNTS 484 (London: Bloomsbury, 2014), p. 189. Whitlark has attempted to show that the author
of Hebrews uses figurative language (a common rhetorical strategy) to critique Roman
imperial culture covertly, so as to encourage his primarily Gentile audience to resist the temptation of giving up their faith in Jesus. Although Whitlark (ibid., p. 17) begins by stating his
method as 'reading with the authorial audience', he eventually equates the audience's
perception with the author's intention of doing so. The latter may not always equate with the
former. As it is oblique, this remains only a possibility, because it is difficult to establish with
certainty whether the author has deliberately done so.

[119] Charles H. Talbert, 'Once Again: The Plan of 1 Peter', in Charles H. Talbert (ed.), *Perspectives on First Peter*, NABPRSSS 9 (Macon: Mercer University Press, 1986), p. 146.

[120] For the sense of the preposition *eis* as purpose, see Jobes, *1 Peter*, p. 67; Dubis, *1 Peter*, p. 3.

last days (1 Peter 1:5) and (3) God will restore and strengthen them when they suffer (1 Peter 5:10). Their grief and suffering from 'all kinds of trials' proves their faith is genuine (1 Peter 1:6). While 'all kinds of trials' is rather broad, the letter mainly addresses the persecution the readers face due to their faith. For Peter, suffering persecution faithfully is a corroboration of their true standing in Christ (1 Peter 1:7). Their genuine faith has greater value than gold and will result in receiving an eschatological eternal 'inheritance' and 'praise, glory and honour' (1 Peter 1:4, 7). He also describes their present suffering as 'a little while' when compared with the eternal (1 Peter 1:6; 5:10). By doing so, Peter seeks to persuade his readers that it is worthwhile suffering for their faith now. He further encourages them not to be ashamed of their suffering for Christ, but to rejoice instead, so they will rejoice also when Christ's glory is revealed (1 Peter 4:12–13, 16).

In line with Jewish tradition, Peter depicts eschatological reward and punishment as two sides of the same coin. Since his readers know that the Father will judge each one's work impartially (1 Peter 1:17; cf. 4:17), they will need to keep away from evil by obeying the truth and live reverently (1 Peter 1:13–22; cf. 2:1, 11–12). Even if they suffer unjustly, they are not to retaliate with evil but to repay evil with blessing instead (1 Peter 2:19–20; 3:9). This concept is developed from Jesus' sayings in the gospel tradition (cf. Matt. 5:10–11, 44–45 // Luke 6:22–23, 27–28).[121]

Peter cites Psalm 32:12–16 as his scriptural basis, in which the psalm emphasizes that the Lord looks after the righteous and punishes those who do evil (1 Peter 3:10–12).[122] He exhorts his audience to follow the example of Christ, who is the exemplar of suffering unjustly but not retaliating, entrusting himself to God because God will judge justly (1 Peter 2:21–23). Although Christ suffered and died, he was resurrected and exalted to the right hand of God, such that all authorities (heavenly and earthly) submit to him (1 Peter 3:18–22). Therefore, since Christ died for the believers' sins, they are to 'arm [themselves] with the same attitude' to overcome sin and evil (1 Peter 4:1). Even if they are to suffer as a Christian, they should continue to do good and entrust themselves to God, because judgment will begin with God's household (1 Peter 4:14–19). This concept of eschatological judgment motivates the readers to persevere in their faith by doing

---

[121] See also France, *Matthew*, p. 170.
[122] See also D. A. Carson, '1 Peter', in G. K. Beale and D. A. Carson (eds.), *Commentary on the New Testament Use of the Old Testament* (Grand Rapids: Baker Academic, 2007), pp. 1036–1037.

good and shunning evil despite facing persecution.[123] For Peter, good works are not just a response to persecutors, but also a motivation to persevere, because their good works may indirectly advance the Christian mission by winning some of their opponents over (1 Peter 2:12; 3:1–2).[124]

Since the end of all things is near, the readers need to have a sober mind, so as to pray and to resist the devil by standing firm in their faith (1 Peter 4:7; 5:8–9). Knowing that other believers throughout the world are also suffering like them helps them to understand that they are not alone in their suffering (1 Peter 5:9b). Peter ends the letter by summarizing his purpose of writing: to encourage them and testify to the 'true grace of God', such that they should '[s]tand fast in it' (1 Peter 5:12).[125]

# Revelation

As apocalyptic literature that has the purpose of persuading its readers to persevere in their faith, the book of Revelation is highly dramatic in its narrative with the use of rich imagery and literary devices, appealing specially to *pathos*, while not lacking in *ethos* and *logos*.[126] The literary and rhetorical devices are knitted closely into the plot of the narrative, within the framework of eschatological judgment and reward, creating a powerful message to convince the audience not to compromise in order to avoid persecution and/or socio-economic losses due to faith in Jesus.[127] John uses dualistic language and contrasts to bring across both positive and

---

[123] See also Oropeza, *Churches Under Siege*, p. 130.

[124] Some scholars have noted 1 Peter's apparently 'over-optimistic' portrayal of opponents 'giving glory to God' (1 Peter 2:12) and 'being won over' (1 Peter 3:1–2), because Peter does not address the possibility of these opponents not being persuaded. See e.g. David G. Horrell, *The Epistles of Peter and Jude*, EC (London: Epworth, 1998), pp. 47–48; Kelhoffer, *Persecution, Persuasion, and Power*, pp. 125–126. Although Kelhoffer thinks that 1 Peter is 'naïve', we must note that (1) Peter is aware of unrepentant opponents despite witnessing their good works (cf. 1 Peter 3:13–17; 4:4) and (2) in my limited experience, I have come across testimonies of such conversion of opponents, albeit not in large numbers.

[125] See also Jobes, *1 Peter*, pp. 232–324.

[126] See deSilva (*Seeing Things John's Way*) for details on how John appeals to *ethos* (pp. 117–145), *pathos* (pp. 175–228) and *logos* (pp. 229–312) in Revelation.

[127] As the focus of this chapter is to understand how New Testament authors encourage their readers to stand firm in their faith despite facing persecution, I will not discuss whether the events in John's visions correspond to specific events in the course of history – historically (preterist, historicist, futurist approach) or analogically (the idealist approach). These are hermeneutical considerations with implications for how the message of the text is relevant or significant to its later readers. For a discussion of my proposed interpretive approach to reading Revelation in the contemporary world, see Chee-Chiew Lee, '"Fire from Their Mouths": The Power of Witnessing in the Face of Hostility and Suffering (Rev 11:3–13)', *CTTSJ* 4 (2013), pp. 210–214.

negative motivations such as honour and shame, so as to achieve his rhetorical goal. The entire apocalypse is replete with allusions to the Jewish Scriptures, especially the Prophets.[128] This reinforces John's identity as a prophet (Rev. 1:1–3; 22:6–9) and shows that his message is in line with what the Prophets had looked forward to and moving towards consummation by the Messiah in the last days.[129] Like the prophets of God before him, his duty is to call God's erring people to repent and to encourage God's faithful people to persevere. John establishes *ethos* by stating that Jesus Christ directly revealed the message he is testifying to (Rev. 1:1).[130] In order to gain his audience's hearing, he also identifies with his audience as a co-participant in the suffering, kingdom and endurance that is in Jesus (Rev. 1:9).

As such, the 'faithfulness' of Christ and his followers is an important motif in Revelation (e.g. Rev. 2:10; 13, 19; 13:10; 14:12; 17:14). 'Conquering' (*nikaō*) is another important motif. In the letters to the seven churches, the faithful saints are frequently referred to as 'the one who conquers' (e.g. Rev. 2:7, 11, 17, 26; 3:5, 12, 21), and will receive their portion of eschatological inheritance in the new heaven and earth in the presence of God and Christ (Rev. 15:2; 21:7). Even though they initially seem to be conquered by their opponents (Rev. 6:2; 11:7; 13:7), they eventually conquer their opponents (Rev. 12:11; 15:2) because Christ has already conquered (Rev. 3:21; 5:5) and will conquer to the very end (Rev. 17:14).[131]

Because structure conveys meaning, a brief introduction to the structure of Revelation here is helpful for us to follow the narrative plot

---

[128] It comes as no surprise that there are a number of monographs and studies on the use of the various prophets in John's apocalypse. See e.g. Jan Fekkes, *Isaiah and Prophetic Traditions in the Book of Revelation: Visionary Antecedents and Their Development*, JSNTSup 93 (Sheffield: JSOT Press, 1994); Matthew A. Dudreck, 'The Use of Jeremiah in the Book of Revelation', PhD diss., Westminster Theological Seminary, 2018; Jean-Pierre Ruiz, *Ezekiel in the Apocalypse: The Transformation of Prophetic Language in Revelation 16,17–19,10*, EUS 23 (Frankfurt: Peter Lang, 1989); Beate Kowalsk, 'Transformation of Ezekiel in John's Revelation', in William A. Tooman and Michael A. Lyons (eds.), *Transforming Visions: Transformations of Text, Tradition, and Theology in Ezekiel* (Cambridge: James Clarke, 2010), pp. 279–307; Marko Jauhiainen, *The Use of Zechariah in Revelation*, WUNT 2.199 (Tübingen: Mohr Siebeck, 2005).

[129] See also deSilva, *Seeing Things John's Way*, pp. 158–174, who shows John's continuity with the Jewish Scriptures in terms of the major theological motifs.

[130] See also ibid., pp. 117–137.

[131] While I agree with Moloney that interpreters of Revelation who over-emphasize the eschatological victory of Christ can easily miss the point that such a victory has already been won, Moloney has unduly dichotomized 'the perennial saving effects of Jesus' death and resurrection' resulting from the already-accomplished victory and 'the definitive eschatological triumph over the wicked'. See Francis J. Moloney, *The Apocalypse of John: A Commentary* (Grand Rapids: Baker Academic, 2020), pp. 21, 24–25.

in the discussion that follows. Revelation 1:1–8 forms the introduction, in which the seven churches in Asia are the primary recipients of Jesus' revelation regarding the imminent future (Rev. 1:3).[132] John sees Christ in a vision, commanding him to write to the seven churches, summarizing their present challenges with calls to repent and persevere, as well as giving warnings and promises of eschatological judgment and rewards (Rev. 1:9 – 3:22). Revelation 4 – 16 forms the major central section in a form of three series of judgments and three interludes. Revelation 17 – 22 wraps up by comparing and contrasting the final outcome of two groups of people: (1) the unrepentant, who identify themselves with the whore and the great city Babylon; and (2) the conquerors, who are identified as the bride and the New Jerusalem. The technique of juxtaposing two entities for comparison and contrast is known as *synkrisis*, which is often used to show which is relatively better or worse.[133]

## Excursus 1: interludes

Scholars have noted that interludes in Revelation have theological significance in relation to the series they 'interrupt'.[134] In the series of the seven seals and the seven trumpets, an interlude with two episodes 'interrupts' the sixth and seventh seals and trumpets respectively. The interlude between the seals emphasizes God's providence for his saints in their suffering (Rev. 7 – 8), while the interlude between the trumpets emphasizes the responsibility of the saints in their suffering (Rev. 10 – 11).[135] Similarly, the parallel structure among the four

---

[132] While these seven churches existed at the time of John's writing, it is also likely that they represent the typical challenges the early church faced in other parts of the Roman Empire. This is evident from the closing of each letter: there is a call to heed 'what the Spirit says to the churches' (Rev. 2:7, 11, 17, 29; 3:6, 13, 22), although each letter is addressed to the church in a specific city. See also John C. Thomas and Frank D. Macchia, *Revelation*, THNTC (Grand Rapids: Eerdmans, 2016), p. 18.

[133] Parsons and Martin, *Ancient Rhetoric*, pp. 231–274; deSilva, *Seeing Things John's Way*, pp. 24–25.

[134] James L. Resseguie, *The Revelation of John: A Narrative Commentary* (Grand Rapids: Baker Academic, 2009), p. 53; Thomas and Macchia, *Revelation*, p. 3.

[135] Koester (*Revelation*, p. 113) explains the function of the interludes as providing 'the reason for the delay' before the last seal and trumpet respectively: 'time has been provided for people to be redeemed' (Rev. 7:1–7) and to bear witness (Rev. 10:1 – 11:14). See also Richard Bauckham, *The Climax of Prophecy: Studies on the Book of Revelation* (Edinburgh: T&T Clark, 1993), pp. 12–13; Peter S. Perry, *The Rhetoric of Digressions: Revelation 7:1–17 and 10:1–11:13 and Ancient Communication*, WUNT 2.268 (Tübingen: Mohr Siebeck, 2009), pp. 209–241.

'seven' series indicates that Revelation 4 – 5 and 12 – 14 are likely also interludes (see Table 3.6).[136]

### Table 3.6 Parallel structure of the four series of sevens in Revelation

| Seven letters (1:9 – 3:22) | Seven trumpets (8:2 – 11:19) |
|---|---|
| *Interlude:* | *Interlude:* |
| Heavenly throne room (4:1 – 5:14) explains why the Lamb is worthy to execute judgments. | Three heavenly signs (12:1 – 15:4) explains the cosmic and spiritual forces behind the warfare of the Lamb and the serpent/beast(s). |
| Seven seals (6:1 – 8:1). | Seven bowls (15:5 – 16:21). |

The first interlude (Rev. 4 – 5) depicts the scene of the heavenly throne room. John describes both God and the Lamb as sitting on the throne, with God ruling over the world as its creator and the Lamb as worthy to initiate the judgment of the seven seals because he has first redeemed people from all the world by his own sacrificial death (Rev. 4:3, 11; 5:6, 11). This scene forms the introduction to the first series of judgments – the seven seals (Rev. 6:1 – 8:1). The second series of judgments – the seven trumpets – proceeds after the seventh seal (Rev. 8:2 – 11:19).[137] The second interlude (Rev. 12 – 14) is the central portion of the narrative, explaining the spiritual and cosmic warfare behind the oppression of the saints on earth (Rev. 12 – 13) and a preview of the final defeat of the beast and the victory of the Lamb with their respective followers (Rev. 14:1 – 15:4).[138] The third series of judgments – the seven bowls – follows in Revelation 15:5 – 16:21.

---

[136] Although Resseguie, Thomas and Macchia note (1) the four series of sevens; and that (2) Rev. 12 – 14 is an interlude between the first two (seals and trumpets) and the last (bowls) series of judgments, they have not mentioned Rev. 4 – 5 as an interlude. See James L. Resseguie, *Revelation Unsealed: A Narrative Critical Approach to John's Apocalypse*, BIS 32 (Leiden: Brill, 1998), p. 162; Thomas and Macchia, *Revelation*, p. 3. Other scholars have noted other interludes; see e.g. Ernst R. Wendland, 'The Hermeneutical Significance of Literary Structure in Revelation', *Neot* 48.2 (2014), p. 450; Koester, *Revelation*, p. 642. However, these series of sevens have clear structural parallels.

[137] It is important to emphasize that I am relating the narrative sequence of the judgments, rather than referring to how these judgments are to be carried out in historical chronology.

[138] Motifs in Rev. 14 fleshed out later in the narrative include trampling of grapes in the eschatological war (Rev. 14:19–20; 19:15), the followers of the beast suffering in the lake of burning sulphur (14:10; 21:8), etc.

Among the various literary devices John uses, I would like to highlight two of them – contrasts and interludes. Using these literary forms, John seeks to persuade his audience in the following ways: (1) by providing warnings and promises with the end in view; (2) by guiding his audience to make a wise choice through comparisons and contrast; (3) by assuring them of God's providence over the suffering saints who faithfully carry out their duties; and (4) by assuring them of God's faithfulness and righteousness in punishing the wicked and unrepentant, rewarding the righteous and avenging the wrongful persecution of his faithful saints.

## Excursus 2: the two women and the two cities

The rest of the narrative from Revelation 17 – 22 fleshes out motifs mentioned earlier in 1 – 16. First, there are thematic links between Jezebel and the great whore in terms of (1) both having led people into sexual immorality (a common metaphor in Jewish writings for unfaithfulness to the true God by worshipping other gods through idolatry); and (2) their final destruction along with those who allied with Jezebel as her 'children' (Rev. 2:22–23; cf. 17:2, 5; 18:21–24; 19:3). Second, the audience is given a 'preview' of the eschatological war with the beast and the serpent and final judgment in the earlier narrative, and then a 'full view' in the later narrative (Rev. 9:13–18; 14:9–11, 20; 16:12–16; cf. 19:11–21; 20:7–15).[139] Structurally, the eschatological war (Rev. 19:11 – 20:15) is sandwiched between the two episodes: the destruction of the great whore (Rev. 17:1 – 19:10) and the marriage of the bride to the Lamb (Rev. 21 – 22).[140] This sandwich structure highlights the eventual defeat of the serpent and the beast, together with all who allied with them, and contrasts it with the ultimate victory of God and the Lamb, together with God's faithful people, those who conquer. John uses similar phrases – a common Jewish literary device – to delineate the two episodes (see Table 3.7).[141]

---

[139] See also Resseguie (*Revelation Unsealed*, pp. 103–104, 136–144), who has shown how 'the mother [in Rev. 12] and the bride are the antithesis of the whore and Jezebel'; ibid., p. 103.

[140] See also Bauckham (*Climax of Prophecy*, p. 5), who sees this section in between as a 'transition' describing 'the events that intervene between the fall of Babylon and the descent of the New Jerusalem'.

[141] On the literary parallels describing the great whore and the bride, see ch. 1, n. 88 above.

**Table 3.7 Comparison between the great whore and the bride in Revelation**

| The great whore as the Great Babylon (Rev. 17:1–3; 19:9–10) | The bride as the New Jerusalem (Rev. 21:9–10; 22:6, 8–9) |
| --- | --- |
| One of the seven angels who had the seven bowls came and said to me, 'Come, I will show you [the great whore] . . .' Then the angel carried me away in the Spirit into a desert [vision of the great whore who is the great Babylon] . . . Then the angel said to me . . . 'These are the true words of God.' At this I fell at his feet to worship him. But he said to me, 'Don't do that! I am a fellow servant with you.' | One of the seven angels who had the seven bowls full of the seven last plagues came and said to me, 'Come, I will show you the bride.' And he carried me away in the Spirit to a mountain [vision of the bride who is the New Jerusalem]. The angel said to me, 'These words are trustworthy and true . . .' And when I had heard and seen them, I fell down to worship at the feet of the angel who had been showing them to me. But he said to me, 'Don't do that! I am a fellow servant with you.' |

## Preliminary warnings and promises with the end in view

In the letters to the seven churches (Rev. 2 – 3), praise from Christ for faithfulness is a form of honour, and rebuke for compromise is a form of shame for the churches in their present earthly life. Reward for those who conquer and punishment for those who do not repent are forms of eschatological honour and shame. It is noteworthy that promises of reward and warnings of punishment made to the churches in Revelation 2 – 3 are depicted as fulfilled in the later narrative (see Table 3.8 on page 136).

While warnings of judgment act as a deterrent, a rebuke and a call to repentance usually accompany them (e.g. Rev. 2:4–5, 15–16; 3:2–3). It is also important to note that if those who have been rebuked and warned do not repent, Jesus' judgment will certainly come upon them (Rev. 2:21–23).

'Whoever has ears' marks the end of each letter (Rev. 2:7, 11, 17, 29; 3:6, 13, 22), echoing Jesus' well-known phrase that marks the end of his sayings in the gospel tradition (Matt. 11:15; 13:9, 43; Mark 4:9, 23; Luke 8:8, 14:35). This phrase appears again in Revelation 13:9, introducing an exhortation

**Table 3.8 Fulfilment of promises and warnings in Revelation 2 – 3 in the later narrative of Revelation**

| | Promise/ warning | Fulfilment |
|---|---|---|
| Tree of life in the paradise. | 2:7 | 22:1–2, 14, 19 |
| Not be hurt by second death. | 2:11 | 21:7–8 |
| Manna and new name.[142] | 2:17 | 19:12; 22:4 |
| Authority to rule over the nations and given the morning star. | 2:26–28 | 4:10; 19:15; 20:4; 22:5c, 16 |
| White garment (robes/linen). | 3:5 | 6:11; 7:9, 13; 19:8, 14; 21:2; 22:14 |
| Name in the book of life. | 3:5 | 13:8; 20:12, 15; 21:27 |
| Pillar in God's temple and Jesus' name written on them. | 3:12 | 21:22–23; 22:4 |
| Wages war on the unrepentant with sword from Christ's mouth. | 2:16 | 19:15 |
| The unrepentant will suffer the same punishment with the woman who seduces others into whoredom; each person will be repaid according to what he or she has done. | 2:21–23 | 18:1–4; 20:12–13 |
| The one who does not heed the 'wake up' call shall face judgment when Jesus comes 'like a thief'. | 3:2–3 | 16:15 |

to persevere despite suffering persecution from the beast. In addition, the phrase describing Jesus' coming 'like a thief' is also a metaphor used in the gospel tradition (Matt. 24:43 // Luke 12:39). It is noteworthy that the context of these two phrases in Revelation is similar to that in the gospel

[142] In Jewish tradition, manna will be given again at the eschaton (*2 Bar.* 29.8). Given the association of Jesus as the 'manna from heaven' (John 6:31–32), the 'hidden manna' and 'unknown name' in Rev. 2:17 very likely refer to Jesus (cf. Rev. 19:12). Thus, the one who conquers partakes in and belongs to Jesus. See also Buist M. Fanning, *Revelation*, ZECNT (Grand Rapids: Zondervan, 2020), pp. 141–142.

tradition.[143] First, the parable of the seeds falling into four types of soil mentions the unfruitful ones who fall away due to persecution or deceitfulness of wealth (Mark 4:17–19 // Matt. 13:21–22 // Luke 8:13–14), which are clearly the challenges faced by the seven churches. Second, God's people who refuse to repent after hearing the message of John the Baptist – the one who is greater than the prophets – will suffer judgment (Matt. 11:7–24). Among the seven churches, those who refuse to heed Jesus' prophetic call to repent will face the same consequence. Third, although the wheat and weeds grow together, the angels will separate them at the eschatological harvest, preserving the grain from the wheat while burning the weeds – which represent the people belonging to the evil one. In contrast, 'the righteous will shine like the sun in the kingdom of their Father' (Matt. 13:24–30, 36–43). The similarity in context is clear because John later provides a glimpse of this eschatological harvest in Revelation 14:4–16. Fourth, Jesus warns that those who do not 'keep watch' will be caught by surprise when he comes at the eschatological judgment. Those who are unfaithful will be caught red-handed and punished accordingly, while the faithful ones will be rewarded (Matt. 24:36–51 // Luke 12:35–48). Similarly, John repeats this warning of Jesus coming 'like a thief' when he describes the eschatological war arising from pouring out the sixth bowl (Rev. 16:15). The concept of Jesus rewarding the faithful and punishing the wicked, giving all according to what they have done, is evident in Revelation 11:18 and 22:12.

If the audience were able to pick up John's allusion to these two phrases from the gospel tradition and recall the original context of these phrases, it would likely create a resonance and an enhanced understanding in them that would steer them to repent.[144] What Jesus warned and promised while on earth has come to fruition in John's apocalyptic visions of the imminent future; these things will take place soon (Rev. 1:1; 22:6).

## Making a choice: compromise or persevere

John uses the literary device of contrast to address who is truly the Lord of the world (God or the beast) and the eventual outcome of those who

---

[143] Contra Koester (*Revelation*, p. 264), who thinks there is 'no trace of the Synoptic contexts in Revelation' for the first phrase. Whether John knows the written Gospels or other forms of oral and written traditions, given the multiple attestations in the Synoptic Gospels of the same pericope, this saying of Jesus is likely transmitted in some form of context.

[144] On the resonance of intertextuality and its effect on enhancing understanding, see Moyise, *Old Testament*, pp. 108–110.

choose to follow their Lord. As mentioned previously, the use of contrast and dualistic language does not allow for 'sitting on the fence'.[145] Also, as mentioned in chapter 1, the Roman emperor was given the title 'the lord of all the world'.[146] God is the true 'Lord of all the world' because he is the creator who sustains life (Rev. 4:11). In contrast, the beast who came out of the sea is able to rule over all the inhabitants of the earth and be worshipped only because it has been 'given authority' to do so (Rev. 13:4, 7–8). All creation worships the Lamb spontaneously, because he willingly sacrificed his life to redeem people from the earth (Rev. 5:9, 13). In contrast, the beast who came out of the earth deceives and coerces the inhabitants of the earth to worship the beast out of the sea with signs and wonders and by threatening them with economic deprivation and death (Rev. 13:17).

Those who receive the mark of the beast (on their foreheads or right hand) may avoid persecution and oppression for the time being, but will eventually be destroyed with the beast in the lake of burning sulphur (Rev. 13:16–17; 14:9–11). They will receive no rest from their suffering eternally (Rev. 14:11). The imagery of the burning sulphur is so vivid that the audience would almost be able to 'smell' it.[147] In contrast, those who refuse to receive the mark of the beast are killed (Rev. 13:15), and their foreheads are marked instead with the names of the Lamb and his Father (Rev. 14:1; cf. 6:3–8). They eventually stand on (the heavenly) Mount Zion before the throne, singing the song of Moses in victory (Rev. 14:1–5; 15:1–4). The imagery of the joyous and triumphant singing is also very vivid, such that the audience almost hear and experience it. They will now enjoy eternal rest from oppression – their toil and faithful resistance to compromise led to economic deprivation and death, but their endurance has paid off and their deeds will follow them (Rev. 14:13).[148] The beast waged war on the saints and conquered them on earth (Rev. 13:7; cf. 11:7). However, the

---

[145] See p. 111 above and Lee, 'Facing Persecution', p. 200.

[146] See p. 43 above.

[147] See deSilva (*Seeing Things John's Way*, pp. 84–85), who notes the 'sensory-aesthetic texture' of Rev. 14:6–13 in evoking the audience's senses, in terms of seeing, hearing, smelling and even touching.

[148] 'Endurance' (*hypomonē*), 'labour' (*kopos*) and 'deeds' (*erga*) in Rev. 14:12–13 link back to Rev. 2, where Jesus praised the church of Ephesus for these three areas, and the church of Thyatira for the first and third. This link helps us to understand that the 'deeds' refer to the churches' faithful resistance to compromise. See Lee, 'Rest and Victory', p. 535; Koester, *Revelation*, p. 211; Ian Boxall, *The Revelation of Saint John*, BNTC 18 (London: Continuum, 2006), p. 211.

faithful have conquered the serpent and the beast by the blood of the Lamb, their testimony for Jesus and not fearing death (Rev. 12:11). The death of the saints in resisting compromise is not just a passive relief from suffering ('rest from toil'), but an active victory over their oppressors ('rest from enemies').[149] This is an additional motivation to help the suffering audience to persevere.

The eschatological judgment will definitely come, as depicted by the Son of Man's coming in the cloud to harvest the grain and grapes of the earth, trampling the grapes in the great winepress of God's wrath (Rev. 14:14–20). So severe is the judgment that the blood flowing from the winepress covers 'the whole earth' (1,600 stadia; Rev. 14:20).[150]

John clearly appeals to *pathos* here: fearful judgment and triumphant hope, and confidence in Christ for his execution of the eschatological judgment.[151] The audience are compelled to make a choice: (1) follow the beast and avoid suffering now but face even greater suffering eternally; or (2) follow the Lamb and suffer intensely now but experience the final victory with greater eternal joy. At three critical junctures, John challenges his audience as to how they should respond, each introduced by the word *hōde* (translated in NIV as 'this calls for'): (1) since captivity and martyrdom are unavoidable, 'this calls for patient endurance and faithfulness on the part of God's people' (Rev. 13:9–10); (2) since deception and temptation to compromise are so strong, 'this calls for wisdom' and 'insight' to recognize what the mark of the beast stands for (Rev. 13:14, 17–18);[152] and (3) since the final end of those who follow the beast or the Lamb is clear: 'This calls for patient endurance on the part of the people of God who keep his commands and remain faithful to Jesus' (Rev. 14:12). The first *hōde* corresponds with the third, while the second *hōde* corresponds with the fourth, which occurs in Revelation 17:9: 'This calls for a mind with wisdom.' The

---

149 Lee, 'Rest and Victory', pp. 357–358.

150 For the symbolic meaning of numbers in Revelation, see Adela Yarbro Collins, 'Numerical Symbolism in Jewish and Early Christian Apocalyptic Literature', in *Cosmology and Eschatology in Jewish and Christian Apocalypticism*, JSJSup 50 (Leiden: Brill, 1996), pp. 55–138; Resseguie, *Revelation of John*, pp. 28–32. In short, the number 4 is associated with 'the earth and creation', 10 represents totality, while multiplication in squares or cubes symbolizes intensity. Thus, $1,600 = 4 \times 4 \times 10 \times 10$ most likely symbolizes the whole earth (Resseguie, *Revelation of John*, p. 29; Thomas and Macchia, *Revelation*, p. 266).

151 See also Oropeza (*Churches Under Siege*, p. 3), who notes 'fear' as one of John's overall rhetorical strategies to steer his audience away from negative consequences.

152 For a summary of the various interpretations of the mark (666) of the beast, see Koester, *Revelation*, pp. 596–599. The point here for the audience is that they must have wisdom to discern the 'powers' pressurizing them to compromise, so that they may not fall into temptation.

audience must be able to recognize who the beast and the whore are and grasp the consequences of worshipping the beast and committing sexual immorality with the whore. They must not buckle under the threat of death nor succumb to the seduction of economic gains.

After contrasting the final end of the two parties with this 'preview', John reiterates the same point through another two contrasts – (1) the whore and the bride; and (2) the eschatological 'portion' (inheritance) of those who identify with the great city and the beast and those who identify with the New Jerusalem and the Lamb. The whore attempts to dress herself luxuriously (Rev. 17:4a), but John exposes her true colours – filth and abominations (Rev. 17:4b) – and her underlying associations with demons and unclean spirits (Rev. 18:2). While she exercises great influence over rulers, merchants and people of the earth, leading them into idolatry (sexual immorality) and giving them great economic gains (Rev. 17:2; 18:3), the rulers eventually turn on her (Rev. 17:16). Her sins are great and she will be punished in full (Rev. 18:5–7a). She proudly assumes her status is permanent, but she will lose everything and be destroyed 'in one day' (Rev. 18:7b–8). In the midst of declaring her imminent destruction, the voice from heaven calls out,

> *Come out of her, my people,*
>> so that you will not share in her sins,
>> so that you will not receive any of her plagues.
> (Rev. 18:4)

Should God's people compromise and remain associated with her, they will not be exempt from suffering the same punishment. John's descriptions of her uncleanness and destruction likely arouse the ancient audience's disgust and fear.[153] In conjunction with the call for God's people to 'come out of her', John's appeal to *pathos* and *logos* steers the audience towards the only wise choice he presents to them: repent from compromise and stay far from the seductive whore, or you will be destroyed with her.[154] The lake of burning sulphur is not just for the

---

[153] See also deSilva, *Seeing Things John's Way*, pp. 219, 293–294.

[154] A common motif in the Prophets is calling God's people to flee from Babylon so they may not partake in her judgment (e.g. Isa. 48:20–22; 52:11–12; Jer. 50:8–10; 51:6–10, 45–48). The call for God's people to 'come out' of Babylon (Rev. 18:4) most likely alludes to Jer. 51:45 and develops from this tradition. See also Beale, *Revelation*, pp. 897–898.

serpent and the beast,[155] but for all their followers – 'the cowardly, the unbelieving, the vile, the murderers, the sexually immoral, those who practise magic arts, the idolaters and all liars' (Rev. 20:10–15; 21:8). According to the narrative plot of Revelation, these followers would include those who compromised their faith (*hoi apistoi*, 'the unfaithful ones') because they were cowardly.[156]

In contrast to the whore, the bride is dressed in fine linen, bright and clean – these are her righteous deeds (Rev. 19:8). She is the one who is truly adorned magnificently – with precious metals and stones, reflecting the glory of God (Rev. 21:11, 18–21). Though she suffered for her faith, her faithful testimony for Jesus brought inhabitants of the earth ('nations' and 'kings') into the fold of God's people (cf. Rev. 21:24–26). There will no longer be any pain or death (Rev. 21:4), and God's people will reign with him for ever (Rev. 21:5; 22:6). In both these episodes, John reiterates the phrase 'faithful [*pistos*] and true [*alēthinos*]' (Rev. 19:11; 21:5; 22:6; cf. 3:14; 19:9), emphasizing Jesus' faithfulness and the certainty of coming to pass what he has revealed (the prophetic words), so that his audience may be encouraged to press on. This is an appeal to *pathos*, stirring up confidence to steer the audience towards the only wise choice he is presenting to them: persevering in faith is worthwhile because Jesus' promises will be fulfilled at the eschaton. The followers of the Lamb – those who conquer – will inherit the new heaven and earth (Rev. 21:7).

## God's providence and the duty of his people

Other than for comparison and contrast, John uses these interludes to emphasize God's providence for his suffering people and their duty to testify for Jesus in the midst of suffering: (1) the 144,000 and the great multitude (Rev. 7:1–17);[157] (2) John eating the scroll, and the two witnesses (Rev. 10:1 – 11:14); and (3) the war between Michael and his angels against

---

[155] The second beast, which rises from the land in Rev. 13:11–16, is identified as the false prophet in Rev. 19:20 and 20:10.

[156] See also Oropeza, *Churches Under Siege*, p. 192.

[157] The 144,000 most likely symbolize the vast and complete number of God's people (12 × 12 × 1,000), as seen in the great multitude. Contra Oropeza (*Churches Under Siege*, pp. 225–226), who thinks that the former refers to Jewish followers. Looking at both Rev. 6 and 13 – 14, it is very unlikely that these twelve tribes refer only to Jewish Christians, but very clearly refer to God's faithful people as a whole (regardless of ethnicity). There is also a Jewish tradition of the twelve tribes as referring to God's faithful people at the eschaton (e.g. *Pss Sol.* 17.26–28; 1QM 3.13–14).

the enormous red serpent and his two beasts, with its implications for God's people (Rev. 12 – 14).

In the first interlude, there are two episodes: (1) an angel sealing God's people – his servants – before the four winds ravage the earth (the land, the sea and the trees) (Rev. 7:1–8); and (2) the deliverance of the great multitude from the tribulation into the throne room of God (Rev. 7:9–17). The imagery of the four winds ravaging the earth alludes to the trumpet and bowl judgments, which affect the land, the sea and the trees.[158] The seal on God's people likely alludes to Ezekiel 9:1–6, which symbolizes God's protection over his faithful people when judgment comes upon the unfaithful people and their city.[159] This seal on the forehead is later identified as the name of the Lamb and his Father (Rev. 14:1). Thus, just as marking with a seal in the ancient world symbolizes ownership, this seal marks God's faithful people as belonging to him. This act of sealing may suggest that God guards his people from harm (cf. Ezek. 9:5–6), but it more likely refers to his keeping his people faithful (cf. Rev. 14:3–5).[160] Although the judgments are not directed at God's faithful people, it does not imply that his people will be spared totally from the devastating effects of the judgment. This is evident in (1) Ezekiel 9:7–11 (though spared from slaughter, the faithful who lament over the sin of the people of Jerusalem have to suffer the consequences of the invasion); (2) Revelation 6:1–11 (God's people are not spared from the acts of evil and oppressive people [war and persecution], nor from the famine and plagues resulting from such evils); and (3) Revelation 7:14 (now that the great multitude has come out of the great tribulation, neither the sun nor any scorching heat will beat down on them, implying that they likely previously suffered their effect; Rev. 7:16; cf. 16:8). *This is an important theological point*: God's protection of his people does not entail their deliverance from all harm all of the time.

The second episode depicts 'a great multitude that no one could count, from every nation, tribe, people and language, *standing [histēmi] before*

---

[158] The devastation of the earth is more obvious in the first three trumpets and the second and third bowls (cf. Rev. 8:7–10; 16:3–4).

[159] See also Beale, *Revelation*, pp. 409–413; Oropeza, *Churches Under Siege*, p. 226.

[160] In the Jewish Scriptures, a 'new song' is sung whenever God's people experience Yahweh's deliverance from and victory over their enemies (Pss 33:3; 40:3; 96:1; 98:1; 144:9; 149:1; Isa. 42:10). See Beale, *Revelation*, p. 736. These faithful people sang a new song (Rev. 14:3; cf. 5:9), implying they had experienced God's deliverance and victory over their enemies.

*the throne and before the Lamb'* (Rev. 7:9).[161] As Lemcio has noted, this scene brings to mind the heavenly throne room in Revelation 4 – 5 (cf. Rev. 7:11) and seems to be the answer to the question exclaimed by those facing the sixth seal judgment: 'Fall on us and hide us *from the face of him who sits on the throne and from the wrath of the Lamb*! For the great day of their wrath has come, and *who can withstand [histēmi] it?*' (Rev. 6:16–17).[162] They are wearing white robes and holding palm branches in their hands (Rev. 7:9) – both symbols of victory. They have emerged victorious from the great tribulation, their robes washed and made white by the blood of the Lamb (Rev. 7:14; cf. 12:11; 22:14). In Revelation, 'garment' symbolizes deeds and 'white' symbolizes both purity and victory.[163] Finally, the imagery in Revelation 7:15–17 alludes to the throne room of the New Jerusalem: (1) Christ gives them 'springs of living water' and thus they thirst no more (Rev. 7:16–17; cf. 21:6; 22:17); and (2) 'God will wipe away every tear from their eyes' (Rev. 7:17; cf. 21:4).[164]

This first interlude comforts God's people and assures them of his providential care in their sufferings and his deliverance from the great tribulation. They will be able to stand firm because God is protecting their faith and they will eventually emerge victorious from their sufferings – a result of their faithful resistance against compromise in the face of persecution. They will enter the sanctuary (throne room) of God's temple – the New Jerusalem.

---

[161] The repetition of this phrase 'from every nation, tribe, people and language' with slight variation throughout the book of Revelation makes the connections as follows: (1) this great multitude is redeemed from this group by the Lamb (Rev. 5:9; 7:9), while the rest of this group is under the rule and influence of the beast and whore respectively (Rev. 13:7; 17:15); and (2) this same group is the audience to whom God's people are to bear witness for Jesus, announce God's impending judgment and call to repentance (Rev. 10:11; 11:9; 14:6). This role is similar to that of God's prophet in the Jewish Scriptures, as seen in (1) John's task to prophesy; (2) the two witnesses bearing the characteristics of the prophets Moses and Elijah; and (3) the angel's (messenger's) call to fear God because of the impending judgment and to worship him because he is the creator. See also Bauckham, *Climax of Prophecy*, pp. 326–337.

[162] Eugene E. Lemcio, *Navigating Revelation: Charts for the Voyage, a Pedagogical Aid* (Eugene: Wipf & Stock, 2011), pp. 19–20.

[163] Lee, 'Rest and Victory', pp. 352–357. Thus, 'white garment' denotes righteous deeds and thus an undefiled and victorious person (Rev. 3:5; cf. 6:11; 19:8); 'soiled garment' denotes tainted with unrighteous deeds and thus defilement (Rev. 3:4); nakedness denotes no worthy deeds at all and thus shameful (Rev. 3:17–18; 16:15). Those who 'washed their robes and made them white in the blood of the Lamb' are those who have been made righteous and victorious by Christ (Rev. 7:14; 22:14).

[164] These descriptions, cited from Isa. 25:8 and 49:10, are depicted as fulfilled in the New Jerusalem. See also G. K. Beale and Sean M. McDonough, 'Revelation', in G. K. Beale and D. A. Carson (eds.), *Commentary on the New Testament Use of the Old Testament* (Grand Rapids: Baker Academic, 2007), pp. 1109–1110.

In the second interlude, there are also two episodes: (1) the angel commands John to eat the little scroll and prophesy to 'many peoples, nations, languages and kings' (Rev. 10:1–11); and (2) the two witnesses are appointed to prophesy and execute judgment on the inhabitants of the earth – 'every people, tribe, language and nation' (Rev. 11:1–14). In the first episode, John sees a mighty angel coming down from heaven with a little scroll in his hand. He announces God's impending judgment – the seventh trumpet is about to sound with no further delay. John is instructed to receive the little scroll and eat it, symbolizing his commission to deliver the prophetic message to 'many peoples, nations, languages and kings' (Rev. 10:11). The sweet then sour taste of the scroll likely symbolizes the privilege of God's calling as his prophet and the prophet's suffering that results from the people rejecting the message.[165] Most likely, John's prophetic role is representative of God's people, because God has also announced to 'his servants the prophets' regarding what God will accomplish (Rev. 10:7) and these prophets are frequently juxtaposed with the saints (cf. 11:18; 16:6; 18:20, 24; 22:9).[166]

In the second episode, John is told to measure God's temple with its worshippers. However, he is to exclude the outer court because 'it has been given to the Gentiles' and '[t]hey will trample on the Holy City for 42 months' (Rev. 11:1–2). The 'temple' here mostly likely refers to God's faithful people and his presence with them, because (1) in Revelation, 'the Holy City' is both 'the bride' and 'the temple' (Rev. 21:2, 22; cf. 3:12); and (2) other New Testament authors have a similar understanding (cf. Mark 14:58; 1 Cor. 3:16; 1 Peter 2:4–5).[167] If this understanding is correct, the altar at the temple with its worshippers symbolizes the provision of a

---

[165] For the various plausible interpretations, see Grant R. Osborne, *Revelation*, BECNT (Grand Rapids: Baker, 2002), pp. 403–404; Koester, *Revelation*, pp. 482–483.

[166] 'God's servants his prophets' would include John and other Christian prophets, who are in the same prophetic tradition as the Old Testament prophets (e.g. Rev. 1:1–3; 22:6, 9; so Mounce; Koester). While prophets may be a subset of God's faithful people, the juxtaposition in Revelation shows both groups suffering the same fate and receiving the same reward and vindication. Robert H. Mounce, *The Book of Revelation*, rev. edn, NICNT (Grand Rapids: Eerdmans, 1998), p. 208; Koester, *Revelation*, p. 481.

[167] Jauhiainen, *Use of Zechariah*, p. 92, n. 141. A detailed discussion of the disagreements among scholars whether these terms should be understood as literal or symbolic is beyond the scope of our study. The more important issue is to understand the theological implications of the text, which may be common between these two approaches, because these two approaches disagree mostly on the referent, rather than the sense, of the text. See Lee, 'Fire from Their Mouths', p. 212. After all, the focus of our study is on how the New Testament authors encourage their audience, rather than on determining the historical referents.

sanctuary for God's people from their persecutors, though, ironically, they are facing persecution at the same time, as 'trampling' of the Holy City implies.[168]

Forty-two months is a period of time associated with the non-believing ('Gentile') persecutors (Rev. 11:2; 13:5), while 1,260 is associated with God's people (Rev. 11:3; 12:6).[169] Both are approximately the same duration, which could imply that the two witnesses are to prophesy as long as the duration of the persecution. The description of the two witnesses abounds with allusions to various prophets in the Jewish Scriptures (Rev. 11:4–6; cf. Exod. 7:17–19; 1 Kgs. 17:1; Jer. 5:14; Zech. 4:1–14), emphasizing their role in the tradition of the prophets.[170] The beast 'made war' (*poieō polemon*) with the two witnesses and 'conquered' (*nikaō*) them (Rev. 11:7), and this same expression also occurs in Revelation 13:7, where the beast does the same to God's faithful people.[171] In view of the above, these two prophets likely symbolize the witness of God's faithful people.[172]

It is noteworthy that the beast kills the two witnesses only after they have finished their testimony (Rev. 11:7a), and God vindicates them by raising them from the dead and taking them up to heaven (Rev. 11:11). In short, 'the story of the two witnesses encourages the church that they are able to complete their task of witnessing to the world despite severe opposition and persecution, because God will protect and empower them'.[173] The message of the second interlude is clear. The role of John and the two witnesses as prophets is likely representative of the role of God's people as a whole. Testifying for Jesus will bring with it suffering, because

---

[168] During Greco-Roman times, temples provided a sanctuary for fugitives. For historical references in antiquity, see Koester, *Revelation*, p. 483.

[169] At times, the early church used the word 'Gentiles' (*ethnoi*) to refer to non-believers in contrast to God's people (cf. Matt. 6:32; Luke 12:30; 1 Peter 2:12; 4:3).

[170] See also Paul S. Minear, *I Saw a New Earth: An Introduction to the Visions of the Apocalypse*, repr. (Eugene: Wipf & Stock, 2003), p. 103, who notes that this is a 'transcendental model . . . describing the common vocation in language drawn from the stories of many prophets'.

[171] There are many other 'verbal and conceptual parallels' between the two witnesses (Rev. 11:1–13) and the two beasts (Rev. 13:1–18); see A. K. W. Siew, *The War Between the Two Beasts and the Two Witnesses: A Chiastic Reading of Revelation 11.1–14.5*, LNTS 283 (London: T&T Clark, 2005), pp. 198–208.

[172] See Koester (*Revelation*, pp. 496–497) for various interpretations of the two witnesses. Whether these two witnesses are understood as symbolic (i.e. they embody what faithful witness for God is like) or literal (i.e. they exemplify faithful witness), the theological implications and appropriation of the text for the audience are similar: God's people are to witness faithfully despite facing persecution (see also n. 167 above).

[173] Lee, 'Fire from Their Mouths', p. 221.

## Excursus 3: Does Revelation encourage violent response?

The two witnesses are empowered by God, such that

> [if] anyone tries to harm them, fire comes from their mouths and
> devours their enemies. This is how anyone who wants to harm
> them must die. They have power to shut up the heavens so that it
> will not rain during the time they are prophesying; and they have
> power to turn the waters into blood and to strike the earth with
> every kind of plague as often as they want.
> (Rev. 11:5–6)

Does Revelation encourage violent retaliation against the persecutors? Is
this how John encourages the faithful saints that they can conquer – by
retaliation?

I have argued elsewhere that the imagery of 'fire from their mouths
to devour their enemies' denotes 'a non-violent action of proclaiming
the message of repentance and God's imminent judgment'.[174] This
imagery alludes to Jeremiah 5:14, in which God put his words into
Jeremiah's mouth as fire to consume the unrepentant people of Israel
and Judah (Jer. 5:1–13). This imagery clearly denotes Jeremiah's proclamation of God's imminent judgment, which was realized during the
Babylonian invasion. This is further supported by a similar use in *4 Ezra*
13.1–11, 21–38, in which the angel explains that the Son of God

> will reproach them to their face with their evil thoughts and with
> the torments with which they are to be tortured (which were
> symbolized by the flames); and he will destroy them without effort
> by the law (which was symbolized by the fire) (*4 Ezr.* 13:38).[175]

This brings to mind Revelation 11:10, which mentions that the two
prophets (i.e. the two witnesses) 'tormented those who live on the
earth'. Indeed, the call to repentance by pointing out the sins of people

---

[174] Lee, 'Fire from Their Mouths', pp. 222–226, 237.
[175] B. M. Metzger, 'The Fourth Book of Ezra', in James H. Charlesworth (ed.), *The Old
Testament Pseudepigrapha*, 2 vols. (Garden City: Doubleday, 1983), vol. 1, p. 552.

and by warning them of their destruction should they not repent would be 'tormenting' to those who rejected this message. Nonetheless, even this should not be regarded as verbal violence, because the message is not malicious but for the good of its hearers.

In addition, the imagery of drought and plague in Revelation 11:6 is an allusion to the miracles of Elijah and Moses, and its purpose is to associate the two witnesses with the Jewish prophetic tradition.[176] Thus, while the images may depict violent retaliation, their symbolic meaning is to the contrary – to witness faithfully in a non-violent manner by calling people to repentance in the tradition of the prophets.[177]

proclaiming the message of repentance and impending judgment to 'many peoples, nations, languages and kings/tribes' (Rev. 10:11; 11:9) will lead to opposition and even persecution from those who reject it. Nonetheless, God will protect and empower them. It is from this same group that the Lamb will redeem his people. Therefore, it is the duty and call of God's people to continue their witness for Jesus, even in the midst of suffering persecution, because their witness will be effective to those whom the Lamb has redeemed.[178]

In the third interlude, John sees three signs from heaven: (1) a woman dressed with the sun, the moon and twelve stars (Rev. 12:1); (2) an enormous red serpent with seven crowned heads and ten horns (Rev. 12:3); and (3) the seven angels with the seven last plagues (Rev. 15:1; i.e. the seven bowls). This woman very likely symbolizes God's people throughout

---

[176] Cf. Exod. 7:17–19; 1 Kgs. 17:1. Beale (*Revelation*, pp. 582–587) notes three important points in favour of a figurative understanding of the drought and plague. First, the preceding context (11:1–5) is likely to be figurative and early Jewish literature also depicts the exodus plagues figuratively. Second, the drought and plagues of the two witnesses are related to the trumpet judgments (Rev. 8 – 9), and these are executed by the angels. Third, Jesus forbade his disciples to destroy their enemies with fire in the way God used Elijah to do (Luke 9:54–62).

[177] For other scholars who also advocate 'active and non-violent resistance', see Richard B. Hays, *The Moral Vision of the New Testament: A Contemporary Introduction to New Testament Ethics* (New York: HarperCollins, 1996), pp. 173–184; David L. Barr, 'Doing Violence: Moral Issues in Reading John's Apocalypse', in David L. Barr (ed.), *Reading the Book of Revelation: A Resource for Students*, RBS 44 (Atlanta: SBL, 2003), pp. 97–108; Sylvie T. Raquel, 'Blessed Are the Peacemakers: The Theology of Peace in the Book of Revelation', in Gerald L. Stevens (ed.), *Essays on Revelation: Appropriating Yesterday's Apocalypse in Today's World* (Eugene: Pickwick, 2010), pp. 50–71; Smith, 'Book of Revelation', pp. 334–371.

[178] See also Bauckham, *Climax of Prophecy*, pp. 291–293; deSilva, *Seeing Things John's Way*, pp. 75–78.

history.[179] The serpent is identified as Satan, who 'leads the whole world astray' (Rev. 12:9). The serpent tries all means to harm the woman but in vain, because God protects the woman time and again (Rev. 12:4–6, 13–17). The serpent and his angels lose the cosmic war against Michael and his angels when the Messiah accomplishes salvation and inaugurates the kingdom of God (Rev. 12:7–10). In his fury, the serpent continues to make war with the rest of the woman's offspring – 'those who keep God's commands and hold fast their testimony about Jesus' (Rev. 12:17). The two beasts in Revelation 13 are the means by which the serpent makes war. Nonetheless, the means by which God's people are able to defeat the serpent are also spelt out clearly: the blood of the Lamb, their testimony for Jesus and not being afraid of death (Rev. 12:11). The songs of deliverance and praise the victorious saints sing before the throne testify that the 'patient endurance' of those 'who keep [God's] commands and remain faithful to Jesus' are effective (Rev. 14:1–5, 12–13; 15:1–4).

This third interlude explains (1) the seven seals: suffering is brought by sinful oppressors to humankind and God's creation, including the killing of God's people, because the serpent has led these oppressors astray (cf. Rev. 12:9); (2) the seven trumpets: judgment on unrepentant people (those who 'did not have the seal of God') comes through suffering from environmental destruction and the dark spiritual forces behind the warfare, because cosmic and spiritual dimensions are involved (cf. Rev. 12:7); and (3) the seven bowls: judgment on the beast's kingdom and his people (those who have the 'mark of the beast') comes through suffering from plagues, further environmental destruction, the eschatological war and the destruction of the great city Babylon, because of their idolatry (worshipping the serpent and the beast; Rev. 13:4, 12–14) and persecution of God's faithful people (Rev. 13:7, 15–16; 16:5–6). *The theology depicted here is significant*: repentance does not result from suffering judgment (Rev. 9:20; 16:9, 11), but from responding positively to the testimony about Jesus and the call to give glory to God (Rev. 11:13; 14:6–7).[180] Therefore, God's people must continue to testify for Jesus.

---

[179] For detailed discussion, see ch. 1, n. 109 above.

[180] As Bauckham notes, in Revelation 'fear' and 'give glory' are associated with worshipping God (Rev. 14:7; 15:4), while 'repent' is also associated with 'give glory' (Rev. 16:9). For his full argument, see Bauckham, *Climax of Prophecy*, pp. 273–283. Beale and McNicol disagree with Bauckham, but see my counter-arguments in Lee, 'Fire from Their Mouths', pp. 227–231. Beale, *Revelation*, pp. 603–605; Allan J. McNicol, *The Conversion of the Nations in Revelation*, LNTS 438 (London: T&T Clark, 2011), pp. 124–125, 129.

The message of the third interlude comforts God's faithful people. Time and again they will suffer at the hands of their persecutors, but God will protect them. They can overcome and be victorious by means of the 'formula' given them (Rev. 12:11). They are given a glimpse of the glorious celebration of victory in the heavenly throne room for those who conquer and the terrible consequences for those who receive the mark of the beast. This motivates them to persevere in their faith despite their suffering.

In summary, God's providence and the duty of his people to persevere in their faith and to testify for Jesus are motifs that connect the three interludes.[181] God will protect his people, keep their faith and deliver them from their suffering into his glorious presence. God will empower them to discharge their duty of testifying faithfully for Jesus. Thus, despite the hardships, they can conquer and emerge victorious. This is an appeal to *pathos*, stirring up the audience's confidence and courage.

## The righteous God avenges his faithful people

The faithful saints cry out, 'How long, Sovereign Lord, holy and true, until you judge the inhabitants of the earth and avenge our blood?' (Rev. 6:10) They were slain because of 'the word of God and the testimony they had maintained' (Rev. 6:9). Nonetheless, they have been rewarded with a conqueror's white robe so that they may 'rest' (*anapauō*) until the full number of fellow martyrs has been reached (Rev. 6:11).[182] This 'rest' is not just referring to the cessation of their outcry, but to the 'rest' in victory from their toilsome resistance to their oppressors (cf. Rev. 14:13).[183]

Prior to the seven trumpet judgments, an angel fills the censer with fire from the altar and hurls it to the earth, resulting in 'peals of thunder, rumblings, flashes of lightning and an earthquake' (Rev. 8:3–5). As the rising smoke of burning incense symbolizes the prayers of the saints (Rev. 8:5; cf. Ps. 141:1–2; *4 Bar.* 9.3–4), the angel's action likely symbolizes God's manifesting his righteous judgments in response to the prayers and cries

---

[181] See also Smith ('Book of Revelation', pp. 355–371), who concludes that Revelation portrays 'the church's mission in a hostile world' as worship of the true God as a form of witness in declaring the creator's sustenance of the world and the salvation he has offered through Christ; it is the destiny of all creatures to worship God and Christ, while waiting patiently for God to consummate his kingdom through Christ's final victory at the eschaton.

[182] On 'white robe' as a symbol of victory, see p. 143 above.

[183] See Lee, 'Rest and Victory', pp. 350–357.

of his saints.[184] This is further corroborated by the rest of the narrative as follows.

First, the victorious saints praise God because his ways – the manifestation of his 'righteous acts' – are 'just and true' (Rev. 15:3–4). This is immediately followed by the judgment of seven bowls. The angel announces that the plague of blood from pouring the third bowl is in response to shedding the blood of God's holy people and prophets, with both the angel and the altar praising God that his judgments are 'true and just' (Rev. 16:4–6). Second, in the vision of the great whore, John describes her as 'drunk with the blood of God's holy people, the blood of those who bore testimony to Jesus' (Rev. 17:6). The heavens, God's people, apostles and prophets are told to rejoice because God's judgment has come upon the whore in her destruction, for

> in her was found the blood of prophets and of God's holy people,
> of all who have been slaughtered on the earth.
> (Rev. 18:20, 24)

Thereafter, John depicts the great multitude in heaven shouting loudly, praising God for his 'true and just' judgments, because he has punished the great whore and has 'avenged on her the blood of his servants' (Rev. 19:2–3).

In addition, John seems to depict the binding of the ancient serpent and the reign of the conquerors as a way by which God avenges his people (Rev. 20:1–6). As Koester notes, the serpent had given authority to the beast to reign over all inhabitants of the earth, such that the beast conquered the faithful saints, captured and killed them (Rev. 13:7, 10). Now, the serpent is the one who is captured and bound in chains (Rev. 20:1–3). Instead, 'those who had been beheaded because of their testimony about Jesus and because of the word of God', whom John identifies as those who 'had not worshipped the beast or its image and had not received its mark', come to life and reign with Christ (Rev. 20:4). The beast had only '42 months' to reign over and oppress them, but they now reign for 'a thousand years' (Rev. 13:5; 20:4). The length of their suffering is very much shorter than the length of their reign.[185]

---

[184] Blount, *Revelation*, p. 184; Koester, *Revelation*, p. 434; Osborne, *Revelation*, p. 346.
[185] Koester, *Revelation*, p. 782.

Though suffering persecution and martyrdom is painful and difficult, God's righteousness and the certainty of his avenging his faithful saints encourage them to persevere. Finally, Revelation's epilogue depicts Jesus addressing the church, reiterating the main points of the prologue, testifying that his coming is imminent (Rev. 1:1; 22:6, 20).[186] John wraps up Revelation with the Spirit, the bride, the one who hears and John himself chorusing the word 'Come!' (Rev. 22:17, 20).[187] They express their hope in Christ's coming to deliver them from suffering oppression, to avenge them by destroying and putting to an end all evil, and establishing eternally God's blessed reign, where they will receive the reward Christ has promised them for persevering (conquering). The hearers who can identify with this hope will be encouraged to persevere despite persecution.

# Summary of theological perspectives

As a framework for our study in this chapter, we began by looking at the first-century Greco-Roman background in terms of how the rhetorical conventions and contemporaneous culture of honour and shame shaped the way the New Testament authors persuaded their audience to remain faithful to Christ despite facing pressures to compromise. Now, I will first summarize the common approaches we have observed across these authors. Thereafter, I will highlight a few unique perspectives of individual authors that have surfaced from our study.

For the New Testament authors, it is clear that redefining what constitutes 'honour and shame' plays a key role in forming the audience's convictions and guiding their actions. This is most obvious in the authors' presentation of the contrast between present versus eschatological suffering and glory. From the perspective of the majority culture, it is shameful to suffer humiliation, ostracization and persecution due to faith in Christ. However, this is redefined as an honour for Christians. While the audience may be able to avoid the shame imposed by the majority culture by denying an association with Christ, this avoidance is only

---

[186] See also Thomas and Macchia, *Revelation*, p. 4.

[187] '[T]hose who hear' refers to people who take heed and obey the prophecies (call to repentance) of Revelation's message (Rev. 1:3; 22:7). There is also an intratextual reference to the call to take heed in the seven letters and in Rev. 13:9, 'Whoever has ears, let them hear.' See also Beale, *Revelation*, p. 1148.

temporary and worthless. This is because they will not escape eternal punishment and will suffer shame at the eschatological judgment.

On the contrary, although they may suffer utmost shame at present when they identify themselves as followers of Christ and persevere in their faith, it is again only temporary but worthwhile. This is because the eschatological reward they will receive is the glorious inheritance of God's kingdom, whose worth is incomparable to any earthly treasure and honour. Besides the hope of receiving eschatological honour from God, receiving praise in the present also serves as an important source of honour and encouragement – Paul and Jesus (as John presents him in Revelation) praise their audience for persevering in suffering for Christ.

The Gospels are distinct in presenting Jesus' teachings on the paradox of losing life (involving shame and humiliation) in order to gain life (relating it to honour and glory). The context of this teaching is rejection by one's own people – immediate family (Matthew and Mark) and ethnic community (John). This paradox addresses the audience's cultural needs as family ties are highly treasured. This paradox is further developed in Revelation, in which faithful saints who have been martyred are resurrected to reign with Christ. They seem to be defeated on earth by their oppressors but have in fact gained victory over them.

The authors of Hebrews and Revelation are unique in motivating their audience by emphasizing that God will avenge his faithful people and vindicate them before their oppressors.[188] While these two authors mention the eschatological inheritance, Hebrews directly contrasts it with the audience's loss of property due to persecution, so as to address the economic loss suffered due to faith in Jesus.

The authors of the Gospels portray Jesus warning his disciples of impending persecution due to their faith in him. They are to rejoice (because of their eschatological reward) and continue their witness for him before their persecutors. They also present Jesus' promise of the Holy Spirit's empowerment in bold witness despite persecution. While continuing to develop these traditions both in his Gospel and in Revelation, John further presents Jesus' promise that God will guard the disciples from falling away. Paul continues this gospel tradition in terms of (1) reiterating

---

[188] Although Paul quotes Deut. 32:35 regarding leaving vengeance to God (Rom. 12:19), his emphasis is not on the vindication of the saints, but on repaying evil with kindness.

how one should persevere in persecution with joy and courage; as well as (2) forewarning about persecution whenever he proclaims the gospel to a new community, as seen in his letters to the Philippians and Thessalonians. He also shares as an exemplar his experience of suffering for Christ. Unlike Paul, Hebrews and Revelation, Luke does not mention any instances of apostasy in Acts, but only portrays the early disciples as exemplars of desired responses to persecution – obeying the teachings of Jesus to be his faithful witnesses despite persecution. Through them, Luke shows how Jesus' promises in Luke's Gospel are fulfilled in Acts. These testimonies of experiencing the Holy Spirit's empowerment and God's deliverance in real life, as depicted by Paul and Luke, serve to motivate their audience that (1) the words of Jesus are true; and (2) the audience will themselves also experience these realities.

The New Testament authors also present suffering for Christ as a worthy cause to motivate perseverance. First, it is a corroboration of one's good standing before God. Matthew presents Jesus as proclaiming the blessedness of suffering persecution and this is a mark of a true disciple. Paul claims that anyone who lives a godly life will be persecuted. Second, both Paul and 1 Peter emphasize that such suffering results in forming positive character traits. Although the author of Hebrews expresses this similar concept, he is unique in associating persecution with 'non-punitive' discipline. Besides these, by identifying themselves as co-sufferers in Christ, Paul and the authors of Hebrews, 1 Peter and Revelation appeal to *ethos* to gain a hearing from their audience with regard to their exhortations. This creates social cohesion among them and brings comfort to their suffering audiences.

Helping their audience to manage the fear of persecution is an important issue for the New Testament authors. Other than exhorting them not to fear, either directly or indirectly by presenting Jesus' similar exhortation, they also explain how their fear may be overcome. As mentioned above, the fear of pain, shame and economic loss can be overcome by a sure hope of eschatological honour and reward. The fear of authorities in inflicting punishment can be overcome by the conviction of God and Jesus as sovereign over all authorities – God is to be feared more than humans and the evil spiritual powers behind the opposition. There is also the promise of divine protection and peace to guard their hearts against fear by approaching God for his grace and help. Nonetheless, this protection refers more to the protection of their faith and sometimes entails physical protection and deliverance from harm; it is by no means a promise of protection against all harm.

In addressing the issue of fear, John's Gospel is unique in his view of secret discipleship. It is noteworthy that John does not deny the reality of fear and seems to empathize with such fear. Although he is consistent with the Synoptic Gospels' teaching that denying Jesus in order to avoid shame is unacceptable (cf. John 12:42–43), he gives more leeway to disciples who have to hide their association with Jesus (e.g. Nicodemus, Joseph of Arimathea). He seems to be ambiguous and withholds his judgment with regard to whether he agrees or disagrees with such secrecy.

Using rhetoric as a tool of persuasion seems natural and more obvious in some New Testament authors, such as Paul and the authors of Hebrews and Revelation, than others. These authors exhibit a rather well-balanced approach in their use of contrasts when appealing to *logos* (e.g. punishment/reward, temporary/eternal, vengeance/vindication, suffering/relief) and *pathos* (e.g. shame/honour, fear/confidence, empathy/indignance). For example, arousing fear (e.g. eschatological punishment for unfaithfulness) is balanced with confidence (e.g. eschatological reward for faithfulness), and rebuke to induce shame (e.g. only able to consume milk and not solid food) is balanced with praise and assurance to give honour (e.g. the audience is better than his previous description of the land that produces thistles after receiving rain). These are frequently accompanied by calls to repentance. Such use of rhetoric demonstrates the intention towards positive moral formation in the audience, rather than ill-intentioned degradation of the audience.

Hebrews is distinct in its emphasis on group solidarity and mutual encouragement. While the other New Testament authors address their audience as a group, their exhortation is usually directed at individual perseverance and is not as obvious in terms of community perseverance.[189] However, the author of Hebrews attempts to create community perseverance not only by direct exhortation, but also by arousing his audience's empathy towards fellow saints who are suffering for their faith, so as motivate towards 'love and good deeds' by supporting one another through practising hospitality.

---

[189] Although there is a sense of supporting others when Paul exhorts his audience to 'encourage the disheartened, help the weak [and] be patient with everyone' in 1 Thess. 5:14, the sense of solidarity and empathy is not as pronounced as in Hebrews.

Revelation's message is strongly subversive, portraying Christ as the King of kings (17:14; 19:16) who will overthrow all opposing earthly political powers at the eschaton. The concepts of 'love your enemies' and 'quiet submission' to authority in the letters of Paul and 1 Peter are absent from Revelation. Also, while Revelation is the most blatant in its anti-imperial rhetoric, others, such as Paul, Matthew, Luke and the author of Hebrews, are indirect.[190] While their audience might associate the use of certain titles of Jesus (e.g. Great High Priest, Son of God) as anti-imperial, we need to be aware of the difference between authorial intentions and the hearers' perceptions when we describe the theological views of these authors on the relationship between Christ and Caesar, even though realistically we may not have certainty in distinguishing between the two. This distinction will have implications for our contemporary reflections, as we will see in the epilogue.

---

[190] For detailed discussions on anti-imperialism in the New Testament, see e.g. Harrison, *Paul and the Imperial Authorities*; Scot McKnight and Joseph B. Modica (eds.), *Jesus Is Lord, Caesar Is Not: Evaluating Empire in New Testament Studies* (Downers Grove: InterVarsity Press, 2013); Anders K. Petersen, 'Imperial Politics in Paul: Scholarly Phantom or Actual Textual Phenomenon?', in Michael Labahn and Outi Lehtipuu (eds.), *People Under Power: Early Jewish and Christian Responses to the Roman Empire* (Amsterdam: Amsterdam University Press, 2015).

# Conclusion

In this concluding chapter, I will attempt to delineate the New Testament authors' theology of facing persecution, in which I will not only synthesize common views but also highlight some of the unique views of certain authors. A more detailed and comprehensive description of the unique perspectives is in the summary of theological perspectives at the end of each preceding chapter.

## Causes of persecution

We began this study by first defining what persecution entails and noting that it is important not simply to identify opposition, suffering for Christ in general and social pressure as persecution. In chapter 1, I asked why early Christians were persecuted for worshipping Jesus. My analysis of the historical background and New Testament texts shows that a web of 'ideological conflicts, misunderstandings, negative ramifications from adopting Christian beliefs and lifestyle' led to opposition and at times persecution.[1]

The Gospels preserve the tradition of Jesus explaining to his disciples that they will be persecuted because of their association with him. From a sociological perspective, the fundamental cause of persecution stems from opposition against the claims about Jesus – the promised Messiah and its correlated theology. From a religious perspective, attributing divinity to Jesus as the promised Messiah caused great offence to the Jews, while monotheism and monolatry caused great offence to the pagans. From a political perspective, as messianic claims had political overtones, the Christian proclamation of Jesus as the Messiah can be easily perceived as seditious to pagans. These claims clashed with dearly held traditional values of the society at large. From an economic perspective, losses of income due to people becoming Christians (e.g. former patrons no longer provide benefactions to synagogues, not buying sacrificial meat from the

---

[1] See pp. 52–53 above.

market) were real and can pose a threat to the livelihood of some people. Among the New Testament authors, Luke stands out as one who uncovers, according to his understanding, the hidden motives of the opponents (such as jealousy and self-serving political motives) in the book of Acts.

For the New Testament authors, they reckon that there are evil spiritual forces behind such opposition, a theological perspective that is unique and not explicitly mentioned by the outsiders. Revelation further portrays Satan as the instigator behind the persecution from authorities. While Christians may regard evil spiritual forces behind the opposition as theological truth, their opponents reckon this as a form of vilification. Therefore, considering all the above perspectives, it is no wonder that early Christians were a threat to social stability from both the Jewish and pagan (outsiders') perspectives.

# Responses to persecution

We have seen that early Christians in the New Testament mostly faced persecution from groups of individuals who felt threatened by the effects of the Christian movement. In order to stamp out this movement, these opponents would typically press charges, sometimes underhandedly, against Christians before the local authorities. At other times, they opposed Christians with mob behaviour. From Luke's perspective, only the Jewish local authorities in Jerusalem were persecuting the Christians on a systematic basis. For him, even though some of the other local authorities punished Christians, they were carrying out their duties to maintain order in society, though their attitude could range from being helpful to indifferent to abusive. John is similar in depicting local Jewish authorities as persecutors in his Gospel. Nonetheless, Revelation portrays imperial and local authorities as persecutors of the saints. This difference could be due to a slightly different period of time they were referring to, rather than a theological perspective.[2]

Early Christians responded to these persecutions in a variety of ways. For the New Testament authors (the insiders' perspective), they perceive suffering persecution due to their faith in Jesus as an honour. Despite this, fear of persecution is real and Christians coped with such fear in a variety of ways. Some showed resilience and perseverance, while others

---

[2] See pp. 34–35 above.

apostatized in order to avoid such shame and sufferings. Still others tried to accommodate by adapting their practices while not compromising their faith.

Acts and Revelation portray faithful believers who boldly testify for Jesus despite persecution and are even willing to die for the Lord Jesus. In Acts, the empowerment of the Holy Spirit generates not only boldness but also wisdom. On the one hand, Luke portrays the disciples and Paul fleeing from persecution but also spreading the gospel along the way. On the other hand, there are also times when Paul was convicted not to escape from persecution due to special revelation from Jesus. In Paul's epistles, we can also see such resilience to continue testifying and persevering in Paul himself and some of the churches he wrote to (e.g. Philippians and Thessalonians). They held fast to the conviction of the good that such perseverance brings: salvation of the people through the proclamation of the gospel, as well as character building of the suffering saints.

Although Acts and Revelation tend to portray faithful Christians taking a strong stance due to their boldness, Matthew 10:16 and 1 Peter 3:4, 16 emphasize gentleness and 1 Peter, in addition, reverence. We have also seen how 1 Peter reflects mindfulness of the outsiders' perspectives of Christians as evil-doers (disrespect and insubordination to those in authority) by advocating 'good works' as a response to persecution.

Hardships from persecution can certainly cause certain Christians to give up their faith in Christ. However, there are others who would respond by cultural assimilation with theological justifications for their actions, rather than apostatizing. The major issues leading to cultural assimilation in response to Jewish and Gentile opposition respectively were: (1) Torah obedience as the means of inclusion into the people of God; and (2) participation in pagan cultic activities (cf. Gal. 6:12; 1 Cor. 8 – 10). These two issues were critical because they created many social and economic pressures, and conflicts for Christians at that time. For Paul, both such attempts are unacceptable and have compromised core Christian beliefs – justification by faith through the salvific work of Jesus and monotheism. However, it is noteworthy that while Paul distinguishes between conscious (unacceptable) and unconscious (acceptable; cf. 1 Cor. 10:25–28) eating of food sacrificed to idols, Acts (15:20) and Revelation (2:14, 20) make no such distinction.

Fear of persecution can easily lead to denial of Jesus. The Synoptic Gospels clearly state that disciples who are ashamed of Jesus and deny him will eventually be denied and shamed before God. Nonetheless, for all four Gospels, Peter's denial, repentance and restoration is a paradigm for accommodating weak but repentant disciples. However, it is important to note that while John's Gospel depicts negatively certain characters who are afraid to confess their faith publicly, he seems deliberately ambiguous in his depiction of Joseph of Arimathea and Nicodemus. Thus, this may be John's way of accommodating certain exceptions to public confession of faith.

Paul (Rom. 13:1–7) and 1 Peter 2:13–17 advocate honour and submission to the authorities. This could likely be their response to accusations of political sedition against Christians. The exhortation to pray for ruling authorities in 1 Timothy 2:1–2 is very likely an adaptation of the contemporaneous Jewish practice of praying and honouring the emperor in place of the pagan imperial cult, though with a clear distinction that Christ, rather than the emperor, is the only mediator between God and people (1 Tim. 2:5).

# Persuasions towards perseverance

In this study, we focused on how the New Testament authors use their cultural conventions of rhetoric, as well as their cultural system of honour and shame, in their persuasion towards perseverance. Some of them continue to develop and adapt Jesus' teachings on persecution in their writings (e.g. Luke, Matthew, Paul and Peter on 'love your enemies', 'bless those who curse you' and 'doing good' to enemies).

There are a number of common motifs that run across the New Testament. First, the redefinition of honour: (1) shame suffered for Christ is redefined as worthiness and blessedness; and (2) comparatively, it matters more to be honoured or shamed by God than by people. Thus, there is also the paradox: (1) those who avoid shame (to gain their lives) by denying Christ seem to be better off now, but they will eventually be ashamed (or lose their lives) before God eternally; and (2) those who suffer shame (or lose their lives) for Christ seem to be worse off now, but will eventually receive glory and honour (or gain their lives) from God eternally. This steers their audience towards making the wiser choice in the long run.

Second, the righteousness and vengeance of God function like a double-edged sword. On the one hand, it arouses fear and serves as a deterrent to those who are tempted to be unfaithful to God, because God will punish both the oppressors of his people and those who are unfaithful. It is also noteworthy how the author of Hebrews explains in detail how unfaithfulness to God constitutes ingratitude and sometimes even rebellion, and is thus an unacceptable response to God's gracious gift of salvation through his Son. On the other hand, it arouses confidence and hope, and comforts God's faithful people who suffer unjustly and have been accused of wrongdoing due to their faith in Christ. Their faithful suffering and perseverance have an end and it is not in vain. God will vindicate them and will not allow the wicked to be unpunished.

Third, the faithfulness of God in fulfilling his promises gives hope to the suffering Christians to persevere. These promises include: (1) the empowerment of the Holy Spirit to witness and overcome when facing persecution; (2) God's power to guard their faith until the end; (3) eschatological reward for faithful followers of Jesus; and (4) God's vengeance on their oppressors. We have summarized (3) and (4) in the previous paragraph. For (1), in accord with Jesus' promises in the gospel tradition, Luke depicts the Holy Spirit in Acts empowering the disciples not only with boldness but also with wisdom to face persecution, enabling them to fulfil their responsibility to persevere in their faith and to continue to witness for Christ. Luke's depiction clearly shows Jesus' promises being fulfilled and experienced in the lives of the disciples. This would encourage his audience that they too could indeed have the same experience and persevere to the end when they relied on God's empowerment. Nonetheless, Revelation does not directly associate such empowerment with the Holy Spirit. New Testament authors depict (2) in a variety of ways, such as the seal on the foreheads (Rev. 7:3; 14:1, 4–5), Jesus as the 'perfecter' of faith who can save 'completely' (Heb. 7:25; 12:2), Jesus interceding for them (John 17:11; Heb. 7:25) and guarding them from falling away (John 10:28; 17:12).

Fourth, exemplars also encourage their audience in that, if others can persevere by faith despite suffering, likewise they can too. Paul frequently shares his personal testimony of suffering for Christ as well as his experience of God's empowerment and deliverance as a form of exemplar. While most of the New Testament authors (e.g. John, Paul, the author of Hebrews) cite both positive and negative examples, Luke depicts only positive ones.

The following are distinctives of a few New Testament authors, rather than motifs that run across all of them. Paul and 1 Peter underscore the value of suffering in terms of corroboration of their true standing in

Christ (Phil. 1:28–29; 1 Thess. 1:4–6; 2 Tim. 3:12; 1 Peter 1:6–7), while Paul also reckons its value in character building (Rom. 5:3–5). Both Paul and 1 Peter stress the importance of integrity (Titus 2:7–8; 1 Peter 3:16), so that their opponents will not have admissible evidence against Christians, while Peter adds an indirect missional value to it (1 Peter 2:12; 3:1–2). These values become the motivation to persevere for those who can identify with them.

Hebrews is most distinctive in its emphasis on empathy. Jesus' empathy functions as an encouragement to suffering Christians to approach Jesus for help in the midst of their struggles. The author also attempts to arouse feelings of empathy from his audience, so that they may be stirred up to help those who are suffering in their faith to persevere. This emphasis on community support in perseverance is not prominent among other New Testament authors.

It is important for us to note that the New Testament authors not only use logical reasoning to persuade their audience to persevere in faith. They also aptly stir up the audience's emotions (such as fear, confidence, hope, empathy, honour, shame) as an additional push towards taking the appropriate action the author is persuading them to take.

# Conclusion: when Christians face persecution today

This study aimed at describing a theology of the New Testament authors when Christians faced persecution during the first century AD: how they understood the causes of persecution, their description of various responses to persecution of others and of themselves, as well as how they persuaded their audience to persevere in the Christian faith. We also saw how they interpreted, developed and reapplied Jesus' teachings about persecution to their own contexts. Through this, we attempted to delineate the theological perspectives that are reflected in their writings. Nonetheless, whether in the academy or among evangelical Christians, this exercise need not end here. As mentioned in the introduction,[3] there is value in appropriating our biblical-theological understanding gained from this exercise for contemporary reflections. How do the theological perspectives of the New Testament authors help us in our own context

---

[3] See p. 7 above.

when Christians face persecution today? With this, I would like to encourage readers of this book to continue with the exercise of reflection for their own context.

# Epilogue:
# some contemporary reflections

This section presents some of my personal reflections. Although I do not live in a context where there is significant persecution, my friends and students come from regions where they face significant persecution, though in varying degrees. Interacting with them has been a humbling learning experience. I do not pretend to have all the answers to the difficulties that they face. Neither do I imply that all the suggestions below would work and have a positive outcome in every situation. Rather, by asking questions, I hope to think together with readers how we may possibly appropriate the theological perspectives of the New Testament authors to our own context. In order to make sense of these reflections, it will be good for readers to refer back to the related sections of this book.

## What constitutes persecution

Having a nuanced understanding of what constitutes persecution is important.[1] At one extreme, failure to identify persecution may trivialize unjust suffering and lead to neglecting social justice while unjust discrimination and harm against Christians (among other vulnerable groups) continue to pervade some regions. At the other extreme, simplistic identification of opposition with persecution may result in neglecting to reflect more objectively on the possible causes of opposition, including the possibility of one's own responsibility. Neither extreme is desirable.

Although New Testament authors such as John may use dualistic terms to delineate faithful followers of Jesus from the rest of the world, it is important for us to understand John's approach as some form of literary device,[2] so that we do not extrapolate it to conclude that all who oppose

---

[1] See pp. 1–4 above, 'Understanding persecution: definition and scope'.
[2] See ch. 1, n. 91 above.

Christians are persecutors. Luke's more even-handed approach is a sober reminder for us to keep our perspectives in balance.[3]

It is also helpful to remind ourselves constantly that Christians are not the only group of people who face persecution.[4] If we can identify with persecuted non-Christian groups, it may help us analyse common reasons underlying these persecutions, which will help us formulate our response strategies accordingly. Also, caring for these persecuted groups can be a form of Christian testimony.

# Appropriating biblical exemplars and teachings

It is important that we consider carefully how to emulate biblical exemplars and apply biblical teachings to our own context. We need to be mindful of the cultural differences and gaps that exist between the ancient world and us, and even among our own cultures. It will be helpful for us to think of analogous forms in our own culture, or of how to adjust them to our culture, rather than always directly applying the ancient forms to our situation. We also need to avoid 'showing favouritism' by frequently employing the teachings of one or a few of the New Testament authors to the neglect of others. The following are a few examples for our consideration.

We have seen how God-centred eschatological honour and shame can help Christians persevere despite persecution.[5] Before we attempt to utilize this moral formative function of 'shame', we need to analyse the similarities and differences of how shame is understood in our context compared with that of the first-century Greco-Roman world. What challenges do we need to overcome in reshaping our culture's understanding of honour and shame in order to avoid overly simplistic applications that could involve wrong cultural assumptions? Lau's attempt to apply the moral formation of 'shame' to the Chinese context provides a good reference for us.[6]

---

[3] See pp. 3, 31–32 above.

[4] See pp. 17–18 above, 'Christians among other persecuted groups: a bigger picture'. It may also be worthwhile to consider the painful lessons from history, and specifically how some Christians, after the cessation of persecution in the fourth century, morphed to become persecutors of pagans and Jews. See Cook, *Roman Attitudes Toward the Christians*, pp. 281–293. What factors could have caused these Christians to do so? While it is beyond the scope of this study, it is an important issue that warrants another study.

[5] See pp. 97–98, 151–152 above.

[6] Lau, *Defending Shame*, pp. 173–233.

Christ Jesus has promised to provide wisdom to his disciples by the Holy Spirit, so that we may know how to respond to our opponents.[7] Revelation also reminds us that wisdom is needed to discern the circumstances that tempt Christians to compromise their faith.[8] On the one hand, we may learn from Peter, Stephen and Paul in terms of their wisdom in capitalizing on the culture of defence in refuting false accusations, and in Paul's exercising of his legal rights as a citizen at the appropriate time.[9] On the other hand, we will also need wisdom to know how to emulate them appropriately. For example, considering the gentle approach Matthew 10:16 and 1 Peter 3:4, 15 advocate, when is it legitimate for Christians to imitate Paul and Stephen in their non-conciliatory approach during their charges against opponents?

Also, the message of the gospel and the proclamation of truth are offensive to many, because they confront people with their sins and call them to repentance. However, does this give us the licence to present the gospel truth recklessly or to be disrespectful to others, for example, by applying the rhetorical vilification used by New Testament authors to our opponents, thereby demonizing them?[10] How can theological truths be expressed in a respectful manner? While we do not seek to please people and win their approval by refraining from speaking the truth in order to avoid conflicts (cf. Gal. 1:10; 1 Thess. 2:4), there is a fine line between not being afraid to speak the truth even if it leads to conflict and the lack of wisdom in speaking the truth (cf. 1 Peter 2:17; 3:15). We need wisdom and humility to distinguish between opposition that arises as a consequence of proclaiming the gospel and that which is a result of our own lack of wisdom and respect. As Boring notes, 'Believers are encouraged to speak up appropriately as witnesses to the faith, but not to pose unnecessary or false stumbling blocks in its communication nor to kindle opposition for the wrong reasons.'[11]

As we have seen, New Testament authors and Christians have differing perspectives on how one should respond to persecution.[12] To have a

---

[7] See p. 65 above.

[8] See p. 139 above.

[9] See pp. 65–68 above.

[10] On rhetorical vilification, see pp. 48–50 above. Recognizing that evil forces are behind persecutions (see pp. 35–36 above) is not the same as our contemporary understanding of 'demonizing' opponents – vilifying them and portraying them as worthy of contempt.

[11] Boring, *I & II Thessalonians*, p. 241.

[12] See pp. 89–93 above.

balanced view, it is helpful to keep in mind the diversity of the New Testament authors' perspectives. Over-emphasis on any one view, whether it be Revelation's strongly subversive message or 1 Peter's 'quiet conformity' and 'polite resistance', will not do us any good.[13]

The Gospel of John is a fine example of expressing one's view on being a secret disciple of Jesus while accommodating others who differ. While John commends the healed blind man for his public confession of faith in Jesus and criticizes his parents and the Jewish leaders who dare not confess their faith in Christ publicly, he withholds his judgment on Joseph of Arimathea and Nicodemus.[14] In our own context, while some may choose secrecy over public proclamation of their faith, others may choose peaceful demonstrations or may attempt to hold dialogues with their opponents, and so on.[15] As King notes, in the history of Christianity persecution of Christians did not always bring unity, but at times 'could tear churches apart and incite divisions that lasted for decades if not centuries'.[16] This goes against Jesus' prayer for unity among his disciples when they face persecution (John 17:11, 14–15, 21–22). While the bottom line of the New Testament's teaching is to persevere to the end in our faith, we need to accept the diverse responses to persecution among Christians, withhold our judgment on others who differ from us and try to put ourselves in their shoes.[17]

# Understanding perspectives and formulating responses

What one perceives as good and true, others may perceive as bad and false. This is not to conclude that there are no truths based on evidence or that only relative perspectives exist. However, understanding perspectives and

---

[13] See pp. 75, 155 above.

[14] See pp. 83–87 above.

[15] The same approach may work for one context but not for another. For example, peaceful demonstrations are frequently used in Western contexts and may to some extent work in getting the authorities to act in accord with the protestors' appeal. However, in some Asian contexts, this method is not tolerated by the authorities.

[16] King, 'Rethinking the Diversity', pp. 65–66. King does a good job in presenting the diverse opinions and responses to persecution among Christians during the first few centuries. She also cites examples of splits that had long-lasting effects (p. 65, n. 19).

[17] For a thought-provoking reflection, see Shūsaku Endō, *Silence: A Novel*, repr. (New York: Picador, 2016). This is a theological fiction written in the 1960s about how various missionaries and local Christians responded to persecution in seventeenth-century Japan. A 2016 film with the same name, directed by Martin Scorsese, was based on this book.

concerns of opponents is important for Christians to formulate relevant responses to them.[18] How do Christians help their opponents see that they are not a real threat to society or are not seditious? How would Christians address real economic losses due to the adoption of Christian faith?

For example, Christians' refusal to participate in ancestor worship is regarded as disrespectful and impious in some Asian and African cultures.[19] Therefore, such Christians face opposition and at times even persecution. In these cultures, worship is a form of expressing veneration to their ancestors. In addition, there is a belief that deceased ancestors are able to provide providential guidance to their living descendants. The main concern likely lies in upholding the *traditional values* (such as honour, respect and filial piety) as well as the *form of expressing such values*, frequently equating form with values – if one does not perform ancestor worship (form), one does not honour the ancestors (value). While there may be commonalities among these cultures, there are also distinctives Christians need to analyse in order to formulate appropriate responses. How then can Christians in these cultures address these concerns and demonstrate their respect and filial piety towards their living elders in the family as well as their ancestors? What forms besides worship can such a demonstration take? New Testament authors such as Paul and Peter, or even the way some Jews during the first half of the first century AD responded to the imperial cult, may provide us with ideas.[20]

Even now, some governments and communities perceive certain Christian values and practices as a threat to the stability of the society and state. Some families see the adoption of Christian faith as an unacceptable abandonment or even a betrayal of their esteemed traditional family religion, at times leading to harsh measures to force non-compliant family members to give up their Christian faith. It is important to analyse the reasons behind such perceptions (e.g. ideological clashes) as well as the rationale behind imposed measures (e.g. prohibition of Christian

---

[18] See pp. 39–40, 158 above.

[19] On Asian and African ancestor worship, see e.g. Anthony Ephirim-Donkor, *African Religion Defined: A Systematic Study of Ancestor Worship Among the Akan*, 3rd edn (Lanham: Hamilton, 2017); Nobushige Hozumi, *Ancestor Worship and Japanese Law* (London: Routledge, 2016); Roger L. Janelli and Ton-hǔi Im, *Ancestor Worship and Korean Society* (Stanford: Stanford University Press, 1982); William Lakos, *Chinese Ancestor Worship: A Practice and Ritual Oriented Approach to Understanding Chinese Culture* (Newcastle upon Tyne: Cambridge Scholars, 2010); Jacob K. Olupona, *African Religions: A Very Short Introduction* (New York: Oxford University Press, 2014).

[20] E.g. Rom. 13:1–6; 1 Tim. 2:1–6; 1 Peter 2:11–13. See pp. 87–89, 159 above.

gatherings, excommunication from the family and their related community, access to the Internet and social media, the frequency and size of gatherings), as we did in chapter 1 regarding the Greco-Roman and Jewish backgrounds. Whether in the ancient or contemporary world, governing authorities impose(d) restrictions to curb the spread of perceived political dissension, and communities impose(d) certain measures to curb the perceived abandonment of tradition and betrayal of members. From their perspective, restrictions in response to Christians are for the good of 'non-compliant' Christian citizen(s) or family member(s), as well as for the greater good of the society and state. Having said that, we must not dismiss the fact that some persecute Christians primarily, or even solely, for their own self-interest.[21] How then can Christians under such circumstances formulate adequate responses?[22] How can Christian apologetics be done amicably and respectfully?

While we try to understand our opponents' perspectives and keep in mind the biblical principle of loving one's enemies, non-retaliation, leaving vengeance to God and overcoming evil with good, we also acknowledge the reality of pain from suffering persecution. It is already not easy to love those who do not love us, let alone those who hurt us (cf. Luke 6:32–36). Nonetheless, just as there are no clauses in the fifth commandment for God's people to exclude honouring non-loving (e.g. either negligent or even abusive) parents (Exod. 20:12; Deut. 5:16; Eph. 6:2), there are no clauses to exclude honouring harsh slave masters (cf. 1 Peter 2:18) or unjust ruling authorities. But is silent suffering (e.g. 1 Peter 2:21–23) or blind submission the best response? Probably not always. How do we honour despite being misunderstood or even wronged? Are there areas where persecutors have nevertheless done relatively well (e.g. parents who still provide for their children, or ruling authorities who still crack down on some criminal activities), which we can acknowledge and for which we can honour them? In what other ways can we continue to do good to them (e.g. physical and financial care for family members, contribution to civic benefactions) despite their opposition to our Christian faith or even persecution?[23] In our context, what mode of expressing honour and doing good would be appropriate (e.g. social media, charitable

---

[21] See p. 39 above.

[22] See pp. 31–32, 92, 104 above.

[23] See p. 88 above.

organizations)? Perhaps our actions may help to counterbalance their perceived threat and have indirect missional value in helping them understand that Christian faith is not inherently bad.

# Empathizing with the persecuted

In Hebrews, we have seen how empathy plays an important role in the community to help believers persevere in their faith despite persecution.[24] Neither John nor the author of Hebrews denied the reality of fear when facing persecution, but sought rather to help their audience overcome their fears.[25] This was these authors' way of empathizing with those stricken with fear due to persecution.

It is also important to note that while fear is a predominant emotion Christians struggle with when persecuted, other kinds of emotions can also be intense. For those in cultures where the abandonment of dearly held traditions is regarded as betrayal, the pain of being misunderstood by non-Christian family members can be more intense than fear, especially when there was previously a strong bond of love in the family. The pain of betrayal felt by these non-Christian family members whose loved one(s) have become Christians can be just as intense.

Empathizing with the persecuted is important for both the persecuted and for the empathizer. We have seen that empathy functions as a catalyst and is a prelude that induces a person to help others.[26] Also, many who are suffering will concur that they find most comfort from those who can empathize with them and find least comfort from those who only 'tell them what to do'. The author of Hebrews emphasizes the way Jesus is able to empathize with his audience's suffering and will not meet them with 'outbursts' of anger, such that they need not be afraid to approach Jesus for help.[27] Empathy opens an avenue for sufferers to share their pain, seek help and be supported, without the fear of being criticized or condemned for being 'weak'.

Both Greco-Roman rhetoricians and modern psychology have noted that emotions affect decisions and actions more than logical reasoning.[28]

---

[24] See pp. 122, 124–126 above.
[25] See pp. 83–87, 113–114, 119–124, 153–154 above.
[26] See pp. 124–125 above.
[27] See p. 122 above.
[28] Lee, 'Rhetoric of Empathy', pp. 205, 217–218, nn. 16, 73.

Therefore, when ministering to those who are suffering from persecution, in what ways can we empathize with them, rather than only telling them what to do? How does Greco-Roman rhetoric help us in the proper use of *pathos* when ministering to them and in our effort to encourage community support when facing persecution?

## Concluding remarks

Christians need to continue the task of reflection for their own contexts based on the Bible's teachings. A biblical-theology approach is a helpful tool for understanding the Bible from various perspectives. Sharing our reflections with one another within similar or across different contexts may also bring fresh insights to help Christians respond to persecution. As fellow Christians, may we support and encourage one another to remain true to our Lord and Saviour Jesus Christ by the empowerment of God's Holy Spirit.

# Bibliography

Achtemeier, Paul J., *1 Peter*, Hermeneia (Minneapolis: Fortress, 1996).

Adewuya, J. Ayodeji, 'The Sacrificial-Missiological Function of Paul's Sufferings in the Context of 2 Corinthians', in Trevor J. Burke and Brian S. Rosner (eds.), *Paul as Missionary: Identity, Activity, Theology, and Practice*, LNTS 420 (London: T&T Clark, 2011), pp. 88–98.

Adkins, Lesley, and Roy Adkins, *Handbook to Life in Ancient Rome*, updated edn (New York: Facts on File, 2004).

Anderson, Ralph, 'New Gods', in Esther Eidinow and Julia Kindt (eds.), *The Oxford Handbook of Ancient Greek Religion* (Oxford: Oxford University Press, 2015), pp. 309–323.

Ascough, Richard S., Philip A. Harland and John S. Kloppenborg, *Associations in the Greco-Roman World: A Sourcebook* (Waco: Baylor University Press, 2012).

Attridge, Harold W., *The Epistle to the Hebrews: A Commentary on the Epistle to the Hebrews*, Hermeneia (Philadelphia: Fortress, 1989).

Aune, David E., *Revelation 1–5*, WBC 52A (Dallas: Word, 1997).

Balch, David L., *Let Wives Be Submissive: The Domestic Code in 1 Peter*, SBLMS 26 (Chico: Scholars Press, 1981).

Barr, David L., 'Doing Violence: Moral Issues in Reading John's Apocalypse', in David L. Barr (ed.), *Reading the Book of Revelation: A Resource for Students*, RBS 44 (Atlanta: SBL, 2003), pp. 97–108.

Barrett, C. K., *A Commentary on the Second Epistle to the Corinthians*, BNTC (London: Black, 1973).

——, *A Critical and Exegetical Commentary on the Acts of the Apostles*, ICC, 2 vols. (London: T&T Clark, 2004).

Barrett, David B., George T. Kurian and Todd M. Johnson (eds.), *World Christian Encyclopedia: A Comparative Survey of Churches and Religions in the Modern World*, 2nd edn (Oxford: Oxford University Press, 2001).

Bassler, Jouette M., 'Mixed Signals: Nicodemus in the Fourth Gospel', *JBL* 108.4 (1989), pp. 635–646.

Bateman, Herbert W. (ed.), *Four Views on the Warning Passages in Hebrews* (Grand Rapids: Kregel, 2007).

Bateman, Herbert W., Darrell L. Bock and Gordon H. Johnston, *Jesus the Messiah: Tracing the Promises, Expectations, and Coming of Israel's King* (Grand Rapids: Kregel, 2012).

Bauckham, Richard, *The Climax of Prophecy: Studies on the Book of Revelation* (Edinburgh: T&T Clark, 1993).

——, *Gospel of Glory: Major Themes in Johannine Theology* (Grand Rapids: Baker Academic, 2015).

——, *Jesus and the Eyewitnesses: The Gospels as Eyewitness Testimony*, 2nd edn (Grand Rapids: Eerdmans, 2017).

——, *Jesus and the God of Israel: God Crucified and Other Studies on the New Testament's Christology of Divine Identity* (Grand Rapids: Eerdmans, 2008).

——, 'What if Paul Had Travelled East Rather Than West?', *BibInt* 8.1–2 (2000), pp. 171–184.

Bauman, Richard A., *Crime and Punishment in Ancient Rome* (London: Routledge, 1996).

——, 'The Suppression of the Bacchanals: Five Questions', *Historia* 39.3 (1990), pp. 334–348.

Beale, G. K., *The Book of Revelation: A Commentary on the Greek Text*, NIGTC (Grand Rapids: Eerdmans, 1999).

——, *The Use of Daniel in Jewish Apocalyptic Literature and in the Revelation of St. John* (Lanham: University Press of America, 1984).

Beale, G. K., and Sean M. McDonough, 'Revelation', in G. K. Beale and D. A. Carson (eds.), *Commentary on the New Testament Use of the Old Testament* (Grand Rapids: Baker Academic, 2007), pp. 1081–1158.

Beasley-Murray, George R., *John*, rev. edn, WBC 36 (Dallas: Word, 1999).

Belle, Gilbert van, 'Peter as Martyr in the Fourth Gospel', in J. Leemans (ed.), *Martyrdom and Persecution in Late Antique Christianity: Festschrift Boudewijn Dehandschutter* (Leuven: Uitgeverij Peeters, 2010), pp. 281–309.

Benko, Stephen, *Pagan Rome and the Early Christians* (Bloomington: Indiana University Press, 1984).

Bennema, Cornelis, *Encountering Jesus: Character Studies in the Gospel of John*, 2nd edn (Minneapolis: Fortress, 2014).

Bernier, Jonathan, *Aposynagōgos and the Historical Jesus in John: Rethinking the Historicity of the Johannine Expulsion Passages*, BibInt 122 (Boston: Brill, 2013).

——, 'Jesus, Ἀποσυνάγωγος, and Modes of Religiosity', in R. Alan Culpepper and Paul N. Anderson (eds.), *John and Judaism: A Contested Relationship in Context*, RBS 87 (Atlanta: SBL, 2017), pp. 127–134.

Blomberg, Craig L., 'Matthew', in G. K. Beale and D. A. Carson (eds.), *Commentary on the New Testament Use of the Old Testament* (Grand Rapids: Baker Academic, 2007), pp. 1–109.

Blount, Brian K., *Revelation: A Commentary*, NTL (Louisville: Westminster John Knox, 2009).

Bock, Darrell L., *Acts*, BECNT (Grand Rapids: Baker Academic, 2007).

——, *Luke*, 2 vols., BECNT (Grand Rapids: Baker, 1994).

Boring, M. Eugene, *I & II Thessalonians: A Commentary*, NTL (Louisville: Westminster John Knox, 2015).

Botha, Pieter J. J., 'The Verbal Art of the Pauline Letters: Rhetoric, Performance and Presence', in Stanley E. Porter and Thomas H. Olbricht (eds.), *Rhetoric and the New Testament: Essays from the 1992 Heidelberg Conference*, JSNTSup 90 (Sheffield: Sheffield Academic Press, 1993), pp. 409–428.

Bovon, François, *Luke*, tr. James E. Crouch, 3 vols., Hermeneia (Minneapolis: Fortress, 2002).

Boxall, Ian, *The Revelation of Saint John*, BNTC 18 (London: Continuum, 2006).

Bradley, Ritter, 'The Stasis in Alexandria in 38 CE and Its Aftermath', in *Judeans in the Greek Cities of the Roman Empire*, JSJSup 170 (Leiden: Brill, 2015), pp. 132–183.

Brown, Raymond E., *The Gospel According to John*, 2 vols., AB 29 (Garden City: Doubleday, 1966).

Bryan, Steven M., *Jesus and Israel's Traditions of Judgement and Restoration*, SNTSMS 117 (Cambridge: Cambridge University Press, 2002).

Bultmann, Rudolf, *Theology of the New Testament*, tr. Kendrick Grobel, 2 vols. (Waco: Baylor University Press, 2007).

Campbell, W. Gordon, 'Bride-City and Whore-City', in *Reading Revelation: A Thematic Approach* (Cambridge: James Clarke, 2012), pp. 225–260.

Carroll, John T., *Luke: A Commentary*, NTL (Louisville: Westminster John Knox, 2012).

Carson, D. A., '1 Peter', in G. K. Beale and D. A. Carson (eds.), *Commentary on the New Testament Use of the Old Testament* (Grand Rapids: Baker Academic, 2007), pp. 1015–1048.

——, *The Gospel According to John*, PNTC (Grand Rapids: Eerdmans, 1991).

Carter, Warren, 'Going All the Way?: Honoring the Emperor and Sacrificing Wives and Slaves in 1 Peter 2.13–3.6', in Amy-Jill Levine and Maria Mayo Robbins (eds.), *A Feminist Companion to the Catholic Epistles and Hebrews*, FCNTECW 8 (London: T&T Clark International, 2004), pp. 14–33.

Chan, Chi-Yee, 'The Interpretation of the "Rest" Tradition in the Epistle to the Hebrews', ThM thesis, Singapore Bible College, 2016 (in Chinese).

Ciampa, Roy E., 'Suffering in Romans 1–8 in Light of Paul's Key Scriptural Intertexts', in Siu Fung Wu (ed.), *Suffering in Paul: Perspectives and Implications* (Eugene: Pickwick, 2019), pp. 7–28.

Clarke, Kent D., 'The Problem of Pseudonymity in Biblical Literature and Its Implications for Canon Formation', in Lee Martin McDonald and James A. Sanders (eds.), *The Canon Debate* (Peabody: Hendrickson, 2002), pp. 440–468.

Cockerill, Gareth L., *The Epistle to the Hebrews*, NICNT (Grand Rapids: Eerdmans, 2012).

Collins, Adela Y., *Crisis and Catharsis: The Power of the Apocalypse* (Philadelphia: Westminster, 1984).

——, 'Feminine Symbolism in the Book of Revelation', in Amy-Jill Levine and Maria Mayo Robbins (eds.), *A Feminist Companion to the Apocalypse of John*, FCNTECW 13 (London: T&T Clark, 2010), pp. 121–130.

——, 'Numerical Symbolism in Jewish and Early Christian Apocalyptic Literature', in *Cosmology and Eschatology in Jewish and Christian Apocalypticism*, JSJSup 50 (Leiden: Brill, 1996), pp. 55–138.

Collins, John J., *Daniel: A Commentary on the Book of Daniel*, Hermeneia (Minneapolis: Fortress, 1993).

Collins, Raymond F., *1 & 2 Timothy and Titus: A Commentary*, NTL (Louisville: Westminster John Knox, 2012).

Colman, Andrew M., 'Conformity', in *Dictionary of Psychology*, 4th edn (Oxford: Oxford University Press, 2015), p. 158.

Cook, John G., *Roman Attitudes Toward the Christians: From Claudius to Hadrian*, WUNT 261 (Tübingen: Mohr Siebeck, 2010).

Cousar, Charles B., *Philippians and Philemon: A Commentary*, NTL (Louisville: Westminster John Knox, 2013).

Croy, N. Clayton, *Endurance in Suffering: Hebrews 12:1–13 in Its Rhetorical, Religious, and Philosophical Context*, SNTSMS 98 (Cambridge: Cambridge University Press, 1998).

Cunningham, Scott, *'Through Many Tribulations': The Theology of Persecution in Luke-Acts*, JSNTSup 142 (Sheffield: Sheffield Academic Press, 1997).

De Villiers, Pieter G. R., 'Persecution in the Book of Revelation', *AcT* 22.2 (2002), pp. 47–70.

DeSilva, David A., *Honor, Patronage, Kinship and Purity: Unlocking New Testament Culture* (Downers Grove: InterVarsity Press, 2000).

——, *The Letter to the Galatians*, NICNT (Grand Rapids: Eerdmans, 2018).

——, *Perseverance in Gratitude: A Socio-Rhetorical Commentary on the Epistle 'to the Hebrews'* (Grand Rapids: Eerdmans, 2000).

——, *Seeing Things John's Way: The Rhetoric of the Book of Revelation* (Louisville: Westminster John Knox, 2009).

DiCicco, Mario M., *Paul's Use of Ethos, Pathos, and Logos in 2 Corinthians 10–13*, MBPS 31 (Lewiston: Mellen Biblical Press, 1995).

Donelson, Lewis R., *I & II Peter and Jude: A Commentary*, NTL (Louisville: Westminster John Knox, 2010).

Doole, J. Andrew, 'To Be "An Out-of-the-Synagoguer"', *JSNT* 43.3 (2021), pp. 389–410.

Dubis, Mark, *1 Peter: A Handbook on the Greek Text*, BHGNT (Waco: Baylor University Press, 2010).

Dudreck, Matthew A., 'The Use of Jeremiah in the Book of Revelation', PhD diss., Westminster Theological Seminary, 2018.

Duff, Paul, 'The "Synagogue of Satan": Crisis Mongering and the Apocalypse of John', in David L. Barr (ed.), *The Reality of Apocalypse: Rhetoric and Politics in the Book of Revelation*, SBLSymS 39 (Atlanta: SBL, 2006), pp. 147–168.

Dunn, James D. G., *The Epistle to the Galatians*, BNTC (Peabody: Hendrickson, 1993).

——, *New Testament Theology: An Introduction*, LBT 3 (Nashville: Abingdon, 2009).

——, *Romans 9–16*, WBC 38B (Dallas: Word, 1988).

——, *The Theology of Paul the Apostle* (Grand Rapids: Eerdmans, 1998).

Dunne, John A., *Persecution and Participation in Galatians*, WUNT 2.454 (Tübingen: Mohr Siebeck, 2017).

Du Toit, Andreas B., 'Vilification as a Pragmatic Device in Early Christian Epistolography', *Bib* 75.3 (1994), pp. 403–412.

Du Toit, Sean, 'Negotiating Hostility Through Beneficial Deeds', *TynBul* 70.2 (2019), pp. 221–243.

——, 'Practising Idolatry in 1 Peter', *JSNT* 43.3 (2021), pp. 411–430.

Dyer, Bryan R., *Suffering in the Face of Death: The Epistle to the Hebrews and Its Context of Situation*, LNTS 568 (London: Bloomsbury, 2017).

Edwards, James R., *The Gospel According to Luke*, PNTC (Grand Rapids: Eerdmans, 2015).

Elliott, John H., *1 Peter: A New Translation with Introduction and Commentary*, AB 37B (New York: Doubleday, 2000).

——, review of *Persecution in 1 Peter: Differentiating and Contextualizing Early Christian Suffering*, by Travis B. Williams, *BTB* 46.4 (2016), pp. 211–212.

Ellis, E. Earle, *The Old Testament in Early Christianity: Canon and Interpretation in the Light of Modern Research* (Eugene: Wipf & Stock, 2003).

Elmer, Ian J., *Paul, Jerusalem and the Judaisers: The Galatian Crisis in Its Broadest Historical Context*, WUNT 2.258 (Tübingen: Mohr Siebeck, 2009).

Endō, Shūsaku, *Silence: A Novel*, repr. (New York: Picador, 2016).

Engberg, Jakob, *Impulsore Chresto: Opposition to Christianity in the Roman Empire c. 50–250 AD*, tr. Gregory Carter, ECCA 2 (Frankfurt am Main: Peter Lang, 2007).

Ephirim-Donkor, Anthony, *African Religion Defined: A Systematic Study of Ancestor Worship Among the Akan*, 3rd edn (Lanham: Hamilton, 2017).

Evans, Craig A., 'Evidence of Conflict with the Synagogue in the Johannine Writings', in R. Alan Culpepper and Paul N. Anderson (eds.), *John and Judaism: A Contested Relationship in Context*, RBS 87 (Atlanta: SBL, 2017), pp. 135–154.

Fanning, Buist M., *Revelation*, ZECNT (Grand Rapids: Zondervan, 2020).

Fee, Gordon D., *The First Epistle to the Corinthians*, rev. edn, NICNT (Grand Rapids: Eerdmans, 2014).

Fekkes, Jan, *Isaiah and Prophetic Traditions in the Book of Revelation: Visionary Antecedents and Their Development*, JSNTSup 93 (Sheffield: JSOT Press, 1994).

Fishwick, Duncan, *The Imperial Cult in the Latin West: Studies in the Ruler Cult of the Western Provinces of the Roman Empire*, 2nd edn, EPRO 108 (Leiden: Brill, 1993).

Fitzmyer, Joseph A., *The Acts of the Apostles: A New Translation with Introduction and Commentary*, AB 31 (New York: Doubleday, 1998).

——, *Romans: A New Translation with Introduction and Commentary*, AB 33 (New York: Doubleday, 1993).

Fotopoulos, John, 'Arguments Concerning Food Offered to Idols: Corinthian Quotations and Pauline Refutations in a Rhetorical Partitio (1 Corinthians 8:1–9)', *CBQ* 67.4 (2005), pp. 611–631.

France, R. T., *The Gospel of Mark: A Commentary on the Greek Text*, NIGTC (Grand Rapids: Eerdmans, 2002).

——, *The Gospel of Matthew*, NICNT (Grand Rapids: Eerdmans, 2007).

Frankfurter, David, 'Jews or Not?: Reconstructing the "Other" in Rev 2:9 and 3:9', *HTR* 94.4 (2001), pp. 403–425.

Frend, W. H. C., *Martyrdom and Persecution in the Early Church: A Study of a Conflict from the Maccabees to Donatus* (Oxford: Blackwell, 1965; repr. Cambridge: James Clarke, 2008).

Friesen, Steven J., 'Sarcasm in Revelation 2–3: Churches, Christians, True Jews, and Satanic Synagogues', in David L. Barr (ed.), *The Reality of Apocalypse: Rhetoric and Politics in the Book of Revelation*, SBLSymS 39 (Atlanta: Society of Biblical Literature, 2006), pp. 137–144.

Fritz, Graf, 'Asclepius', in Simon Hornblower, Antony Spawforth and Esther Eidinow (eds.), *The Oxford Classical Dictionary*, 4th edn (Oxford: Oxford University Press, 2012), doi: 10.1093/acref/9780199545568.013.0853.

Gager, John G., *The Origins of Anti-Semitism: Attitudes Toward Judaism in Pagan and Christian Antiquity* (New York: Oxford University Press, 1983).

Gager, John G., with E. Leigh Gibson, 'Violent Acts and Violent Language in the Apostle Paul', in Shelly Matthews and E. Leigh Gibson (eds.), *Violence in the New Testament* (New York: T&T Clark, 2005), pp. 13–21.

Gardner, Paul, *1 Corinthians*, ZECNT (Grand Rapids: Zondervan, 2018).

Garland, David E., *1 Corinthians*, BECNT (Grand Rapids: Baker Academic, 2003).

——, *Luke*, ZECNT (Grand Rapids: Zondervan, 2012).

Garnsey, Peter, and Richard P. Saller, *The Roman Empire: Economy, Society and Culture*, 2nd edn (London: Bloomsbury Academic, 2014).

Gizewski, Christian, 'Coercitio', in Hubert Cancik and Helmuth Schneider (eds.), *Brill's New Pauly* (Leiden: Brill, 2006), vol. 3, pp. 508–509.

Gorman, H., 'Persuading Through *Pathos*: Appeals to the Emotions in Hebrews', *ResQ* 54.2 (2012), pp. 77–90.

Grabbe, Lester L., *An Introduction to Second Temple Judaism: History and Religion of the Jews in the Time of Nehemiah, the Maccabees, Hillel and Jesus* (London: T&T Clark, 2010).

Gradel, Ittai, *Emperor Worship and Roman Religion*, OCM (Oxford: Clarendon, 2002).

Gray, Patrick, *Godly Fear: The Epistle to the Hebrews and Greco-Roman Critiques of Superstition*, SBLAcBib 16 (Atlanta: Society of Biblical Literature, 2003).

Gruen, Erich S., *Diaspora: Jews Amidst Greeks and Romans* (Cambridge, Mass.: Harvard University Press, 2002).

Gundry, Robert H., *Matthew: A Commentary on His Handbook for a Mixed Church Under Persecution* (Grand Rapids: Eerdmans, 1994).

Guthrie, George H., *2 Corinthians*, BECNT (Grand Rapids: Baker Academic, 2015).

——, 'Hebrews', in G. K. Beale and D. A. Carson (eds.), *Commentary on the New Testament Use of the Old Testament* (Grand Rapids: Baker Academic, 2007), pp. 919–995.

Hardin, Justin K., *Galatians and the Imperial Cult: A Critical Analysis of the First-Century Social Context of Paul's Letter*, WUNT 2.237 (Tübingen: Mohr Siebeck, 2008).

Hare, Douglas R. A., *The Theme of Jewish Persecution of Christians in the Gospel According to St. Matthew*, SNTSMS 6 (Cambridge: Cambridge University Press, 2005).

Harris, Murray J., *The Second Epistle to the Corinthians: A Commentary on the Greek Text*, NIGTC (Grand Rapids: Eerdmans, 2005).

Harrison, James R., *Paul and the Imperial Authorities at Thessalonica and Rome: A Study in the Conflict of Ideology*, WUNT 273 (Tübingen: Mohr Siebeck, 2011).

——, 'The Persecution of Christians from Nero to Hadrian', in Mark Harding and Alanna Nobbs (eds.), *Into All the World: Emergent Christianity in Its Jewish and Greco-Roman Context* (Grand Rapids: Eerdmans, 2017), pp. 266–300.

Harrod, Kenneth, *Promise and Persecution: A Biblical Theology of Suffering for Christ* (Orpington, Kent: Release International, 2018).

Hatina, Thomas R., *New Testament Theology and Its Quest for Relevance: Ancient Texts and Modern Readers* (London: Bloomsbury T&T Clark, 2013).

Hays, Richard B., *The Moral Vision of the New Testament: A Contemporary Introduction to New Testament Ethics* (New York: HarperCollins, 1996).

Heil, John Paul, *The Letters of Paul as Rituals of Worship* (Eugene: Cascade, 2011).

Hillard, Tom W., 'Vespasian's Death-Bed Attitude to His Impending Deification', in Matthew Dillon (ed.), *Religion in the Ancient World: New Themes and Approaches* (Amsterdam: A. M. Hakkert, 1996), pp. 197–198.

Horrell, David G., 'Between Conformity and Resistance: Beyond the Balch–Elliott Debate Towards a Postcolonial Reading of First Peter', in Robert L. Webb and Betsy J. Bauman-Martin (eds.), *Reading First Peter with New Eyes: Methodological Reassessments of the Letter of First Peter*, LNTS 364 (London: T&T Clark, 2007), pp. 111–143.

——, *The Epistles of Peter and Jude*, EC (London: Epworth, 1998).

Hozumi, Nobushige, *Ancestor Worship and Japanese Law* (London: Routledge, 2016).

Hurtado, Larry W., *One God, One Lord: Early Christian Devotion and Ancient Jewish Monotheism*, 3rd edn, CS (London: Bloomsbury, 2015).

Janelli, Roger L., and Ton-hŭi Im, *Ancestor Worship and Korean Society* (Stanford: Stanford University Press, 1982).

Jauhiainen, Marko, *The Use of Zechariah in Revelation*, WUNT 2.199 (Tübingen: Mohr Siebeck, 2005).

Jipp, Joshua W., *Divine Visitations and Hospitality to Strangers in Luke-Acts: An Interpretation of the Malta Episode in Acts 28:1–10*, NovTSup 153 (Leiden: Brill, 2013).

Jobes, Karen H., *1 Peter*, BECNT (Grand Rapids: Baker Academic, 2005).

Johnson, Luke T., *Hebrews: A Commentary*, NTL (Louisville: Westminster John Knox, 2012).

——, 'The New Testament's Anti-Jewish Slander and the Conventions of Ancient Polemic', *JBL* 108.3 (1989), pp. 419–441.

Johnston, Sarah I., 'Oracles and Divination', in Esther Eidinow and Julia Kindt (eds.), *The Oxford Handbook of Ancient Greek Religion* (Oxford: Oxford University Press, 2015), pp. 477–489.

Keener, Craig S., *Acts: An Exegetical Commentary*, 4 vols. (Grand Rapids: Baker Academic, 2012–15).

——, *The Gospel of John: A Commentary*, 2 vols. (Peabody: Hendrickson, 2003).

Kelhoffer, James A., *Persecution, Persuasion, and Power: Readiness to Withstand Hardship as a Corroboration of Legitimacy in the New Testament*, WUNT 270 (Tübingen: Mohr Siebeck, 2010).

Kierspel, Lars, *The Jews and the World in the Fourth Gospel: Parallelism, Function, and Context*, WUNT 2.220 (Tübingen: Mohr Siebeck, 2006).

King, Karen L., 'Rethinking the Diversity of Ancient Christianity: Responding to Suffering and Persecution', in Eduard Iricinschi, Lance Jenott, Nicola Denzey Lewis and Philippa Townsend (eds.), *Beyond the Gnostic Gospels: Studies Building on the Work of Elaine Pagels*, STAC 82 (Tübingen: Mohr Siebeck, 2013), pp. 60–78.

Klink III, Edward W., *John*, ZECNT 4 (Grand Rapids: Zondervan, 2016).

——, 'The Overrealized Expulsion in the Gospel of John', in Paul N. Anderson, Felix Just and Tom Thatcher (eds.), *John, Jesus, and History*, vol. 2: *Aspects of Historicity in the Fourth Gospel*, SBLSymS 44 (Atlanta: SBL, 2007), pp. 175–184.

——, *The Sheep of the Fold: The Audience and Origin of the Gospel of John*, SNTSMS 141 (Cambridge: Cambridge University Press, 2007).

Kloppenborg, John S., 'Disaffiliation in Associations and the Ἀποσυνάγωγος of John', *HTS* 67.1 (2011), pp. 1–16.

Koester, Craig R., *Hebrews: A New Translation with Introduction and Commentary*, AB 36 (New York: Doubleday, 2001).

——, *Revelation: A New Translation with Introduction and Commentary*, AB 38A (New Haven: Yale University Press, 2014).

——, 'Theological Complexity and the Characterization of Nicodemus in John's Gospel', in Christopher W. Skinner (ed.), *Characters and Characterization in the Gospel of John*, LNTS 461 (London: Bloomsbury T&T Clark, 2013), pp. 165–181.

Köstenberger, Andreas J., *John*, BECNT (Grand Rapids: Baker Academic, 2004).

Kowalsk, Beate, 'Transformation of Ezekiel in John's Revelation', in William A. Tooman and Michael A. Lyons (eds.), *Transforming Visions: Transformations of Text, Tradition, and Theology in Ezekiel* (Cambridge: James Clarke, 2010), pp. 279–307.

Kraft, Heinrich, *Die Offenbarung des Johannes*, HNT 16a (Tübingen: Mohr, 1974).

Kruse, Colin G., 'The Price Paid for a Ministry among Gentiles: Paul's Persecution at the Hands of the Jews', in Michael J. Wilkins and Terence Paige (eds.), *Worship, Theology and Ministry in the Early Church*, JSNTSup 87 (Sheffield: JSOT Press, 1992), pp. 260–272.

Laansma, Jon, 'Titus', in Philip W. Comfort (ed.), *1–2 Timothy, Titus, Hebrews*, CBC (Carol Stream: Tyndale House, 2009), pp. 221–302.

Lakos, William, *Chinese Ancestor Worship: A Practice and Ritual Oriented Approach to Understanding Chinese Culture* (Newcastle upon Tyne: Cambridge Scholars, 2010).

Lane, William L., *Hebrews 9–13*, WBC 47B (Nashville: Thomas Nelson, 1991).

Latham, Jacob A., '"Honors Greater Than Human": Imperial Cult in the *Pompa Circensis*', *Performance, Memory, and Processions in Ancient Rome: The Pompa Circensis from the Late Republic to Late Antiquity* (Cambridge: Cambridge University Press, 2016), pp. 105–145.

Lau, Te-Li, *Defending Shame: Its Formative Power in Paul's Letters* (Grand Rapids: Baker Academic, 2020).

——, review of *Galatians and the Imperial Cult: A Critical Analysis of the First-Century Social Context of Paul's Letter*, by Justin H. Hardin, *BBR* 20.1 (2010), pp. 130–131.

Lee, Chee-Chiew, *The Blessing of Abraham, the Spirit, and Justification in Galatians: Their Relationship and Significance for Understanding Paul's Theology* (Eugene: Pickwick, 2013).

——, '"Fire from Their Mouths": The Power of Witnessing in the Face of Hostility and Suffering (Rev 11:3–13)', *CTTSJ* 4 (2013), pp. 204–237.

——, '*Gôyim* in Genesis 35:11 and the Abrahamic Promise of Blessings for the Nations', *JETS* 52.3 (2009), pp. 467–482.

——, 'Rest and Victory in Revelation 14:13', *JSNT* 41.3 (2019), pp. 344–362.

——, 'The Rhetoric of Empathy in Hebrews', *NovT* 62.2 (2020), pp. 201–218.

——, 'Scripture as God's Word', in Roland Chia (ed.), *Dei Verbum: The Bible in Church and Society* (Singapore: Sower, 2020), pp. 5–22.

——, 'A Theology of Facing Persecution in the Gospel of John', *TynBul* 70.2 (2019), pp. 189–204.

——, 'The Use of Scriptures and the Rhetoric of Fear in Hebrews', *BBR* 31.2 (2021), pp. 191–210.

Lemcio, Eugene E., *Navigating Revelation: Charts for the Voyage, a Pedagogical Aid* (Eugene: Wipf & Stock, 2011).

Lesbaupin, I., *Blessed Are the Persecuted: Christian Life in the Roman Empire, AD 64–313*, tr. R. R. Barr (Maryknoll: Orbis, 1987).

Levene, D. S., 'Defining the Divine in Rome', *TAPA* 142.1 (2012), pp. 41–81.

Levine, Lee I., *The Ancient Synagogue: The First Thousand Years*, 2nd edn (New Haven: Yale University Press, 2005).

Lim, Kar Yong, *'The Sufferings of Christ Are Abundant in Us' (2 Corinthians 1:5): A Narrative-Dynamics Investigation of Paul's Sufferings in 2 Corinthians*, LNTS 399 (London: T&T Clark, 2009).

Lincoln, Andrew T., *The Gospel According to Saint John*, BNTC 4 (Peabody: Hendrickson, 2005).

Lindars, Barnabas, 'The Persecution of Christians in John 15:18–16:4a', in William Horbury and Brian McNeil (eds.), *Suffering and Martyrdom in the New Testament* (Cambridge: Cambridge University Press, 1981), pp. 48–69.

Litwak, Kenneth D., 'Synagogue and Sanhedrin', in Joel B. Green and Lee Martin McDonald (eds.), *The World of the New Testament: Cultural, Social, and Historical Contexts* (Grand Rapids: Baker Academic, 2013), pp. 264–271.

Longenecker, Richard N., *The Epistle to the Romans: A Commentary on the Greek Text*, NIGTC (Grand Rapids: Eerdmans, 2016).

——, *Galatians*, WBC 41 (Dallas: Word, 1990).

Lyons, William J., 'Joseph of Arimathea: One of "the Jews," but with a Fearful Secret!', in Steven A. Hunt, D. F. Tolmie and Ruben Zimmermann (eds.), *Character Studies in the Fourth Gospel: Narrative Approaches to Seventy Figures in John*, WUNT 314 (Tübingen: Mohr Siebeck, 2013), pp. 646–657.

MacBride, Timothy, 'Aliens and Strangers: Minority Group Rhetoric in the Later New Testament Writings', in Mark Harding and Alanna Nobbs (eds.), *Into All the World: Emergent Christianity in Its Jewish and Greco-Roman Context* (Grand Rapids: Eerdmans, 2017), pp. 301–333.

McGrath, James F., *The Only True God: Early Christian Monotheism in Its Jewish Context* (Urbana: University of Illinois Press, 2009).

McIntyre, Gwynaeth, *Imperial Cult*, AH (Leiden: Brill, 2019).

Mackie, Scott D., *Eschatology and Exhortation in the Epistle to the Hebrews*, WUNT 2.223 (Tübingen: Mohr Siebeck, 2007).

McKnight, Scot, and Joseph B. Modica (eds.), *Jesus Is Lord, Caesar Is Not: Evaluating Empire in New Testament Studies* (Downers Grove: InterVarsity Press, 2013).

McNicol, Allan J., *The Conversion of the Nations in Revelation*, LNTS 438 (London: T&T Clark, 2011).

Maier, Harry O., *New Testament Christianity in the Roman World*, EBS (New York: Oxford University Press, 2018).

Malherbe, Abraham J., *Moral Exhortation: A Greco-Roman Sourcebook*, LEC 4 (Philadelphia: Westminster, 1986).

Marshak, Adam, 'Idumea', in John J. Collins and Daniel C. Harlow (eds.), *The Eerdmans Dictionary of Early Judaism* (Grand Rapids: Eerdmans, 2010), pp. 759–762.

Marshall, I. Howard, 'Acts', in G. K. Beale and D. A. Carson (eds.), *Commentary on the New Testament Use of the Old Testament* (Grand Rapids: Baker Academic, 2007), pp. 513–606.

Marshall, I. Howard, and Philip H. Towner, *A Critical and Exegetical Commentary on the Pastoral Epistles*, ICC (London: T&T Clark International, 2004).

Martin, Dale B., *Inventing Superstition: From the Hippocratics to the Christians* (Cambridge, Mass.: Harvard University Press, 2004).

Martin, Troy W., 'Invention and Arrangement in Recent Pauline Rhetorical Studies: A Survey of the Practices and the Problems', in J. Paul Sampley and Peter Lampe (eds.), *Paul and Rhetoric* (London: T&T Clark, 2010), pp. 48–118.

Martyn, J. Louis, *Galatians: A New Translation with Introduction and Commentary*, AB 33A (New York: Doubleday, 1997).

——, *History and Theology in the Fourth Gospel*, 3rd edn, NTL (Louisville: Westminster John Knox, 2003).

Matera, Frank J., *II Corinthians: A Commentary*, NTL (Louisville: Westminster John Knox, 2003).

Matthews, Shelly, 'The Need for the Stoning of Stephen', in E. Leigh Gibson and Shelly Matthews (eds.), *Violence in the New Testament* (New York: T&T Clark, 2005), pp. 124–139.

Mayo, Philip L., *'Those Who Call Themselves Jews': The Church and Judaism in the Apocalypse of John*, PTMS (Eugene: Pickwick, 2006).

Metzger, B. M., 'The Fourth Book of Ezra', in James H. Charlesworth (ed.), *The Old Testament Pseudepigrapha*, vol. 1 (Garden City: Doubleday, 1983), pp. 517–560.

Michaels, J. Ramsey, *The Gospel of John*, NICNT (Grand Rapids: Eerdmans, 2010).

Minear, Paul S., *I Saw a New Earth: An Introduction to the Visions of the Apocalypse*, repr. (Eugene: Wipf & Stock, 2003).

Moloney, Francis J., *The Apocalypse of John: A Commentary* (Grand Rapids: Baker Academic, 2020).

Moo, Douglas J., *The Epistle to the Romans*, 2nd edn, NICNT (Grand Rapids: Eerdmans, 2018).

——, *Galatians*, BECNT (Grand Rapids: Baker Academic, 2013).

Moore, Michael S., 'Civic and Voluntary Associations in the Greco-Roman World', in Joel B. Green and Lee Martin McDonald (eds.), *The World of the New Testament: Cultural, Social, and Historical Contexts* (Grand Rapids: Baker Academic, 2013), pp. 149–155.

Morwood, James (ed.), *Pocket Oxford Latin Dictionary: Latin–English*, 3rd edn (Oxford: Oxford University Press, 2005).

Moss, Candida R., *The Myth of Persecution: How Early Christians Invented a Story of Martyrdom* (New York: HarperOne, 2013).

Mounce, Robert H., *The Book of Revelation*, rev. edn, NICNT (Grand Rapids: Eerdmans, 1998).

Mounce, William D., *Pastoral Epistles*, WBC 46 (Dallas: Word, 2000).

Moyise, Steve, *The Old Testament in the Book of Revelation*, JSNTSup 115 (Sheffield: Sheffield Academic Press, 1995).

Murray, Michele, *Playing a Jewish Game: Gentile Christian Judaizing in the First and Second Centuries CE*, SCJ 13 (Waterloo, Ont.: Wilfrid Laurier University Press, 2004).

Newsom, Carol A., and Brennan W. Breed, *Daniel: A Commentary*, OTL (Louisville: Westminster John Knox, 2014).

North, Wendy S., 'John for Readers of Mark?: A Response to Richard Bauckham's Proposal', *JSNT* 25.4 (2003), pp. 449–468.

Nystrom, David P., 'We Have No King but Caesar: Roman Imperial Ideology and the Imperial Cult', in Scot McKnight and Joseph B. Modica (eds.), *Jesus Is Lord, Caesar Is Not: Evaluating Empire in New Testament Studies* (Downers Grove: InterVarsity Press, 2013), pp. 23–37.

Olbricht, Thomas H., and Jerry L. Sumney (eds.), *Paul and Pathos*, SBLSymS 16, (Atlanta: SBL, 2001).

Olupona, Jacob K., *African Religions: A Very Short Introduction* (New York: Oxford University Press, 2014).

Orlin, Eric M., *Foreign Cults in Rome: Creating a Roman Empire* (Oxford: Oxford University Press, 2010).

——, *Temples, Religion, and Politics in the Roman Republic* (Boston: Brill Academic, 2002).

Oropeza, B. J., *Churches Under Siege of Persecution and Assimilation: The General Epistles and Revelation*, ANTC 3 (Eugene: Cascade, 2012).

Osborne, Grant R., *Matthew*, ZECNT (Grand Rapids: Zondervan, 2010).

——, *Revelation*, BECNT (Grand Rapids: Baker, 2002).

Osiek, Carolyn, '*Diakonos* and *Prostatis*: Women's Patronage in Early Christianity', *HTS* 61.1/2 (2005), pp. 347–370.

Oswalt, John N., *The Book of Isaiah: Chapters 1–39*, NICOT (Grand Rapids: Eerdmans, 1986).

Parsons, Mikeal C., *Acts*, Paideia (Grand Rapids: Baker Academic, 2008).

Parsons, Mikeal C., and Michael W. Martin, *Ancient Rhetoric and the New Testament: The Influence of Elementary Greek Composition* (Waco: Baylor University Press, 2018).

Penner, Glenn M., *In the Shadow of the Cross: A Biblical Theology of Persecution and Discipleship* (Bartlesville: Living Sacrifice, 2004).

Peppard, Michael, *The Son of God in the Roman World: Divine Sonship in Its Social and Political Context* (Oxford: Oxford University Press, 2011).

Perry, Peter S., *The Rhetoric of Digressions: Revelation 7:1–17 and 10:1–11:13 and Ancient Communication*, WUNT 2.268 (Tübingen: Mohr Siebeck, 2009).

Pervo, Richard I., *Acts: A Commentary*, Hermeneia (Minneapolis: Fortress, 2009).

Petersen, Anders K., 'Imperial Politics in Paul: Scholarly Phantom or Actual Textual Phenomenon?', in Michael Labahn and Outi Lehtipuu (eds.), *People Under Power: Early Jewish and Christian Responses to the Roman Empire* (Amsterdam: Amsterdam University Press, 2015), pp. 101–127.

Peterson, David, *The Acts of the Apostles*, PNTC (Grand Rapids: Eerdmans, 2009).

Phua, Richard L.-S., *Idolatry and Authority: A Study of 1 Corinthians 8:1–11:1 in the Light of the Jewish Diaspora*, LNTS 299 (London: T&T Clark, 2005).

Pobee, J. S., *Persecution and Martyrdom in the Theology of Paul*, JSNTSup 6 (Sheffield: JSOT Press, 1985).

Porter, Stanley E., 'Pauline Chronology and the Question of Pseudonymity of the Pastoral Epistles', in Stanley E. Porter and Gregory P. Fewster (eds.), *Paul and Pseudepigraphy*, PS 8 (Leiden: Brill, 2013), pp. 65–88.

Prokhorov, A. V., 'Taking the Jews out of the Equation: Galatians 6.12–17 as a Summons to Cease Evading Persecution', *JSNT* 36.2 (2013), pp. 172–188.

Raquel, Sylvie T., 'Blessed Are the Peacemakers: The Theology of Peace in the Book of Revelation', in Gerald L. Stevens (ed.), *Essays on Revelation: Appropriating Yesterday's Apocalypse in Today's World* (Eugene: Pickwick, 2010), pp. 55–71.

Reimer, Andy M., 'The Man Born Blind: True Disciple of Jesus', in Steven A. Hunt, D. F. Tolmie and Ruben Zimmermann (eds.), *Character Studies in the Fourth Gospel: Narrative Approaches to Seventy Figures in John*, WUNT 314 (Tübingen: Mohr Siebeck, 2013), pp. 428–438.

Reimer, Ivoni R., *Women in the Acts of the Apostles: A Feminist Liberation Perspective* (Minneapolis: Fortress, 1995).

Resseguie, James L., 'A Narrative-Critical Approach to the Fourth Gospel', in Christopher W. Skinner (ed.), *Characters and Characterization in the Gospel of John*, LNTS 461 (London: Bloomsbury T&T Clark, 2013), pp. 3–17.

——, *Narrative Criticism of the New Testament: An Introduction* (Grand Rapids: Baker Academic, 2005).

——, *The Revelation of John: A Narrative Commentary* (Grand Rapids: Baker Academic, 2009).

——, *Revelation Unsealed: A Narrative Critical Approach to John's Apocalypse*, BIS 32 (Leiden: Brill, 1998).

Reumann, John, *Philippians: A New Translation with Introduction and Commentary*, AYB 33B (New Haven: Yale University Press, 2008).

Rhodes, Peter J., and Beate Ego, 'Synhedrion', in Hubert Cancik and Helmuth Schneider (eds.), *Brill's New Pauly*, vol. 14 (Leiden: Brill, 2019), pp. 26–28.

Richard, Earl, *Reading 1 Peter, Jude, and 2 Peter: A Literary and Theological Commentary*, RNTS (Macon: Smyth & Helwys, 2000).

Robinson, O. F., *The Criminal Law of Ancient Rome* (London: Duckworth, 1995).

Rogers, T. J., 'Shaking the Dust off the Markan Mission Discourse', *JSNT* 27.2 (2004), pp. 169–192.

Rohrbaugh, Richard L., 'Honor: Core Value in the Biblical World', in Dietmar Neufeld and Richard E. DeMaris (eds.), *Understanding the Social World of the New Testament* (Milton Park: Routledge, 2009), pp. 109–125.

Rothaus, Richard M., *Corinth, the First City of Greece: An Urban History of Late Antique Cult and Religion*, RGRW 139 (Leiden: Brill, 2000).

Ruiz, Jean-Pierre, *Ezekiel in the Apocalypse: The Transformation of Prophetic Language in Revelation 16,17–19,10*, EUS 23 (Frankfurt: Peter Lang, 1989).

Runesson, Anders, *The Origins of the Synagogue: A Socio-Historical Study*, CBNTS 37 (Stockholm: Almqvist & Wiksell, 2001).

——, 'Synagogue', in Joel B. Green, Jeannine K. Brown and Nicholas Perrin (eds.), *Dictionary of Jesus and the Gospels*, 2nd edn (Downers Grove: IVP Academic, 2013), pp. 903–911.

Sauer, Christof, and Richard Howell (eds.), *Suffering, Persecution and Martyrdom: Theological Reflections*, RSF 2 (Johannesburg: AcadSA, 2010).

Schirrmacher, Thomas, *The Persecution of Christians Concerns Us All: Towards a Theology of Martyrdom*, 3rd edn, WEAGIS 5, repr. (Eugene: Wipf & Stock, 2018).

Schnabel, Eckhard J., *Acts* (Grand Rapids: Zondervan, 2012).

——, 'The Persecution of Christians in the First Century', *JETS* 61.3 (2018), pp. 525–547.

Schnelle, Udo, *Theology of the New Testament*, tr. M. Eugene Boring (Grand Rapids: Baker Academic, 2009).

Schreiner, Thomas R., *Commentary on Hebrews*, BTCP (Nashville: B&H, 2015).

——, *Galatians*, ZECNT (Grand Rapids: Zondervan, 2010).

——, *Paul, Apostle of God's Glory in Christ: A Pauline Theology*, 2nd edn (Downers Grove: IVP Academic, 2020).

Seifrid, Mark, 'Romans', in G. K. Beale and D. A. Carson (eds.), *Commentary on the New Testament Use of the Old Testament* (Grand Rapids: Baker Academic, 2007), pp. 607–694.

Shelton, W., review of *The Myth of Persecution: How Early Christianity Invented a Story of Martyrdom*, by Candida Moss, *JETS* 57.1 (2014), pp. 210–214.

Shogren, Gary S., *1 and 2 Thessalonians*, ZECNT (Grand Rapids: Zondervan, 2012).

Siew, A. K. W., *The War Between the Two Beasts and the Two Witnesses: A Chiastic Reading of Revelation 11.1–14.5*, LNTS 283 (London: T&T Clark, 2005).

Sim, David C., 'Gentiles, God-Fearers and Proselytes', in David C. Sim and James S. McLaren (eds.), *Attitudes to Gentiles in Ancient Judaism and Early Christianity*, LNTS 499 (London: Bloomsbury, 2015), pp. 9–27.

——, 'Jews, Christians and Gentiles: Observations and Some Concluding Remarks', in David C. Sim and James S. McLaren (eds.), *Attitudes to Gentiles in Ancient Judaism and Early Christianity*, LNTS 499 (London: Bloomsbury, 2015), pp. 259–266.

Smallwood, E. Mary, *The Jews Under Roman Rule: From Pompey to Diocletian*, 2nd edn, SJLA 21 (Leiden: Brill, 1981).

Smith, Gary V., *Isaiah 1–39*, NAC 15A (Nashville: B&H, 2007).

Smith, Ian K., 'The Letter to the Hebrews', in Mark Harding and Alanna Nobbs (eds.), *Into All the World: Emergent Christianity in Its Jewish and Greco-Roman Context* (Grand Rapids: Eerdmans, 2017), pp. 184–207.

Smith, Murray J., 'The Book of Revelation: A Call to Worship, Witness, and Wait in the Midst of Violence', in Mark Harding and Alanna

Nobbs (eds.), *Into All the World: Emergent Christianity in Its Jewish and Greco-Roman Context* (Grand Rapids: Eerdmans, 2017), pp. 334–371.

Smith, Ralph L., *Micah–Malachi*, WBC 32 (Waco: Word, 1984).

Stambaugh, John E., and David L. Balch, *The New Testament in Its Social Environment*, LEC 2 (Philadelphia: Westminster, 1986).

Stamps, Dennis L., 'The Use of the OT in the NT as a Rhetorical Device: A Methodological Proposal', in S. E. Porter (ed.), *Hearing the Old Testament in the New Testament*, MNTS (Grand Rapids: Eerdmans, 2006), pp. 9–37.

Stanley, Christopher D., 'The Rhetoric of Quotations: An Essay on Method', in Craig A. Evans and James A. Sanders (eds.), *Early Christian Interpretation of the Scriptures of Israel: Investigations and Proposals*, JSNTSup 148 (Sheffield: Sheffield Academic Press, 1997), pp. 44–58.

Stein, Robert H., *Mark*, BECNT (Grand Rapids: Baker Academic, 2008).

Stiebing, William H., and Susan N. Helft, *Ancient Near Eastern History and Culture*, 3rd edn (London: Routledge, 2017).

Strauss, Mark L., *Four Portraits, One Jesus: An Introduction to Jesus and the Gospels*, 2nd edn (Grand Rapids: Zondervan, 2020).

——, *Mark*, ZECNT (Grand Rapids: Zondervan, 2014).

Streib, Heinz, 'Deconversion', in Lewis R. Rambo and Charles E. Farhadian (eds.), *The Oxford Handbook of Religious Conversion* (Oxford: Oxford University Press, 2014), pp. 271–296.

Sumney, Jerry L., *'Servants of Satan', 'False Brothers' and Other Opponents of Paul*, JSNTSup 188 (Sheffield: Sheffield Academic Press, 1999).

——, 'Studying Paul's Opponents: Advances and Challenges', in Stanley E. Porter (ed.), *Paul and His Opponents*, PS 2 (Leiden: Brill, 2005), pp. 7–58.

Sun, J.-W., 'Conquering Idolatry: John's Literary Creativity and Purpose in His Depiction of Babylon the Whore', ThM thesis, Singapore Bible College, 2020 (in Chinese).

Takács, Sarolta A., *Isis and Sarapis in the Roman World*, RGRW 124 (Leiden: Brill, 1995).

Talbert, Charles H., 'Once Again: The Plan of 1 Peter', in Charles H. Talbert (ed.), *Perspectives on First Peter*, NABPRSSS 9 (Macon: Mercer University Press, 1986), pp. 141–151.

Taylor, Tristan S., 'Social Status, Legal Status and Legal Privilege', in Paul J. du Plessis, Ando Clifford and Tuori Kaius (eds.), *The Oxford Handbook of Roman Law and Society* (Oxford: Oxford University Press, 2016), pp. 349–359.

Thayer, Anne, review of *The Myth of Persecution: How Early Christians Invented a Story of Martyrdom*, by Candida Moss, *Int* 68.1 (2014), pp. 81–83.

Thielman, Frank, *Romans*, ZECNT (Grand Rapids: Zondervan, 2018).

Thiessen, Matthew, *Contesting Conversion: Genealogy, Circumcision, and Identity in Ancient Judaism and Christianity* (Oxford: Oxford University Press, 2011).

——, 'Hebrews 12.5–13, the Wilderness Period, and Israel's Discipline', *NTS* 55.3 (2009), pp. 366–379.

Thiselton, Anthony C., *The First Epistle to the Corinthians*, NIGTC (Grand Rapids: Eerdmans, 2000).

Thomas, John C., and Frank D. Macchia, *Revelation*, THNTC (Grand Rapids: Eerdmans, 2016).

Thompson, Leonard L., *The Book of Revelation: Apocalypse and Empire* (New York: Oxford University Press, 1990).

Thompson, Marianne Meye, *John: A Commentary*, NTL (Louisville: Westminster John Knox, 2015).

Thornhill, A. Chadwick, *The Chosen People: Election, Paul, and Second Temple Judaism* (Downers Grove: InterVarsity Press, 2015).

Thrall, Margaret E., *A Critical and Exegetical Commentary on the Second Epistle of the Corinthians*, 2 vols., ICC (London: T&T Clark International, 2000).

Thurén, Lauri, *Derhetorizing Paul: A Dynamic Perspective on Pauline Theology and the Law*, WUNT 124 (Tübingen: Mohr Siebeck, 2000).

Tieszen, Charles L., 'Minding the Gaps: Overcoming Misconceptions of Persecution', *IJRF* 2.1 (2009), pp. 59–72.

——, 'Towards Redefining Persecution', *IJRF* 1.1 (2008), pp. 67–80.

Tolmie, D. Francois, 'The Ἰουδαῖοι in the Fourth Gospel: A Narratological Perspective', in Gilbert van Belle, Jan G. van der Watt and Petrus Maritz (eds.), *Theology and Christology in the Fourth Gospel*, BETL 184 (Leuven: Leuven University Press, 2005), pp. 377–399.

——, *Persuading the Galatians: A Text-Centred Rhetorical Analysis of a Pauline Letter*, WUNT 2.190 (Tübingen: Mohr Siebeck, 2005).

Towner, Philip H., 'Romans 13:1-7 and Paul's Missiological Perspective: A Call to Political Quietism or Transformation?', in Sven K. Soderlund and N. T. Wright (eds.), *Romans and the People of God* (Grand Rapids: Eerdmans, 1999), pp. 149–169.

Trebilco, Paul R., *Self-Designations and Group Identity in the New Testament* (Cambridge: Cambridge University Press, 2012).

Turner, David L., *Matthew*, BECNT (Grand Rapids: Baker Academic, 2008).

Vinciane, Pirenne-Delforge, and André Motte, 'Aphrodite', in Simon Hornblower, Antony Spawforth and Esther Eidinow (eds.), *The Oxford Classical Dictionary*, 4th edn (Oxford: Oxford University Press, 2012), doi: 10.1093/acref/9780199545568.013.0582.

Vinson, Richard B., *Luke*, SHBC (Macon: Smyth & Helwys, 2008).

Wahlde, Urban C. von, 'Narrative Criticism of the Religious Authorities as a Group Character in the Gospel of John: Some Problems', *NTS* 63.2 (2017), pp. 222–245.

Wallace, Daniel B., *Greek Grammar Beyond the Basics: An Exegetical Syntax of the New Testament* (Grand Rapids: Zondervan, 1996).

Wang, Lian, 'Johannine View of Persecution and Tribulation', *LMM* 25.2 (2017), pp. 359–370.

Watson, Alan, *The State, Law, and Religion: Pagan Rome* (Athens, Ga.: University of Georgia Press, 1992).

Watson, Duane F., 'The Role of Style in the Pauline Epistles: From Ornamentation to Argumentative Strategies', in J. Paul Sampley and Peter Lampe (eds.), *Paul and Rhetoric* (London: T&T Clark, 2010), pp. 119–140.

Weima, Jeffrey A. D., *1-2 Thessalonians*, BECNT (Grand Rapids: Baker Academic, 2014).

Wendland, Ernst R., 'The Hermeneutical Significance of Literary Structure in Revelation', *Neot* 48.2 (2014), pp. 447–476.

Whitlark, Jason A., *Resisting Empire: Rethinking the Purpose of the Letter to 'the Hebrews'*, LNTS 484 (London: Bloomsbury, 2014).

Wilder, Terry L., 'Pseudonymity and the New Testament', in David Alan Black and David S. Dockery (eds.), *Interpreting the New Testament: Essays on Methods and Issues* (Nashville: B&H, 2001), pp. 296–355.

Wilken, Robert L., *The Christians as the Romans Saw Them*, 2nd edn (New Haven: Yale University Press, 2003).

Williams, Travis B., *Good Works in 1 Peter: Negotiating Social Conflict and Christian Identity in the Greco-Roman World*, WUNT 337 (Tübingen: Mohr Siebeck, 2014).

——, *Persecution in 1 Peter: Differentiating and Contextualizing Early Christian Suffering*, NovTSup 145 (Leiden: Brill, 2012).

Wilson, S. G., *Related Strangers: Jews and Christians, 70–170 C.E.* (Minneapolis: Fortress, 1995).

——, 'Voluntary Associations: An Overview', in John S. Kloppenborg and Stephen G. Wilson (eds.), *Voluntary Associations in the Graeco-Roman World* (London: Routledge, 1996), pp. 1–15.

Winter, Bruce W., *Divine Honours for the Caesars: The First Christians' Responses* (Grand Rapids: Eerdmans, 2015).

——, 'Divine Imperial Cultic Activities and the Early Church', in Mark Harding and Alanna Nobbs (eds.), *Into All the World: Emergent Christianity in Its Jewish and Greco-Roman Context* (Grand Rapids: Eerdmans, 2017), pp. 237–265.

——, *Seek the Welfare of the City: Christians as Benefactors and Citizens*, FCCGRW (Grand Rapids: Eerdmans, 1994).

Witherington, Ben, III, *The Acts of the Apostles: A Socio-Rhetorical Commentary* (Grand Rapids: Eerdmans, 1998).

——, *New Testament Rhetoric: An Introductory Guide to the Art of Persuasion in and of the New Testament* (Eugene: Cascade, 2009).

Workman, Herbert B., *Persecution in the Early Church: A Chapter in the History of Renunciation* (London: Epworth, 1906; repr. Oxford: Oxford University Press, 1980).

Zeev, Miriam Pucci Ben, 'Jews Among Greeks and Romans', in John J. Collins and Daniel C. Harlow (eds.), *The Eerdmans Dictionary of Early Judaism* (Grand Rapids: Eerdmans, 2010), pp. 237–256.

Zerbe, Gordon M., *Non-Retaliation in Early Jewish and New Testament Texts: Ethical Themes in Social Contexts*, BAC (London: Bloomsbury Academic, 2015).

# Index of Scripture references

# Index of Scripture references